Be Creative

Be Creative

Making a Living in the New Culture Industries

Angela McRobbie

polity

First published in 2016 by Polity Press
Reprinted 2016

Polity Press
65 Bridge Street
Cambridge CB2 1UR, UK

Polity Press
350 Main Street
Malden, MA 02148, USA

ISBN-13: 978-0-7456-6194-0 (hardback)
ISBN-13: 978-0-7456-6195-7 (paperback)

A catalogue record for this book is available from the British Library.

Library of Congress Cataloging-in-Publication Data

McRobbie, Angela.
   Be creative: making a living in the new culture industries / Angela McRobbie.
      pages cm
   ISBN 978-0-7456-6194-0 (hardback) – ISBN 978-0-7456-6195-7 (paperback)
1. Cultural industries.   2. Cultural industries–Employees.   3. Arts–Economic aspects.
I. Title.
   HD9999.C9472M37 2015
   650.1–dc23
         2015010073

Typeset in 10.5 on 12 pt Sabon
by Toppan Best-set Premedia Limited
Printed and bound in Great Britain by Clays Ltd, St Ives PLC

For further information on Polity, visit our website: politybooks.com

Contents

Acknowledgements

My first thanks must go to the Berlin-based artist and academic Marion von Osten. In the early 2000s Marion arranged for some of my earlier work on UK fashion designers to be translated and published in German. Round about the same time she had a show in Zurich which she called 'Be Creative', and I have borrowed the phrase from her for the title of this book. In 2002 Marion invited me to join a project funded by the German Cultural Ministry 'Atelier Europa' and this collaboration also crystallized many of the ideas I subsequently followed up in this book. Chapter 1 was first presented tentatively at the Bauhaus Dessau, followed by the Munich Kunstverein. Indeed this whole book maps a series of exchanges and collaborations between London and Berlin and so I would also like to thank the following people in Berlin: Kerstin Drechsel, Rita Eichelkraut, Maria Exner, Marte Henschel, Ares Kalandides, Bastian Lange, Oliver MacConnell, Bettina Springer, Tatjana Turanskyj, Agnes Zelei and, in both Berlin and Spoleto, Monika Savier. In addition I am grateful to Nana Adusei-Poku, Sabine Hark and Ulrike Ottinger for such great friendship and support in Berlin.

So much of what I write about here has been formulated in the course of my working days, weeks and years at Goldsmiths, University of London. Always on a small budget, we have nevertheless managed to host events, seminars and talks, which have brought academics from across the world and this has helped us all in turn to develop our own research programmes. These invitees have included the late Ulrich Beck, Judith Butler, Angela

Davis, Michel Feher, Maurizio Lazzarato and Bernard Stiegler. Many of my former students have become busy creative professionals, while others are by now established academics; thanks then to Bridget Conor, Kerstin Forkert, Onur Komurcu, Guido del Ponzo and Sharmadean Reid. My Goldsmiths colleagues have also been inspiring and I offer warm thanks to them, especially Sara Ahmed, Lisa Blackman, Matt Fuller, Sarah Kember, Scott Lash, Gerald Lidstone, Carrie Paechter, Sian Prime and Joanna Zylinska. Thanks also to Goldsmiths for providing funding, which has enabled much of this current work to be undertaken in London and Berlin, as well as in Italy. These funds have been supplemented in recent years by an Arts and Humanities Research Council grant titled CREATe, based in Glasgow University School of Law. I wish to express my deep gratitude for this support and for the collegiality of participants.

This book has taken longer to complete than expected and for this reason I want to thank several journals and publishers for granting permission for the following chapters. Chapter 1 was originally published in 2002 in *Cultural Studies* vol. 16, no 4; thanks to Taylor and Francis for permission to reprint here. Sections of Chapter 4 were first tried out in *New Formations* 70, in 2011; thanks to Lawrence and Wishart for allowing me to make use of them here. A much shorter version of Chapter 5 was published in *Cultural Studies* in 2013; thanks again to Taylor and Francis. A few short segments from Chapter 6 were published in 2012 in a *Festschrift* volume for Ulrich Beck; I would like to express my thanks to Transcript Verlag in Hamburg for using them again here.

Various international colleagues have invited me to present chapters from this book and I would especially like to thank Norma Rantisi and Matt Soar at Concordia University, Montreal, where I spent several days in 2013; likewise Chelsey Hauge, Mary K. Bryson and Janice Stewart at the University of British Columbia, Institute for Gender, Race, Sexuality and Social Justice in Vancouver. In 2012 I spent a week in residence at McMaster University, Hamilton, as Hooker Visiting Professor, and I am also grateful to Priya Kapoor for inviting me to speak at Portland State University during my times in Oregon between 2011 and 2013. I was honoured to present an early draft of Chapter 6 at the *Festschrift* for Ulrich Beck at the Ludwig Maximilians University in Munich in 2011. Like so many others, I feel the recent loss of both Ulrich Beck and Stuart Hall deeply and the influence of both these thinkers flows across the pages of this book.

Finally, I want to thank my personal friends and family. Paul Gilroy and Vron Ware have been my neighbours in North London for so long; likewise, Shelley Charlesworth, Denise Riley and Irit Rogoff. In Birmingham I would like to thank Mo White, who also provided the cover photograph. Now in San Francisco, I would like to thank Sarah Thornton and her family, and my sister Ros Lambert in Edinburgh. As ever, I thank my daughter Hanna and I dedicate this book to two small boys – Joseph McGhee and Gabriel McGhee.

Introduction: Pedagogical Encounters and Creative Economy

For more than a decade now I am generally, on Wednesday afternoons through the Spring term, sitting in my office from midday onwards, seeing the Master's students to discuss their research dissertations. What I have seen unfolding in front of my eyes during these supervisions is a microcosm of the new creative labour market, taking into account also the impact of the Euro-crisis and the global financial recession since 2008. The lives and times of these young people reflect many of the themes in this book. In my university department and across the institution we offer a whole assortment of one-year Master's courses. These include Media and Communications, Brand Development, Transnational Media, Culture Industries, Cultural and Creative Entrepreneurship, Gender, Media and Culture and so on. Students have to pay fees and there are only a handful of bursaries, but this does not mean our constituency is from the international wealthy classes; but rather they are the children of the middle classes from various countries across the world. The parents are, as far as I can surmise, teachers, civil servants, small publishers, doctors, sometimes themselves from the arts and creative worlds. The students come from Brazil and from Portugal, from Bulgaria and Lithuania, from Russia, Germany, Italy and Spain, from Greece and Turkey, from Croatia, Montenegro and Slovenia, from Poland and from the Middle East. They also come from China, Korea and from southeast Asia. To enter the courses they must reach a high level of competence in English to ensure they are able to write four 6,000-word essays and a 12,000-word dissertation in line with the Bologna regulations for Master's courses across EU countries. We also have a sprinkling of UK students and some from other countries, including those above, but who have been resident in the UK for many years and have already completed a BA in a UK university.

Typically the students are in their twenties – often their mid to late twenties. They are very dedicated, exceptionally hard working. Many have done a few years work at least following their first degree. From southeast Asia, Japan and Korea it is more common that they have actually held down a job as a journalist or brand manager or fashion stylist and, having saved up enough money, and with some help from their parents, are taking a year off to improve and update their academic skills. This entire cohort has a good deal of work experience behind them, which can range from events management in Athens, to working behind the counter in a fashion chain like *Zara* in Madrid, to having an internship on a women's magazine, to working in a gallery in Istanbul. Of the thirty or so whom I usually get to know well, there are usually two or three planning an academic career and hoping for success in gaining a place to study for a PhD and funding to go with it. So, with this as a backdrop, part and parcel of my own working life, what are the sociological themes that can be extrapolated from these actual pedagogic encounters?

The students are disproportionately female and child-free. They are part of a global demographic of young women determined to live a 'life of one's own' as Ulrich Beck in his treatises on individualization processes, put it. What is not on their minds at all is the question of motherhood and the idea of grappling with a career and children. And given the adverse circumstances of the labour market for well-qualified young women like these, they are stretching out the training period even longer than might have been the case in the past, for the reason that nowadays training can itself be considered a job of sorts. It is anticipative of gainful employment or risk-laden self-employment. There is both the need constantly to enhance their CVs in order to have any chance in the job market, as well as the long-term need to find a decently paid job. Many will consider the idea of self-employment or of setting up some sort of small creative business as a realistic option, not because young people like this are natural-born entrepreneurs, but because, when weighing up their options, this emerges as a hope for a more productive and perhaps exciting future (Neff 2012). There is a time-space stretch mechanism in place that in effect disallows consideration of motherhood as anything other than a very future prospect for the reason that mobility is also a defining feature of the career pathway. These young women envisage moving city and country even if the job contract is only for a year or two. This also militates against the idea of having children, since maternity means having a more fixed abode, usually in proximity to extended family for help with childcare. On the one hand, being able to travel and fund themselves for a Master's course in London is of course a privileged position to occupy; on the other hand, there is also pressure to make good use of the expenditure and the students feel obligated to pay back to parents what has been borrowed; for this reason work takes precedence, and relationships occupy the second place in the agenda of 'life planning'. Work becomes akin to a romantic relationship. Feminism is relevant insofar as it analyses the gender inequities in the precarious career pathways into which these young women find themselves locked. But the immediate socio-economic environment militates against an ethos of solidarity and collectivity. Across several chapters of this book I ruminate on these issues, reflecting on the creative economy options for those who have children and need to stay put in a city like Berlin (the same could apply to other European cities), which is child-friendly, but with such a weak labour market that highly qualified mothers, now in their forties, have the hard choice of looking for a job, perhaps in London and commuting, or remaining *in situ* and opting for some form of creative entrepreneurship. On the one hand there is a sheer determi-nation to make something of a working life and to come up with a viable business plan; on the other hand such conditions as these also precipitate a sense of acute crisis of identity for a generation of young women who sought gender equality through acquiring what once were the risk-proof kind of qualifications linked with degrees and post-graduate training. Unfailingly the spreadsheet mindset of the life-plan, such a recurrent feature of neoliberal everyday life, shows itself to be implausible. The feature film by the feminist director Tatjana Turanskyj titled *Eine Flexible Frau* (2010) reflects on this crisis condition from the viewpoint of an unemployed architect and single mother job-seeking in Berlin. The film shows vividly what is more often a hidden or deeply privatized dimension of creative labour anxiety, that is a spiral into alcoholism and despair. The woman who had, as the film's narrative suggests, been one of the rising talents of her profession, finds herself being scolded by friends for not using her unemployment time to devote herself more to her young son. One female friend, a fellow architect who has given up her job to stay home with the children, appears to have the upper hand since she has embraced the neoliberal ethos of what she calls 'team-work' with her husband who is, perhaps temporarily, now the breadwinner.[1] At the same time Greta's pain is offset by a deep love of the urban space, and an anger about its rapid gentrification and the selling off of plots of land for private gated-communities. The figure of Greta re-plays

debates about the female *flâneuse* as she adamantly inhabits the city's
open-spaces such as the Tempelhof airport, or at the city limits where
fields take over the landscape at Schoenefeld. Turanskyj is also
re-telling the history of previous Berlin-based feminist and queer film-
makers such as Ulrike Ottinger who deliberately put female pleasures
of the urban gaze at the heart of her cinematic practice. *Eine Flexible
Frau* re-iterates some of the key moments in Ottinger's *Bildnis Einer
Trinkerin* from 1980 but in this case by 2010 'the sky is not so blue'.[2]

What I observe during my Wednesday supervisions is something
like a euphoria of imagined success, relatively untainted by a reality
of impediments and obstacles in the creative labour market. The
options are seen as either full-time employment or freelance self-
employment, or indeed short-term jobs that entail moving from one
project to the next. This new kind of working life introduces some
dilemmas for feminist social scientists who must re-think the sociology of employment to engage more fully with entrepreneurial culture
and with the self-employment ethos now a necessity for survival. It
is hardly a choice in countries like Greece and Italy and Spain and
for this reason I make the case later in the book that the current
debate about cultural and creative economy, including the critique of
neoliberalism from the perspective of the *précarité* movements that
have sprung up in recent years, needs urgently to spend time on this
topic of job creation: how to develop new forms of community and
cultural economy, which produce some sort of income streams and
which produce livelihoods allowing people to contribute to neighbourhood and locality, including taking care of children, the elderly
and the vulnerable. The question will be how to finance activities that
in the past were part of the public sector. How might it be possible
to make a living from working with unemployed or 'at risk' youths
in the community? How can social work be re-invented, aided and
supported by the rise of the creative economy? Can the current discourse of social enterprise be re-inflected away from the individualistic
rhetoric of charismatic entrepreneurs who 'want to make a difference'
in favour of a more grounded or grass-roots approach to community-
building? What would it mean to bring a feminist perspective to bear
on social and cultural entrepreneurship in the light of the current
crisis of unemployment for young people across and beyond the Eurozone?[3] What kind of new vocabulary can be developed to replace the
seemingly stale or over-used terms of the grass-roots and the community and how can culture play a role in this re-imagination process?
Arguably the European Commission has invested for many years in
this kind of terrain. Through the huge range of projects it supports
it has been possible for those experiencing forms of semi-employment

or interrupted under-employment nevertheless to maintain and update skills and to have a sense of self-worth in regions of high unemployment. Here too the vocabulary of self-entrepreneurship has a strong presence, as I show in the concluding chapter of this book, but it is modified, less shaped by the heroic vocabulary of enterprise associated with US Business Schools and more measured, reflecting the residual presence of social democratic elements within the Commission.

The second theme that emerges is that we see an upscaling (by degree conferment) of what in the past would have been considered vocational training or life-long learning. Smaller organizations, often from the so-called third sector, which in the past provided such training in the form of short courses, are gradually being squeezed out and replaced by the generic Master's undertaken in a university environment with the relevant accreditation process, which also carries the value of a degree rather than a certificate or diploma. This shift is acknowledged in the recent development of the ERASMUS Plus programmes supported by the European Commission. In effect, many different forms of youth training are now rolled into an umbrella of provision led by the university sector. It stands to reason, since only large universities can bear the risks, invest in technical infrastructure (e.g. computing and digital studios) and can have installed the complex accounting systems to make this kind of provision cost effective. Such a role also forces the universities to fulfil more fully the requirement to ensure employability, while also *de facto* enforcing the 'links with industry' agenda set by national governments.[4] At a policy-level this upskilling dimension also appears to match the needs of the new creative economy, especially with the increasingly important role of social media and e-commerce. A key term here is training or *ausbildung* and, as I argue in this book, this is at the heart of the project of current governmentality that aims to transform the modern work regime. Training programmes ensure that the workforce is in a constant state of readiness (or employability) while also having their hopes pinned to the stars of the new economy. The word 'training' also has a long and honourable tradition within social democratic and this gives it a strategic value in terms of gesturing to some idea of social justice.

My Wednesday afternoons reveal two further elements, each of which throws light on the pathways of creative economies and the extent to which the university plays an increasingly central role in managing and overseeing this terrain. One element is the role of London as a global city and the detrimental impact this has for local and national job markets (Sassen 1991). One student in his thirties tells me how the Northern Italian fashion company he had worked for as a sourcing manager was increasingly downscaling local manufacturers in favour of cheaper off-shore outfits now set up in Cambodia and Vietnam. His own job security was looking uncertain so, with savings and some support from his family, he took a risk and moved to London, where his wife, a fashion graduate, quickly found a job in the charity-shop sector. Midway through the Master's course, the young man was offered a job by a big fashion company sourcing suppliers in Italy, that is, doing exactly what he had been doing back in Italy, but premised on his now seemingly permanent location in London. He got the job on the basis of his know-how and contacts in the region where he had grown up and worked; he was interviewed for the job in Italian, by a team of Italians in London already working for the UK company, and he was pleased to be offered the post, despite the travel back and forth to Italy and the high cost of living, especially rental costs in London. This -same pattern emerges across my cohort, including young women who had worked in publishing in Greece and Portugal but for whom the economic crisis, along with the decline in book sales, put their jobs at risk or made them disappear altogether. The possibilities for work became improved in the network environment to which they were exposed in London, including the chances for internships in companies already adjusting to the digital transformations in publishing. The same holds true for journalists coming from the world of magazine publishing. For students who have recently completed an undergraduate degree there is also the expectation of developing transferable skills. A student with a degree in Art and Technology from Denmark tells me that not seeing herself as a visual artist has led to a range of career options, especially with a Master's degree from London under her belt. 'I know exactly what is needed to undertake large-scale events management, such as what is entailed in staging a city fashion week,' she says. This raises inevitable questions about who can take such risks and those for whom it is quite impossible. Those who can somehow afford to live in London and who have the cultural capital and the time to access its dense creative networks. Those who are healthy and energetic enough to undertake a Master's while also doing an internship while working nights in a cocktail bar. In my observations this portfolio of weekly activities is quite normal. However, such a skewered global city job market has adverse consequences for those unable to be mobile, as well as for smaller cities across the UK. It is almost impossible to set up a new fashion business in the UK outside London, with any hope of survival, despite the large numbers of universities training students to a high level from the north of Scotland (Aberdeen) to the southwest corner of England

(Falmouth), the reason being the concentration of big brands in London and the powerful role their 'transaction rich networks' play in creating small-scale casual or part-time job opportunities even as sales assistants (Lash and Urry 1994). Micro-fashion enterprises need publicity and they need to be talked about by influential bloggers. The network is both virtual and live; people need to see and be seen out and about and smaller cities can only provide this infrastructure with a lot of government support and regional funding. It is not impossible to create this kind of fashion hub (Montreal and Berlin are good examples) but the spell of the fashion conglomerates is such that they need not look far afield; the expectation is that people come to them. Likewise, stores and retail spaces will only locate to cities where there are guaranteed high-income consumers. Therefore the pervasive inequality and competition that underpins the growth of the new creative economy at a time when the public sector is being dramatically shrunk reduces the capacity for poorer regions and cities to respond with long-term policies for job creation, and this means they are often looking for a quick fix and will seek image enhancement through bolstering the marketing and branding departments in the often forlorn hope of attracting investment from the big brands. The overwhelming power of the global cities insofar as they are home to major companies and in this case vast retail spaces, produces hugely imbalanced labour markets, not least in the creative economy, putting paid to Florida's ideas that smaller towns and cities can somehow create an infrastructure to attract the right calibre of talented people (Florida 2002). This means that a key question for consideration is how local economies can be developed separately from the agglomeration effect of the big brands and the job creation capacity therein.[5]

Another question arising from my Wednesday afternoons is that of pedagogy. 'Cultural studies', with its history in the UK to include the writing of Richard Hoggart, Raymond Williams and Stuart Hall (adding to this Dick Hebdige and Paul Gilroy), has become a field with almost unlimited potential for what Gayatri Spivak referred to as the 'teaching machine'. One additional and unanticipated consequence of the idea of 'cultural studies' has been the immense commercial value emerging out of 'subcultural theory'. The pathway here could be traced through the idea of bricolage, 'cut ups' and the subversion of style, as theorized by Hebdige, finding its way out of the classroom or seminar room of the art school into the hands of the fashion designers, the graphic designers and communications graduates able to translate the ideas of the street and of 'authentic' working-class culture or even of revolt into the very stuff of collections, or for the 'edgy' visual image of global labels such as Dior or YSL[6] (Hebdige 1978). For many years I myself stopped teaching subcultural theory for this reason. The vocabulary could too easily be translated into a snazzy pitch. Instead what was needed was a meta-critique, one that, like the writing of Boltanski and Chiapello, could show how capitalism replenishes itself by conceding ground and by admonishing itself under the impact of the social or artistic critique now extended, as I would argue, to include a pop or subcultural critique (Boltanski and Chiapello 2005). In various articles dating back (in French) to the mid 1990s, these authors claim that what they call the artistic critique (an off-shoot of the student movement of the late 1960s, whose more political counterpart they label the 'social critique') is absorbed by media and creative practitioners in the commercial world such as advertising and it becomes part of their own professional vocabulary. In short they can use artistic or avant-garde theories of society, to bolster their careers in advertising. This suggests instead a wholescale absorption of the counter-cultural critique by capitalism in its post-Fordist phase. It also suggests that creative professionals are largely de-politicized and concerned only with their own self-advancement. The awkward reality is that the political leanings and affiliations of those working in the creative and cultural sector are so diverse as to make it difficult to draw any generalizations. Often professionals themselves have to bear the brunt of working against the grain of their own inclinations for the sake of an income in a highly competitive and difficult economic climate, architects being an obvious example but also actors and musicians. There is both co-option and critique across the cultural landscape. However there are also times of embedded conservatism and likewise periods of seemingly sudden politicization and organization. In this book I speak of the 'Damien Hirst moment' to refer to the former, while more recently in the aftermath of the Occupy movement there is a resurgence of activism. What has been unexpected is the way in which cultural studies has become the privileged conduit for this double and paradoxical movement of instrumentalization and politicization. The commercial value of what Sarah Thornton called 'subcultural capital' cannot be underestimated but this does not mean its field of influence is totally depleted of political value, despite my own past reservations in the classroom. In the course of this book I return to this dilemma. There is a further irony at the heart of the tradition of British popular culture, which is that what was being done or being made by young 'creative practitioners' – musicians, artists, graphic designers – typically from a working-class background and within the direct orbit of the art school (e.g. The Beatles, Roxy Music, The Sex Pistols) provided the raw materials upon which writers like Dick Hebdige were able to develop such elaborate theoretical models. We would not be here without them, making such outstanding cultural artefacts. Stuart Hall et al. were right to emphasize that these were youth-culture offshoots of working-class culture, as Hebdige and Gilroy also emphasized the role of race and ethnicity as it intersected with these white class formations (Hall and Jefferson 1976). Such phenomena could not so easily come into being in countries like Italy or Germany where working-class culture did not have the same established place, one that in the UK had been gained through struggle. This leads Italian sociologists Arvidsson and Malossi to 're-read' youth subcultures retrospectively merely as 'effervesence' connected with the new consumption possibilities brought about by post-Fordism, where in contrast the original Birmingham CCCS work stressed the politics of working-class culture (Arvidsson and Malossi 2010). But for our purposes here the unexpected outcome of cultural studies is to have found itself canonized as a curriculum for the new creative economy, alongside and even conjoined with the more mainstream staple of business studies as it adapted itself to the needs of trainee artists and designers. When we bring these developments into the space of the new 'entrepreneurial university' it becomes clear how a good deal is at stake inside the 'teaching machine'. This does not mean that what we teach will inevitably merely shore up, replenish and re-invigorate the cultural agenda of contemporary capitalism. Instead we can put the teaching machine to work in order to interrogate how its own critical thought is taken on board and turned into an instrument for economic growth and renewal. In the context of the imperative to have 'industry links' this is perhaps totally predictable. And in fact such processes have long been the subject of attention by social theorists such as Bourdieu and Ulrich Beck under the heading of 'reflexive sociology'. In this case I am undertaking an exercise in reflexive cultural studies, although in fact my overall argument in this book reflects more widely much of Foucault's emphasis on 'pastoral care' now translated into 'pedagogic practice' as the privileged site for guidance and instruction within the field of contemporary governmentality (Foucault 2008)[7]. We live in a work regime of constant training. This education-training complex takes formal shape as curriculum, and informal shape as 'edutainment'. Amid this panoply of instructive discourses the kind of critical pedagogy that is associated with the cultural studies tradition permits, or so I argue, 'shards of light' to emerge as prefigurative forms of

social understanding and political consciousness. However the environment within which this happens is one defined by the intensity
and embeddedness of individualization. How a capacity to resist
comes into being in the context of such an array of forces, which
would tend to extinguish this potential, is a recurring theme in the
pages that follow.

Middle-classification

In the title of this book, I retain the words 'culture industries' to
signal a lineage from the Frankfurt School and Adorno in particular
through to the Birmingham CCCS, where I started my own academic
career (Adorno and Horkheimer 1976; Hall et al. 1976). The alle-
giance to the former is oblique in that, for Adorno, while the dream
factory of the culture industries was indeed a place of production,
employing legions of writers and artists, it was paced according to a
relentless assembly line of economies of scale such that cultural artefacts took on the semblance of sameness, uniformity and mind-
numbing banality. The Birmingham CCCS under the influence of
Gramsci disputed this analysis of inevitable banalization, making a
strong case for critical participation at both producer and consumer
ends in the context of the social history of popular culture as a site
of class struggle. Birmingham scholars extended this to include struggles of ethnicity (citing *pace* Gilroy the idea of a black musical genius
such as Bob Marley) and the importance of gender struggles also
with reference to the subversive ways in which items of commercial
femininity could be deployed in un-imagined ways, an argument
more recently developed by Lauren Berlant (Gilroy 1987, McRobbie
1976, Berlant 2010). However in both the cases of Frankfurt and
Birmingham it was the outcome of cultural production, the artefacts
themselves, which took precedence over the social conditions of their
inception. In this current book my emphasis is on the latter processes
and with how changing conditions militate against the kinds of collective identities that help produce political art and popular culture.
Nevertheless, I retain the term 'culture industry' because it stands as
a counter to the more pragmatic ideas of creative industries adopted
by the policy-makers and advisers in the late 1990s to designate a
preference for the ways in which creativity as an individual activity
could be economized. Indeed, I argue that the word 'creativity' dis-
places and supplants the word 'culture', since it is less contaminated
by the Marxist legacy that in the space of British public debate at
least still lingers round the edges of many such debates. Creativity

becomes something inherent in personhood (childhood, adolescence and young adulthood; less often, old age), which has the potential to be turned into a set of capacities. The resulting assemblage of 'talent' can subsequently be unrolled in the labour market or 'talent-led economy'. The creativity *dispositif* comprises various instruments, guides, manuals, devices, toolkits, mentoring schemes, reports, TV programmes and other forms of entertainment.[8] I see these come together as a form of governmentality, as Foucault would define it, with a wide population of young people within its embrace. In the book I trace the illustrious inception of the creativity *dispositif* from the UK New Labour government to its coming of age under the auspices of the EC to include small social projects in Italy and Germany and elsewhere across member states. I see two things happen together: the expansion of higher and further education from the mid 1990s in the UK with particular reference to the arts, humanities and media fields, and with this the directing of such young people so that they adjust themselves to the idea of enterprise culture. Middle-classification processes come to be linked directly to self-entrepreneurship as an ideal. This is not, however, upward mobility; instead, it is an ideological effect, giving young people, especially young women, the feel of being middle class and aspirational. For instance, from studying dance and theatre arts, they will go on to set up their own small company providing dance classes and stage school for children in different neighbourhoods as after-school activities. Or else they may set up a pilates studio with ballet classes, and so on. As I discuss in Chapter 3, this kind of process shows the *dispositif* to be an instrument of 'de-proletarianization' as the Ordo-liberal economists stressed. Neo-liberalism succeeds in its mission in this respect if a now very swollen youthful middle class bypasses mainstream employment with its trade unions and its tranches of welfare and protection in favour of the challenge and excitement of being a creative entrepreneur. Concomitantly, when in a post-industrial society there are fewer jobs offering permanent and secure employment, such a risk-taking stance becomes a necessity rather than a choice. The two come together in a kind of magic formula. This raises the question: what kind of entrepreneur with what kind of 'project'? The role of the *dispositif* is to manage and oversee the seemingly exciting and rewarding aspects of this transition, which in effect means that it does some of the work of labour reform under the rubric of the encouragement to 'be creative'. This making of a new young middle class is also the making of a 'risk class' as Ulrich Beck would put it; it works as a future template for being middle class and learning to live without welfare protection and social security. The realm of this *dispositif* is education and the media and entertainment environment, which nowadays wraps itself around all of our social lives. For example, on Saturday 15 February 2015 on BBC Radio 4, the successful young cook and pastry-maker Rachel Khoo described her path from studying fashion, starting off in fashion public relations, then deciding it was important to follow her dreams, which meant moving to Paris and holding down several jobs at one time in order to take a Cordon Bleu cookery course. Khoo's enthusiasm on air reflected everything this book is about in terms of the girlish romance of following your dreams. As she put it, 'If it doesn't work out, at least you have tried.' Khoo was employed as an au pair, a perfume assistant in a department store, and ended up working as a cook-book store assistant, organizing launches for successful food writers, which took her into an extended network of editors and publishers and eventually landed her a book contract. Her TV series, filmed from a tiny Paris kitchen, where she exuded a joyful enthusiasm about cooking for friends while living in a tiny attic, all helped to create a successful brand identity, with one contract leading to another. The point, of course, is that we the audience only hear about these success stories, and about how all the hard work eventually paid off. Here the *dispositif* is embedded in the broadcasting of the narrative itself and the production decisions underpinning it. Entering the risk class and embarking on a creative career means listening to the voice of the *dispositif* as it says, 'Here is your chance; take it now and prove to yourself that making films or baking cakes or knitting jumpers is something you can do.'

Précarité?

With such encouragement to become a creative practitioner[9] questions about making a living fade into the margins and the value of sheer hard work and constant activity takes over. It therefore requires a whole new vocabulary to raise questions about livelihoods, about payment for freelance work, and about earning enough money to support a family, never mind funding a private pension plan. This switching of registers is also a political process, one that may well be resisted by those within the professional field for whom it is the work itself that matters. This difficulty is marked in the UK fashion design sector. Policy matters tend to be conducted at what we might call the top end of CEOs, lobbyists and global retailers like Sir Philip Green of *Topshop*. Where very recently the idea of *Made In Britain* with the revival of small-scale manufacture has re-emerged in policy debate (such as that conducted at the Westminster Media Forum),[10] the glamour image of the industry as a whole, and the emphasis on public relations means that voices that reflect the kind of issues in this book tend not to be heard and they must seek out other avenues for debate. This focus on fashion as a culture industry provides a key thread throughout the book, with a long-term interest on my own part in livelihoods and in how critical fashion practices, which stand as something of a counter to the dominance of the big brands, can survive and defend their right to existence, perhaps again by looking to the field of art and the gallery world for recognition and support. This possibility has a different meaning in London from what happens in Berlin. In London, fine-art fashion (under the heading of 'emerging talent') can only survive if it finds support from a major label or from a leading fashion house. In Berlin, as I show in Chapter 5, fashion designers struggle to keep their own labels going, but do so with a glance towards the art world in the city and the strategies of artists for keeping their own studio practice going while also working as a lecturer in a range of different art schools and colleges.

This book is not one that engages closely with cultural policy, although in Chapter 3 it does offer some reflections on how colleagues in the field have responded to and intervened in discussions about the present status and the future of the creative economy. Drawing however most directly on Foucault, I dissect the incitement to 'be creative'. My emphasis is on the mix of pleasure and discipline in these various addresses and the way in which they undertake labour reform by stealth and without even drawing attention to the old ways of organized labour. Being expected to work without workplace entitlements severs a connection with past generations who not only had such protection (in the form of sick pay, pensions, maternity leave etc.) but also fought hard to get them. And once these go, if indeed they do, it becomes difficult to imagine them being reinstated, especially since they took almost a century of struggle to win. It is therefore all the more important to reclaim the 'w' word (i.e. welfare-in-work). How then to resist this imperative to become creative? By adamantly remaining un-creative? In some ways this is the logic of Richard Sennett's fine body of writing on the modern work society, and I reflect on his trilogy of books in Chapter 6, where I also take issue, however, with some of his ideas on craft. In effect, it stands in for creativity in his opus and I have some misgivings about the special slow and recalcitrant qualities of craft-work and the joy of practising and rehearsal, which Sennett emphasizes as suggestive of a more harmonious relationship between people and working life. But there is also a tendency to upgrade more monotonous tasks in Sennett's books, and this makes him seemingly immune to the sheer hard work and the exhausting repetition of daily cleaning, washing and cooking for a family, as well as taking care of the children.

In recent years many other scholars have also reflected on this governmental imperative to become creative, especially the Italian social theorist Maurizio Lazzarato. But the work that stands most closely to this current endeavour is Isabell Lorey's recent book *The State of Insecurity* (2015). Where I argue that the call to be creative is a potent and highly appealing mode of new governmentality directed to the young in the educational environment, whose main effect is to do away with the idea of welfare rights in work by means of eclipsing normal employment altogether, Lorey's argument complements this by proposing that this mode of neoliberal governmentality is also a general and widespread process of precarization. She deftly makes a series of theoretical connections between her use of this term and the writing of Judith Butler (who posits precarity as a feature of all living beings through their essential vulnerability and dependency) by showing how this new form of governmentality makes us all precarious and thus seemingly in need of more extensive and heightened forms of security, since we are also made fearful of those who seem to threaten the now fragile security to which we struggle to hold on. Precarization for Lorey works by summoning the spectre of outside dangers. She stresses that this is not entirely an invention of our neoliberal times but has a much longer historical trajectory through the development of modern liberal government and the contract into which it enters with its citizens (subject to strict criteria) through providing some means of protection from the dangers or risks outside the jurisdiction of this protectionist 'embrace'. In particular Lorey refers to the welfarist entitlements offered, against a backdrop of labour struggle, from the early years of the twentieth century, to sectors of the male, white, working class, taking the form of the 'family wage' and forms of support and subsidy that were predicated on the nuclear family with a dependent wife and children. This kind of wage labour, offered only to sections of the population, was able to provide a kind of bulwark against the dangers of destitution. Lorey shows how good self-governance had the imaginary effect of reducing vulnerability while also permitting entitlement to protection. But this changes with the advent of post-Fordism alongside the rise of neoliberal forms of governmentality, which increasingly normalizes forms of precarization across the population, including those designated middle class, while also seeing through the 'demolition of workers' rights'. Lorey stresses the paradox at the heart of this precarization process, which is that the subject is promised freedom (to self-actualize) while also being subjugated to this normalization (and privatization) of risk and uncertainty. She also reflects on what it would mean or entail to provide security for all, predicated *pace* Butler on our inherent vulnerability. In contrast, in my own more localized case, l show how a concerted effort is made to encourage the unleashing of an inner creativity, which brings the tantalizing promise of self-reward, thereby almost negating the threat of insecurity. Or at least, the risk is written into the excitement of the undertaking. The *dispositif* is encouraging rather than coercive, and the imperative to 'be creative' is an invitation to discover one's own capabilities, to embark on a voyage of self-discovery, for example by joining a creative-writing class. It is an immensely pedagogic invitation – one that again seems far removed from the hard facts of self-employment. Insecurity is seen as part of the adventure. There are two final concerns also shared by Lorey, though with different inflections. The first of these is the focus on the possibilities of a new 'care community' as an organizational tool for the politics of *précarité* and an antidote to the marketization and privatization of care. The reinstatement of care for Lorey is envisaged as part and parcel of what the movement of the 'precarious' will embark on in the course of its search for new ways of living. Pursuing a similar concern, I turn in contrast to the already existing not-for-profit sector and the role of social enterprise as a possible site for marrying care with creative economy, at the same time as I remind readers of the longer history of such small institutions often having emerged from grass-roots feminist social and community work. My intention here is to re-awaken an interest in these modest but valuable ventures, while also seeing possibilities for continuing and refreshing this tradition. In effect, I aim to retrieve and uphold the social democratic tradition embedded in these small organizations. This would be to propose a coming together of older not-for-profit workers with the young campaigners emerging from the European *précarité* movement, especially through a commitment to inter-generational feminism. Lorey, like myself, picks up the Deleuzian line of flight, which, echoing Virno, she sees as permitting a kind of exodus from the stranglehold of capitalist relations. This is not an actual escape to some new outside but rather an immanent flight with the potential to form new alliances on the basis of breaking the binary that currently divides the still (relatively) protected from the unprotected. Lorey rightly does not endorse a call to reinstate protection for the few. But I am not sure that an insistence on the need for social protection and new welfare rights in precarious cultural work implies a privileged prerogative. It could also be seen as a process of re-politicization, in a field that has been subjected to such intensive individualization that the idea of a common cause has for many years been all but lost. This leads to my final point, the idea of line of flight or shard of light. The young people may depart from some point in space, a city or town or community, but there is also continuity and inter-generational transmission inscribed within the movement or flight they undertake. Lorey is correct in seeing the line of flight as a movement 'away'. I envisage this as a mobility that carries within it the traces or memories of the familial point of departure. The shard of light works in the space of pedagogy and mediates between the family as site for memory and belonging, and the movement away. It endeavours to perform a work of historical translation so as to ensure a connectedness in the process of becoming creative. Working in, through and beyond the tropes of individualization, there are eventually some safeguards against precariousness and vulnerability to be wrought from the counter-knowledges of 'reflexive cultural studies' as well as from contemporary social and cultural theory. The question then opens up as to how the actual practice of creative labour is able to mobilize a new radical voice.

1

Clubs to Companies: Notes on the Decline of Political Culture in Speeded-Up Creative Worlds

The 'Arts Labs' of the New Cultural Economy

Creative Industry Sectors as defined in Creative Industries Mapping Document (DCMS 1998). Music, Performing Arts, Publishing Software, TV and Radio, Film, Designer Fashion, Advertising, Arts and Antiques, Crafts, Design, Architecture, Interactive Leisure Software.

Cultural Entrepreneur Club (initiative led by ICA, London, Nesta, Arts Council England, Goldsmiths College London and Cap Gemini Ernst and Young), 2000. Selected 'new job' titles of 400 invited members including Arts Promoter, Incubator, Consultancy for Inventor, Cultural Strategist, Multimedia Artist, Visual Support Consultant, Media Initiatives and Relationships, Digital Design Consultant, Branding and Communications, Arts in Business Consultants, Art-To-Go Sales, Events Organizer, New Media Agent, net casting/e label/cdrom, Music Portal, dance/music/youth culture, Bio-entrepreneur.[1]

This chapter provides a preliminary and thus provisional account of some of the defining characteristics of work and employment in the new cultural sector of the UK economy, and in London in particular.[2] It also describes a transition from what can be labelled 'first-wave' culture industry work as defined by the Department of Culture, Media and Sport Creative Industries 1998 document (see above), to the more economically highly charged and rapidly mutating 'second wave' of cultural activity that has come into being in the last three years. This latter development is marked by de-specialization, by its intersection with internet working, by the utilizing of creative capacities provided by new media, by the rapid growth of multi-skilling in the arts field, by the shrunken role of the sector that I would describe as the 'independents',[3] by a new partnership between arts and business with public sector support, and by government approval as evident in the most recently published Green Paper from the DCMS (2001). (For new job titles see above.) The 'second wave' comes into being as a consequence of the more rapid capitalization of the cultural field as small-scale previously independent micro-economies of culture and the arts find themselves the subject of commercial interest.

The expansion of these sections of employment also brings about, for a more substantial number of people, a decisive break with past expectations of work.[4] As the focus for extensive interest in the media (TV and press), involvement in these fields provides to a much wider section of the population different ideas about how working lives can now be conducted. Through the profusion of profiles and interviews with hairdressers, cooks, artists and fashion designers, the public (especially young people) are presented with endless accounts of the seemingly inherent rewards of creative labour.[5] The flamboyantly *auteur* relation to creative work, which has long been the mark of being a writer, artist, film director or fashion designer, is now being extended to a much wider section of a highly 'individuated' workforce. The media has always glamorized creative individuals as uniquely talented 'stars'. It is certainly not the case that now, in postindustrial Britain, people genuinely have the chance to fulfil their creative dreams. Rather it is the case that there is a double process of individualization. First this occurs in the obsessive celebrity culture of the commercial media, now thoroughly extended to artists, designers and other creative personnel, and second in the social structure itself, as people are increasingly disembedded from ties of kinship, community and social class. They are, in a deregulated environment, 'set free', as Giddens would put it, from both workplace organizations and from social institutions (Giddens 1991).

What individualization means sociologically is that people increasingly have to become their own micro-structures, they have to do the work of the structures by themselves, which in turn requires intensive practices of self-monitoring, or 'reflexivity'. This process where structures (like the welfare state) seem to disappear and no longer play their expected roles, and where individuals are burdened by what were once social responsibilities marks a quite profound social transformation as Bauman, Beck and others have argued (Bauman 2000a, b; Beck 2000). (In response to government initiatives to get people to take out their own pension schemes, a television advertisement for finance company Norwich Union asks 'Are you an actor? Act now and get a stakeholder pension' (C4 and ITV, May 2001).)

Individualization in the UK could summarily be defined as the con-vergence of the forcefulness of neoliberal economics put in place by the Thatcher government from 1979 onwards, with mechanisms of social and demographic change, which result in new social groupings replacing traditional families, communities and class formations. Individualization is not about individuals *per se*, as about new, more fluid, less permanent social relations seemingly marked by choice or option. However, this convergence has to be understood as one of contestation and antagonism. Individualization thus marks a space of social conflict; it is where debates about the direction of change are played out and where new contradictions arise. This is most apparent in the world of work, since it is here that the convergence is most dramatically configured. Capital finds novel ways of offload-ing its responsibility for a workforce, but this relinquishing process no longer is confronted by traditional and organized 'labour'. Instead, the new conditions of work are largely being experienced by 'New Labour' – by sectors of the working population for whom work has become an important source for self-actualization, even freedom and independence. This includes women for whom work is an escape from traditional marriage and domesticity, young people for whom it is increasingly important as a mark of cultural identity, and ethnic minorities for whom it marks the dream of upward mobility and a possible escape from the denigration.

The cultural sphere provides an ideal space for young people to explore such individualized possibilities, just as it also offers govern-ment opportunities for a post-industrialized economy unfettered by the constraints and costs of traditional employment. The impact of this intersection accounts for what I want to propose here as an acceleration in the cultural realm. There is a much expanded work-force comprising freelance, casualized and project-linked persons, and there is also a more fiercely neoliberal model in place with the blessings of government for overseeing the further de-regulation and commercialization of the cultural and creative sector (DCMS 2001). The culture industries are being 'speeded up' and further capitalized as the state steps back and encourages the privatization of previously publicly subsidized cultural provision (for example by buying in freelance arts administrators for single projects, rather than employ-ing full-time staff). Those working in the creative sector cannot simply rely on old working patterns associated with art worlds, they have to find new ways of 'working' the new cultural economy, which increasingly means holding down three or even four 'projects' at once. This becomes a necessity as, in a crowded and competitive field, charges to the client fall (to pick up the business), and consequently to make ends meet the 'cultural entrepreneur' must be running several jobs at once.[6] In addition, since these projects are usually short term there have to be other jobs to cover the short-fall when a project ends. The individual becomes his or her own enterprise, sometimes presiding over two separate companies at the one time.[7] To sum up, if we consider the creative industries in the UK as a kind of experimental site, or case study, or indeed 'arts lab' for testing out the possibilities for 'cultural entrepreneurialism' (see Leadbeater and Oakley 1999), then I would suggest that we can also see a shift from first to second wave, which in turn (ironically) marks the decline of 'the indies' the rise of the creative sub-contractor and the downgrading of creativity.

On the Guest List? Club Culture Sociality at Work

Given the ongoing nature of these developments, the 'authorial' voice of the following pages is tentative, in that I am drawing on observations and trends emerging from my current work in progress on this topic. I propose a number of intersecting and constitutive features. They are as follows: *first* that imported into the creative sector are elements of youth culture, in particular those drawn from the energetic and entrepreneurial world of dance and rave culture; *second* that the realm of 'speeded up' work in the cultural sector now requires the holding down of several jobs at the one time; *third* that such working conditions are also reliant on intense self promotional strategies, and, as in any business world, on effective 'public relations'; and *fourth* that where there is a new relation of time and space there is little possibility of a politics of the workplace, little time, few existing mechanisms for organization, and no fixed workplace for a workplace politics to develop. This throws into question the role and function of 'network sociality' (Wittel 2001). Thus *fifth* and finally we can see a manifest tension for new creative workers, highly reliant on informal networking but without the support of these being underpinned by any institutional 'trade association'. They can only find individual (or 'biographical' as Beck puts it) solutions to systemic problems (Beck 1992).

The dance/rave culture that came into being in the late 1980s as a mass phenomenon has strongly influenced the shaping and contouring, the energizing and the entrepreneurial character of the new culture industries. The scale and spread of this youth culture meant that it was more widely available than its more clandestine, rebellious, 'underground' and style-driven predecessors, including punk.

The level of self-generated economic activity that 'dance-party-rave' organization entailed, served as a model for many of the activities that were a recurrent feature of 'creative Britain' in the 1990s. Find a cheap space, provide music, drinks, video, art installations, charge friends and others on the door, learn how to negotiate with police and local authorities and in the process become a club promoter and cultural entrepreneur. This kind of activity was to become a source of revenue for musicians and DJs first, but soon afterwards for artists, so that the job of 'events organizer' is one of the more familiar of new self-designated job titles. The form of club sociality that grew out of the ecstasy-influenced 'friendliness' of the clubbing years gradually evolved into a more hard-nosed networking, so that an informal labour market has come into being, which takes as its model the wide web of contacts, 'zines', flyers, 'mates', grapevine, 'word of mouth' socializing, which also was a distinctive feature of the 'micro-media' effects of club culture (Thornton 1996). The intoxicating pleasures of leisure culture have now, for a sector of the under thirty-fives, provided the template for managing an identity in the world of work. Apart from the whole symbolic panoply of jargon, clothes, music and identity, the most noted features of this phenomenon were the extraordinary organizational capacities in the setting up and publicizing of 'parties'. Now that the existence of raves and dance parties has become part of the wider cultural landscape having secured the interest and investment of major commercial organizations, it is easy to overlook the energy and dynamism involved in making these events happen in the first place. But the formula of organizing music, dance, crowd and space have subsequently proved to give rise to 'transferable skills', which in turn transform the cultural sector as it is also being opened up to a wider, younger and more popular audience.[8]

The example of the shaping up influence of club culture therefore sets the scene for this chapter. And where patterns of self employment or informal work are the norm, what emerges is a radically different kind of labour-market organization. While inevitably the working practices of graphic designers, website designers, events organizers, 'media office' managers and so on share some features in common with previous models of self-employed or freelance working, we can propose that where in the past the business side of things was an often disregarded aspect of creative identities best looked after by the accountant, now it is perceived as integral and actively incorporated into the artistic identity. This is illustrated in the activities of the Young British artists for whom the commercial aspect of the art world is no longer disparaged but is welcomed and even celebrated. Mentor and tutor to the Goldsmiths graduates, including Damien Hirst,

Professor Michael Craig Martin reputedly encouraged the students to consider the partying and networking they had to do to promote their work as a vital part of the work, not as something separate.[9] He also insisted that artistic values were not incommensurate with entrepreneurial values. To some extent this more openly commercial approach is also part of the logic (though unexpected for leftist critics) of breaking down the divide between high and low culture. If, for example, art is not such a special and exceptional activity, if it ought not to see itself as superior to the world of advertising, then what is to stop the artists from expecting the same kind of financial rewards, expense accounts and fees as the art directors inside the big agencies? The new relation between art and economics marks a break with past anti-commercial notions of being creative. Instead, young people have exploited opportunities around them, in particular their facilities with new media technology and the experience of 'club-culture sociality' with its attendant skills of networking and selling the self and have created for themselves new ways of earning a living in the cultural field.

In this creative economy, older features of working life, including the career pathway, the ladder of promotion, the role of bureaucracy, the 'narrative sociality' of a life spent in a stratified but secure work-place have been rapidly swept away to be replaced by 'network sociality' (Wittel 2001). Work has been re-invented to satisfy the needs and demands of a generation who, 'disembedded' from tradi-tional attachments to family, kinship, community or region, now find that work must become a fulfilling mark of self.[10] In this context more and more young people opt for the insecurity of careers in media, culture or art in the hope of success. In fields like film-making or fashion design there is a euphoric sense among practitioners of by-passing tradition, pre-empting conscription into the dullness of nine to five and evading the constraints of institutional processes. There is a utopian thread embedded in this wholehearted attempt to make-over the world of work into something closer to a life of enthu-siasm and enjoyment. We could also note that for young women, now entering into the labour market as a lifelong commitment instead of a part-time or interrupted accompaniment to family life as a primary career, the expectation that work is satisfying and inherently rewarding has a special significance alongside the need now to be one's own breadwinner.

As one of my own students, who is also a DJ and club promoter, said, it is a matter of asking 'what kind of capitalism does one want to live in?' As she saw it, quoting de Certeau back to me, her own entrepreneurial activities could be seen as a form of 'making do', a means of creating a space within a system that is so all-encompassing that it is difficult to imagine an alternative. To have seemingly circumvented unhappy work and to have come upon a way of earning a living without the feeling of being robbed of identity or of ability is a social phenomenon worthy of sociological attention. But the larger question, of course, is how this fits with the needs of a form of cultural capitalism that is currently re-inventing itself as innocuous or 'soft', at least in its Western forms. For the young woman fashion designer working eighteen-hour days and doing her own sewing to complete an order, 'loving' her work but self-exploiting, she only has herself to blame if things go wrong. After all, she opted for this kind of unstable career choice.[11] This is exactly the scenario described by Bauman in his description of the stealthy ways in which the new capitalism seems to absolve itself from responsibility by creating invisible structures, and by melting down or liquifying the old social order (Bauman 2000a). Self-blame where social structures are increasingly illegible or opaque serves the interests of the new capitalism well, ensuring the absence of social critique.

A further defining feature of new cultural work is that its 'time and space' dynamics, coupled with self-employment, short-term project work and hence an individualized outlook, all contribute to a marked absence of workplace politics in terms of democratic procedures, equal opportunities, anti-discrimination policies and so on. Maybe there can be no workplace politics when there is no workplace, where work is multi-sited. The necessity of speed and the velocity of transaction, along with the mobility and fluidity of individuals, throw into question a defining feature of this kind of work, that is 'reflexivity'. In fact there are several versions of reflexivity currently in circulation. Underpinning both Giddens' and Beck's version is a traditional notion of the unified subject increasingly capable, indeed called upon to undertake self monitoring activities. But in each case reflexivity has retained an abstract character, requiring us to ask, what are the limits of reflexive practice? Is reflexivity applied primarily to the job in hand? Or to put it another way, the socially valuable outcome of reflexivity is yet to reveal itself. We would need some ethnographies of reflexivity before it would be possible to draw any conclusions, or indeed before the actual mechanisms of reflexivity could be assessed. What are its parameters? Under what circumstances does it lead to social critique? If alternately we consider reflexivity as a self-disciplining mode, where subjects of the new enterprise culture are increasingly called upon to inspect themselves and their practices, in the absence of structures of social support (other than individualized counselling services), then reflexivity marks the space of self responsibility, self blame, and is thus a de-politicizing, de-socializing mechanism. 'Where have I gone wrong?'

One way of explaining how and why things go wrong might involve turning to sociology and indeed having recourse to specialist knowledge, which is how Beck actually understands reflexivity as operating. For him it refers to the wider dissemination and application of sophisticated sociological knowledge to the issues with which sociology (or another academic field) has engaged, usually as social problems, and attempted to explain. (In the UK this is most apparent in the concept of the 'moral panic' in relation to youth culture; see McRobbie and Thornton 1995.) Thus with an increasingly highly educated population it might be surmised that critical reflexivity becomes a more widespread practice. But how does this tally with Bauman's argument that the more difficult are the social structures of inequality and injustice to discern, the less likely are people to understand how the society actually operates? At present and in the 'trade press' for the creative sector there is no obvious point of entrance for sociological explanations, since this medium considers such knowledge as old-fashioned or irrelevant. This is partly the result of the pervasive success of neoliberal values, their insinuating presence in the culture and media sector, and their successful discrediting of the political vocabulary associated with the left and with feminism including equal opportunities, anti-discrimination, workplace democracy, trade-union representation etc. The only site for the dissemination of these values is actually the academy, the place of training or education of the creatives. But whether or not these are remembered or acted upon or cast aside is an open question. Only anecdotal evidence exists.[12]

The extent to which the new world of work directly contributes to the decline of political society is a clear gain for the free-market economy. In the cultural sector where, for reasons of its emphasis on the creative and expressive, it might be imagined that this could be the right place for social minorities to succeed and for women to achieve equal participation, it now seems possible that quite the opposite is happening. What we see (although of course clear visibility is obscured in the labyrinthine and endlessly mutating, and thus sociologically hard-to-track, chains of networking) is the emergence of working practices that reproduce older patterns of marginalization (of women and people from different ethnic backgrounds) while also disallowing any space or time for such issues to reach articulation. In a field of power and competition, if there is no representation from subordinate or disadvantaged groups then inevitably dominant groups will happily reproduce their own structures of access and exclusion.[13] In this case the club culture question of 'are you on the guest list?' is extended to recruitment and personnel, so that getting an interview for contract creative work depends on informal knowledge and contacts, often friendships. Once in the know about who to approach (the equivalent of finding where the party is being held), it is then a matter of whether the recruitment adviser 'likes you' (the equivalent of the bouncer 'letting you in'), and all ideas of fairness or equal representation of women or of black or Asian people (not to say the disabled) fly out of the window.

In this new and so-called independent sector (see Leadbeater and Oakley 1999) there is less and less time left in the long-hours culture to pursue 'independent work'. The recent attempts by the large corporations to innovate in this sector means that the independents are in effect dependent sub-contracted suppliers. And where such contracts are to be had, but in a context of increasing competition from so many other creative companies capable of providing similar services, it is hard to imagine there is time and space for private reading never mind wider critical debate. (As Lash and Urry comment '.... information technology can...erode the critical crafts of reading and writing. What Agger calls "fast capitalism" undermines the power of the book' (Lash and Urry 1994, p. 324). And after hours, in the dedicated club/networking space, with free vodka on tap all night, thanks to the sponsorship of the big drinks companies, who would dare to ask 'uncool' questions about the minimal representation of women and non-white young people, about who the big clients are, and what they do with the product, and about the downside of the 'talent-led' economy? In an atmosphere of businesslike conviviality overseen by accomplished public relations people, the emphasis on presentation of self is incompatible with a contestatory demeanour. Personal angst, nihilism or mere misgivings (see Giddens 1991) must be privately managed and, for the purposes of club sociality, carefully concealed.[14] This is a public relations meritocracy where the question of who gets ahead on what basis and who is left behind finds no space for expression, in that speed and risk negate ethics, community and politics.

The Demise of the Indies?

It is incumbent upon we social scientists and cultural studies academics to develop a vocabulary and a methodology for tracing freelance pathways in the cultural sector. We need to be able to understand at the level of experience how this terrain is negotiated. There remains a chasm of difference between middle-aged academics for whom the university sector has provided a single sourced income more or less since graduation and young people whose portfolio careers increasingly mean not serial jobs but multi-tasking. This latter becomes necessary partly because there is no cushion of welfare to cover periods between jobs, also because labour costs are falling in the cultural sector, and finally because creative work, as various studies have shown, is simply low-paid work except for those at the very top.[15] Since 1998 I have been engaged in a tracking research study of freelance, self-employed and contract creative workers, a handful of whom are fashion designers who participated in my earlier study (see McRobbie 1998). For them, the kind of conditions that prevailed in the 'independent' cultural scene in London and in other UK cities between 1986 and 1996, which were detailed in my study, are very much a thing of the past. Despite the hardship faced by the fashion designers I interviewed, including the long hours and the difficulties of maintaining a cash flow, the luxury they had, as my more recent respondents see it, was of being able to concentrate on their 'own work'. This sector of independent fashion design has been swept away as the high-street chains are able to translate the catwalk styles into off-the-peg items literally within days. Likewise, with the spiralling of urban property values there are fewer opportunities for finding cheap centrally located market stalls. By the end of the 1990s the only way to be 'independent' was to be 'dependent' on *Kookai, Debenhams, Topshop*; indeed the only way fashion design could survive was to sign up with a bigger company and more or less relinquish 'creative independence'. The corrosion of creativity was further achieved as the chain stores 'adopted' less than a handful of graduate stars a year and often discarded them within the year. No state-supported infrastructure for young and struggling designers working from tiny outlets now remains, with the demise of 'dole' and its replacement by the Job Seekers' Allowance, and a range of Business Start-Up Schemes that provide advice only. The Prince of Wales Trust only offers a loan scheme for up to £5,000 for the under thirties.

Thus fashion designers become a scattered and disconnected profession. They can no longer be found in key city-centre locations. The small shops are all gone, Hyper Hyper (the unit space for up-and-coming designers situated in Kensington High Street, London), disappeared in 1998, and the question might be asked what happens now to the annual crop of 4,000 fashion graduates? The answer is that they are now advised to play safe and get a job with a high-street retailer. A tiny number are recruited by the European fashion houses or by the American conglomerates and one or two are awarded grants in competition. Hence I think we can surmise that there is a decline in creativity, as the incubation period that was documented in my earlier research becomes increasingly unviable. There is nothing like the vibrancy and the collective (and competitive) spirit that character-ized the earlier period. Fashion-design graduates today must become multi-skilled. If they are doing a collection it will be at weekends, or perhaps in the odd day they can find between other jobs. Typically, magazines like *I-D* find ways of celebrating this new scenario. In a recent article (which actually appeared shortly after I gave a public lecture on this very topic) the journalist wrote, 'Fashion multi-taskers: suddenly they're everywhere...And it's addictive. Once you've tried doing four jobs you'll never want anything less'...'Its no longer necessary to be a full-time anything to be successful and respected' (Rushton 2001).

This well reflects the kind of upbeat business-minded euphoria that is a characteristic of the sector. So much for reflexivity. (This comment might also be counter-posed with that of the student quoted earlier, who saw herself trying to create a modified capitalism by her DJ work.) When it is inconceivable that the main trade magazine shows itself capable of seriously reflecting on conditions in the sector, and on the fact that fashion design could cease to exist if it is more and more difficult to produce, show and sell a collection independently, then magazines like *The Face*, *I-D* and *Dazed and Confused* demon-strate themselves to be remarkably disengaged, complicit with change per se. These changes come from the increased presence of the big brands. The large companies need to innovate and to develop a more experimental youth-driven image, and this is provided by the second wave of young cultural entrepreneurs hiring out their services on a contractual basis. But what is squeezed out in this process is inde-pendence and socially engaged, critical creativity. The same is true for many of the other creative sectors. Freelance economies in the field of film or video production cannot, for example, take the strain of turning down work to free up time to make, let us say, a short documentary film uncommissioned and with no apparent destination. Instead, cultural production is increasingly driven by the imperatives of market and consumer culture, and the banality of pop promos and TV and cinema advertising is concealed by the technological eupho-ria, the association of newness and youthfulness and, of course, by the parties, the celebrity culture and the cheque in the post. Granted, there are still fashion designers, architects, writers, artists, musicians and other creative occupations but being a specialist rather than a multi-skilled 'creative' is becoming a thing of the past and a mark of being over thirty-five.[16] The norm now is a kind of middle-class 'ducking and diving'. In the shift from the first to the second wave

of creative economy in the New Labour enterprise culture, the kind
of small-scale economies of the decade from the mid 1980s to mid
1990s have all but disappeared. Thus we could say that the cultural
entrepreneurialization set in motion during the Thatcher years has in
the Blair period been almost fully accomplished. Of course it is
important to avoid a crude determinism, which first claims there to
be a deterioration in critical creative work and then accounts for this
along the lines described above. It is not therefore my intention to
engage here with questions of cultural value, but rather to point to
a process of creative compromise. There is more and more culture,
more visual work, more novels being published, more music being
produced, more magazines being launched and at the same time the
shift from there being 'independent work' to there being any number
of freelance workers is also a shift in the balance of power from a
social 'milieu of innovation' to a world of individual 'projects'.

The Loneliness of the Long-Distance Incubator

It is as though culture were suddenly embraced by New Labour
coming into office as an unexpected source of economic regeneration
(as in the *Cool Britannia* episode). Here is something (a last gasp of
Empire) that could be packaged cheaply for export (to include some
of its own home-grown post-colonial talent), it didn't seem to be
looking for substantial state hand-outs because, thanks to Mrs
Thatcher, these 'kids' had learnt how to fend for themselves, and
finally of course, this is what 'we' have always been good at: pop
groups, fashion design, pop-art, 'working-class' youth culture. What
good fortune. No need for planning when artistic types have always
enjoyed chaotic and disorganized ways of working. In fact, there are
many issues that New Labour does not want to discuss, including the
lack of social insurance (and the prohibitively high cost of private
insurance), competition from abroad (already the UK's lead in innovative fashion design is in decline), new social, spatial and other
divides regarding access to cultural fields (e.g. the high cost of living
in London), the social consequences of a fully individuated and
network-oriented creative labour market, and the long-term costs and
sociological consequences of Britain's eventually finding as a solution
to the globalization of the economy, its own Post-Fordism on its
doorstep and on the streets.

Let me conclude by rehearsing some of the features that serve to
consolidate new (and never spoken about) structural divides in the
cultural economy. *First* if the club is the hub, then age and domestic

responsibilities define patterns of access and participation. While sociologists have pointed to the increasing impact of age in changing labour markets (especially for women, see Walby 1997) in the creative sector there is simultaneously a stretching out of the contours of youthfulness (i.e. middle youth) through the marketing of lifestyle goods to the under fifties, and also a retrenchment and re-marking of boundaries, in that the new ways of working bear the hallmark of the rave culture generation. The night-time economy of club culture translates directly into the long-hours' culture of new media and creative work. This is obviously incompatible with having children, and certainly incompatible with being, for example, a single parent. Work merges with leisure and when a deadline must be met, friends might lend their support and work through the night (described in McRobbie 1998). The assumed youthfulness and the impregnable space of the club suggests that these are not such 'open-minded' spaces. Of course all occupational groups develop their own ways of working, nor is the club *per se* a novelty for artistic and creative persons. But there is an irony in that alongside the assumed openness of the network, the apparent embrace of non-hierarchical working practices, the various flows and fluidities (see Lash and Urry 1994), there are quite rigid closures and exclusions. The cultural and creative sectors have in the past in the UK been led and administered by the public sector. Academics have also had a role to play. But a close reading of the recent Green Paper 'Culture and Creativity Ten Years On' (DCMS 2001) implies that this will change dramatically, as artists and creative individuals are freed from the constraints of bureaucracy and 'red tape'. As the whole sector is more thoroughly entrepreneurialized there will be less need for the infrastructures of state; indeed, it is argued that it will be to the advantage of the artists that administration will be cut. The result? Artists and cultural personnel will be free to carry on with what they do unhindered. Academics will be kept well out of the picture; indeed, if the recent Cultural Entrepreneur Club is a model, their presence will be occasional and by invitation only. What warrants the presence of those who are not 'good for business'?[17]

The *second* structural dynamic is that of qualification. The conventions associated with the traditional CV and the job application process are nothing short of overturned in the network culture, and yet patterns do re-emerge. Top or 'branded' universities promise graduates better access to big companies seeking to outsource creative work, and the same holds true for appointments with venture capitalists. Universities and colleges become key sites for developing the social skills for the network (once again often as party organizers)

so, for the 45 per cent of young people who at present do not enjoy
three years of higher education, this is a further absence of opportunity. (It is also unlikely that mature students who are concentrated
in poorer universities are in a position to immerse themselves in the
hedonistic and expensive culture of networking.) Third there is the
spatial dynamic, with only a few urban centres providing anything
like the cultural infrastructure for gainful employment in creative
fields. With a handful of private–public partnerships now replacing
the kind of city cultural policies for regeneration pursued in the 1980s
and into the early 1990s, there is the appearance of shadow culture
industries in Glasgow, Manchester and Nottingham (all of which
have large student populations), while, as Leadbeater reports, Cardiff
Bay has also seen the development of a thriving new media sector
(Leadbeater 1999). But this leaves vast tracks of the country more or
less untouched by the work opportunities provided by the cultural
and creative network and it creates an enormous imbalance between
London where, at least in the short term, freelance curators and art-
project managers can have five jobs on the go at once (and thus juggle
the bank balance around the cash-flow) and elsewhere where 'portfolio income' is replaced by at best 'one job at a time', usually with
spaces of no work in between. (Is London also disembedded and
individuated, a city state with its own speeded up economy? What
distortions occur as a result of this 'lifted out' status?)

Age, gender, ethnicity, region and family income re-emerge like
phantoms (or in Beck's terminology 'zombie concepts' dead but still
alive) from the disguised hinterland of this new soft capitalism and
add their own weight to the life chances of those who are attempting
to make a living in these fields (Beck 2000). As Lisa Adkins argues,
new forms of re-traditionalization begin to have an impact on the
participation of disadvantaged social groups and minorities (Adkins
1999). Adkins is suggesting that where state-provided supports disappear and community weakens, and where individuated persons
operate on a more self-reliant basis, in this case in the new cultural
economy, then there will almost inevitably be a process of having to
fall back on traditional forms of support. This can mean a return to
more rigid gender roles for women. For example being excluded from
the network because of children, or finding it difficult to avoid repro-
ducing traditionally patriarchal family forms. Such changes are also
the result of the double process of neoliberal successes in the field of
work and the negating of the values of the left and the women's
movement. *Third* and finally, there is the sheer incommensurability
of working patterns in the creative network with existing official,
governmental and social science paradigms. (Even the recent Green

Paper fails to appreciate the growth of multi-taskers in the arts.) There is as yet no category for the curator/ project manager/ artist/ website designer who is transparently multi-skilled and ever willing to pick up new forms of expertise, who is also constantly finding new niches for work and thus inventing new jobs for him/herself (e.g. incubator/creative agent), who is highly mobile, moving from one job or project to the next, and in the process also moving from one geographical site to the next. Social interaction is fast and fleeting, friendships need to be put on hold, or suspended on trust and when such a non-category of multi-skilled persons is extended across a whole sector of young working people, there is a sharp sense of transience, impermanence and even solitude (Auge 1995).

Research on these areas would have to consider the specifically gendered and ethnic consequences of individualization. The existing methodologies of the social sciences might well be brought into crisis by the fluidity and hyper-mobility of these agents. There are a number of other points of tension or ambivalence, which also throw our older political paradigms into crisis. In the past I have taken issue with those who have considered the ambition and energy, the glamour and desire for success on the part of these young people as evidence of their either being complicit with the aims and ambitions of the project set in motion by Mrs Thatcher, or else of their being ideologically bludgeoned into believing the Hollywood dream (McRobbie 1999). My argument was that it was quite possible to adhere to principles of social justice, and gender and racial equality while working in the seemingly glamorous world of the culture industries. Of course in the absence (yet again) of studies that systematically tracked creative employment with political sensibility, my comments were based on working closely with students who would be entering or who already had entered these fields. The accelerated speed of cultural working in the second wave marks however an intensification of individuation, a more determined looking out for the self. At this point the possibility of a revived, perhaps re-invented, radical democratic politics, which might usefully de-individuate and re-socialize the world of creative work, is difficult to envisage.

To conclude, if the instruments of the social sciences are challenged by the flows of creative individuals, and likewise the vocabularies of social democratic practice seem ill-equipped for the new mobile work-sites of cultural capitalism, so also is it the case that the identity of these cultural workers as bounded by the characteristics of 'British creativity' is a quite profound misnomer. The creative work the government wants to flag up is less British than is assumed.[18] Many are producing for a global market; as mobile subjects the political peculiarities of the nation state begin to look either insular, or restrictive, for example in relation to work practices and migration law. This undermines the value of a vocabulary of political culture bound by nation. The second wavers are redescribing culture and creativity as we know them, transcending and traversing a multiplicity of boundaries that come tumbling down in an 'ecstasy of communication'. We cultural studies academics might teach these young people in the relatively fixed space of the seminar room, but once they enter the world of work, our encounters with 'incubators' and others are increasingly estranged and contingent.

2

Unpacking the Politics of Creative Labour

The Romance of Being Creative

The June 2013 issue of *Vice* magazine attracted a good deal of attention across the UK media for its fashion shoots based on the 'favoured' modes of suicide by a number of famous women writers, including Sylvia Plath and Virginia Woolf. Castigated widely for bad taste as well as for glamorizing suicide, the magazine nevertheless gained extensive publicity while also confirming its outsider, or underground reputation as a media space that speaks directly to a section of youth educated well enough to recognize the narratives and mythologies that have existed for decades around the tragic circumstances and untimely deaths of these women, while also appreciating the dark humour, the editorial risk-taking and the irony, the implied quotation marks saying that 'no harm is intended'. *Vice* magazine has for many years pursued this pathway most infamously with the fashion space it gave to so-called 'wife beating T-shirts' (i.e. worn by working-class /blue-collar male characters in films featuring scenes of domestic violence). In this respect *Vice* is similar to many of the other avant-garde style and fashion magazines, including *Dazed and Confused*, *Tank*, *Another* and *Love*, all of which ride on a tide of masculine hipster kudos, which relishes the opportunity to endorse an anti-political correctness ethos, and which entails a disavowal of feminism as old-fashioned, and holds at bay, editorially, any notion of serious ethical or political engagement, in favour of being ahead of trends, being in touch with the kind of attitude that will eventually translate into consumer lifestyles. In recent years *Vice* magazine has turned

masculine hipster kudos ethos

into a huge media company but, more generally, this bandwagon of 'hipsterdom' is reliant on how well magazines like these generate advertising revenue, or gain a lot of exposure for being 'in the know' and it is this that keeps them afloat and also pays for the salaries or freelance incomes of those who are involved in the production process. Several of these publications are also underwritten by huge corporations such as *LVMH* while masquerading as independent, in much the same way that big record companies often support 'indie' labels without drawing attention to this fact, thereby allowing the label or magazine to act as a kind of trailblazer for new trends or new music, while also garnering cultural credentials on the basis of seeming editorial freedom. These cultural gatekeepers or tastemakers are people whose role is to give unique shape to the consumer landscape of the new culture industries. In many ways the figure of the 'hipster' embodies this constellation of forces that drives the precise forms taken by these urban economies, differing from place to place, while also registering remarkably similar features, pushing up property values in what were inner city areas, contributing to changes in the retail landscape, presenting an image of artistic activity and upmarket nightlife in the form of cuisine and authentic breweries and so on. These spaces become what Sassen called 'urban glamour zones' even when they are located in small and seemingly insignificant outlying neighbourhoods (Sassen 2002).

With the financial crisis of 2008 and with the soaring rates of unemployment across Europe particularly affecting young people, it could be argued that the high expectations about the creative economy are now being played down, and the bubble has burst. On the contrary I propose that instead we see new kinds of pathways being created under the label of innovation, and at the ground level we see young people cling on with more determination than ever to making a living in these alley-way micro-economies.[1] For example, reports in the local Berlin media describe how young unemployed Italians have been coming to live in the city with its relatively cheap accommodation. Then, with help from friends, they find their way through the benefit (or *Hartz IV*) system to which they are entitled as EU citizens. This in turn permits a bridge from welfare to work, and through this pathway they can get set up as internet start-ups, as artists, DJs, or as fashion designers (see Chapter 5).[2] So my contention, developed across the pages of this book, is that there is a *dispositif* that drives the growth of the new creative industries, and this has a triple function. It oversees novel forms of job creation (in times of both unemployment and under-employment), the defining features of which are impermanent, short-term, project-based or temporary positions; it orchestrates an expansion of the middle classes in the light of the policies adopted by most national governments in recent years to increase the numbers of students attending universities and art colleges and at the same time it supports the creative activities of this *arriviste* middle class, allowing them to act as guinea pigs for testing out the new world of work without the full raft of social security entitlements and welfare provision that have been associated with the post-Second World War period. Lazzarato, reflecting from the viewpoint of cultural workers, on the changes to the French welfare system, understands these as a wholesale 'reconstitution of society' (Lazzarato 2012). My argument here is that we see a kind of new assemblage of the middle class, with a wide range of 'instruments' and 'toolkits' coming into play to oversee and manage this transformation. The creative workforce may be relatively small, but it is being trained up to pave the way for a new post-welfare era. Such a workforce might include some of the children of the more privileged middle classes, but my sociological emphasis here will, where possible, look more closely at those who have found themselves within this cohort in recent years, coming from lower middle-class or upper working-class backgrounds.[3] Nowadays we also see a remarkable influx of young women in the direction of these kinds of jobs, from across the boundaries of class. With this inflation of graduates from the fine arts, design, media and humanities subjects entering into this largely self-organized labour market, I ask a number of questions. Are these young people simply taking on the same kind of risks that have always characterized small business entrepreneurship, in which case the absence of benefits and entitlements such as sickness pay are par for the course? Or is this a different kind of undertaking, one that does not quite match with the typical small business model? I look at the self-employment strategies, the freelance work and the new modes of 'self-entrepreneurship', which develop within a recently expanded sector of creative and artistic activity. If it were just a matter of almost self-flagellating patterns of 'new sweated labour' in the name of creativity, we might imagine short bursts of activity in the early years, followed by retreat into something more sustainable. Nowadays retreat is not really an available option in this era of post-industrial society and in times of austerity and high unemployment. As a result, what we find in the longer term are integrated combinations of high and lower-status activities and occupations. The seemingly exciting compensation for work without protection is the personal reward of 'being creative'. One's inner talents and abilities, instead of being lost or expended or unused in the daily grind of office or routine work, never finding an outlet because of nine to five demands, are nowadays used, indeed cultivated, on a daily basis. We can call this passionate work or we can call it working like an artist, but it functions overall as a way of acclimatizing these new social strata to a different kind of existence from that associated with routine work such as administrative or managerial posts in the public sector, including its arts, educational and cultural institutions. That is to say, it provides a set of career pathways away from normal to abnormal work (Beck 2000).

There are several themes introduced in the following pages and developed in the course of this book: there are the actual modes and styles of cultural working in the contemporary urban environment: then there is the way in which in recent years 'business models' have come to dominate the various pathways open to those young people pursuing a career in the arts and culture. In the past, this would have been rather reluctantly adopted by recently graduated fashion designers; now it has become a prerequisite across the whole range from the visual arts, through graphic design, to documentary film-making, stage design to performance art. There is the appearance, mentioned already, of a distinctive social group, or middle-class faction, whose careers, unlike those of their parents, are no longer underwritten by the statutory rights and entitlements associated with the post-war welfare regime. There is a visible interest in the idea of 'passionate work', and the expectation of 'happiness at work' (McRobbie 2002). To some extent middle-class status nowadays rests upon the idea that work is something to which one has a passionate attachment. I first encountered this high degree of affective attachment some years ago when I carried out interviews with young British fashion designers, mostly female, all of whom declared this kind of personal investment in work, despite long hours and low returns (McRobbie 1998). Indeed, the idea of happiness at work or 'pleasure in work', as Donzelot puts it, marks out the institutional terrain for new forms of post-welfare governmentality (Donzelot 1991). The argument posed by Donzelot is that when people love their job the role of the trade unions is diminished, reflecting, as I discuss later, the orchestrations by governments in the UK from Mrs Thatcher onwards to dismantle organized labour. Donzelot sees the enriching 'self-management' strategies developed by employers in the same light. Looking at industrial jobs and at the social-welfare regimes that came into being to counter or compensate for the frustrations of monotonous work, Donzelot charts the problems posed by absenteeism as the 'social cost of productivity', which in effect gives rise to the new science of 'management' developed in the US Business Schools. With a focus still on actual employment (rather than freelance work and self-employment)

Donzelot summarizes and condenses the shift of government and employers attention away from the post-Second World War social democratic question of industrial democracy, to the emergent US-led MBA culture that seeks to develop the individual capacities of the worker, making him 'responsible and autonomous'. In my own previous work on UK fashion designers I stepped right outside the framework of normal work into the much more informal world of small-scale fashion design, showing how in this sphere of self-management there is an expectation of pleasure in the work itself, such that it functions as a rationale for embarking on an otherwise perilous career (McRobbie 1998). These entanglements of desire and 'capture' (a term we find often used by the Italian social theorist Paulo Virno) are critical of how careers are both established and maintained as young women (and men) navigate a way through the offices of the new more flexible institutions of the state, and as they are required to present themselves as potential recipients of internships, work-placement schemes and workfare programmes. What starts as an inner desire for rewarding work is re-translated into a set of techniques for conducting oneself in the uncertain world of creative labour.

Such issues as these apply to a cohort of relatively young people, often, though not always, educated to degree level, with qualifications across the range of social sciences and arts and humanities subjects, for whom career expectations can be characterized by this high level of uncertainty, and for whom jobs and projects seem to be 'permanently transitional'. These young men and women are typically living in cities that have a wide range of institutions, organizations and corporations devoted to arts, media, culture and creative economy. Such cities will also be host to major institutions and whole departments of government concerned with and overseeing activities in the cultural sector. Policies emanating from such offices along with the hiring strategies of major media companies, as well as fashion retailers and a host of other design-related organizations, function to create the kinds of labour markets towards which these same young people nowadays gravitate; there is a magnet effect and a kind of convergence. I have already briefly drawn attention to the question of the class composition as well as the gender of this new urban workforce and I will be interrogating these in the course of the book; let me just here flag up that the raft of equality measures of the type we associate with mainstream normal employment is often suspended if not reversed in this cruel (if also seemingly 'cool') environment where the US 'start-up' mentality prevails, or where the sheer 'pleasure of work' is assumed to compensate for workplace security and protection.

Here we can see how the governmentality aspect of anticipated pleasure or promise of workplace sociability functions to close down awkward issues around race or sex discrimination.

Actually I must quickly offer some qualifications. This is not an account of a particular group of creative practitioners, neither is it a work that pursues an empirical pathway. My subject of investigation, or at least one among several, is rather the more nebulous question of the 'romance' of this style of working, and how this romance is translated at an institutional level so that it functions as a kind of *dispositif*, a self-monitoring, self-regulating mechanism. Foucault describes the *dispositif* as 'a thoroughly heterogenous ensemble consisting of discourses, institutions, architectural forms, regulatory decisions, laws, administrative measures…the system of relations that can be established between the elements' (Foucault 1980, p. 194) Creativity is designated by current modes of biopolitical power, as the site for implementing job creation and, more significantly, labour reform; it is a matter of managing a key sector of the youthful population by turning culture into an instrument of both competition and labour discipline. The word culture fades into the background and is replaced by creativity. It is a deployment of power to encourage self-actualization through being creative. It is a matter of putting creativity to work. With such efforts invested in turning culture into the more productive idea of creativity, the social stage where this creativity is played out is also a site of multiple anxieties. What I offer here is an account of new work where creativity is a practice of self-romanticism. Drawing on the concept of line of flight from Deleuze, 'where mutations and differences produce not just the progression of history but disruptions, breaks, new beginnings', the romance here is the 'line of flight' the desire to escape a lifetime of routine work, let us say in a local taxation office, or in life insurance (albeit with a university degree) and the wish to lead a self-directed life in regard to work and career (Deleuze 1987; Colebrook 2002, p. 57). This motivation towards self-expressive work now intersects with and is nurtured as well as managed by the prevailing governmental discourse of business, entrepreneurship and self-organized work across this particular terrain. This looks like a happy and fortuitous coming together of forces, the desires of young people for self-expressive opportunities in life and work are being taken up by providers of training, and by colleges and universities. In fact this convergence marks out the precise site for labour struggle outside the conventional workplace. From the point of view of the young black British woman from a working-class background who has graduated in media studies, the element of struggle to work in film and television is

articulated through an often family based narrative of s॰
doing the menial and repetitive jobs that her mother
Labour struggle here means the battle to overcome ma
vantage and everyday prejudices in order to get through ॰॰॰॰॰ ॰॰॰
into university and from there into interesting work. The politics is
generated mostly in the home and community, not from any experience of the 'shop-floor'. Family is the 'line of flight'. Although frequently understood as such at a common-sense level, this is not just
a matter of upward mobility.[4] Later in this book I will argue that the
line of flight comprises a distinct mode of individuated, 'deterritorial-
ized' and then 'reterritorialized' labour struggle, as an array of disciplinary technologies descend upon these subjects from so many offices
of the state, working through and with this desire for freedom and
enjoyment in work, and for self-expression. The conditions of such
an individuated state of 'sociality' are themselves the outcome of the
post-Fordist scenario, which I use here as a summary for a multiple
set of profound transformations of production and labour processes
entailing new entanglements of class, race and gender. The invention
of techniques and apparatuses then introduced or unrolled across
various institutions and social spaces, expands upon and enlarges that
process described by Rose as the 'power of freedom' (Rose 1996,
2008). With the aim of transforming 'culture' into creative economy,
arguably a defining feature of the New Labour government, there
was generated a small mountain of government reports, white papers
and various other policies emanating from the UK Department of
Culture, Media and Sport from 1997 onwards.

If the impulse of the line of flight is to work (in the sense of actually earning a living) like an artist, a musician, a writer or a designer,
or in the orbit of art and design and media worlds, then such desires
gather momentum so that they can be seen as distinctive cultural or
subcultural formations (such as punk in the mid 1970s, or artist-
bohemians today). Nowadays these phenomena seem to be formed,
almost from inception, within a wide range of inciting practices of
governmentality, including the prevailing discourses that inform and
give content to the school or academic or 'art school' curriculum. In
recent years these are full of business modules for fine-art students
or 'toolkits' for setting up as a fashion designer. These pedagogic
instruments have a strongly subjectivizing capacity as they are directed
towards individuals in all of their uniqueness and distinctiveness (e.g.
taking the form of one-to-one mentoring), nevertheless there is also
a commonality, a familiar framework emerges, which crystallizes into
ways of speaking, ways of engaging, ways of comporting the self,
expressing enthusiasm, withholding a critical disposition etc., all of

which have their own distinctive rhythms, pleasures and excitements (Bandinelli 2016). There are so many 'opportunities' in these facilitating devices and instruments and they operate through 'capture'; that is to say, something of the wide capacities, enthusiasm and critical intellect of people are precisely what is captured by power and actively used then to replenish and innovate so that capitalist production is seemingly radicalized and made more interesting and exciting and also apparently concessionary or tuned into the demands of its subjects (Virno 2005). These processes produce noticeable subjective outcomes; the toolkit approach, for example, is highly normative, offering little space for negative subjective states such as moodiness or bad temper, ironically the 'depths' historically associated with the artistic temperament, so there is an ironing out of 'bad affect' and a flattening effect. The correctly trained artist is no longer expected to be shy or retiring or even too quiet. And the whole point of customized or individualized mentoring means that the line of flight based on coming from a specific family or community background, is brought into play as a defining feature and an attribute, as part of the way in which the pedagogies of entrepreneurial subjectification seek out and do their work of capture. The kind of person you are, the background you come from, your 'story' is the contact point for how the toolkit then unfolds.[5] This current range of programmes, including whole degree programmes, and more often short courses as well as individual learning packages, designed to guide or supervise or support the individual, marks out the terrain of how the *dispositif* of contemporary power works.

Despite periods of disenchantment and uncertainty, both occluded publicly by the imperative to self-present in a cheerful if not exuberant fashion, there is a hard-edged incentive to keep going and maintain a professional stance. This is a key part of the 'middle-classification' process. It also reduces the prospects for the formation of a more oppositional or collective movement of 'creative workers' since these are not workers in the conventional sense. Professionalism, an adjunct to middle-class status, is extended to these informal activities such as freelance and precarious work, where in the past it was associated only with occupations such as teaching, law, medicine etc. Of course there has been in existence the idea of the professional artist or professional writer or musician, and the advertising industry has also played a significant role in professionalizing creative practices such as graphic design and copywriting. Professionalism in these occupations has been synonymous with specialism, expertise, qualification, accreditation and possibly membership of an association. In addition, some of the strongest trade unions, such as BECTU[6] or Equity, do serve as representational bodies for creative workers such as actors, journalists, media technicians and so on. However, this is hard to sustain in a world of fast-evolving specialisms as well as widespread multi-tasking. BECTU, for example, has fought to protect the specialisms of its workforce threatened with the de-skilling impact of digitalization and new social media (Gandini 2014). And in both unions (as well as with *Les Intermittentes* as described by Lazzarato) membership regulations are tightly controlled (Lazzarato 2012). The new creatives themselves are faced with the challenge of formulating an occupational identity that gives weight and status to what they do, in conditions where it is uncertain from where the next job or project is actually coming. The question of a more oppositional stance to the precarious nature of this sort of work emerging is countered by the sheer need to keep going and to maintain the middle-class professionalism and the upbeat demeanour that the toolkits and instruments take for granted under the rubric of having the right kind of 'personality' for the work. At the same time, wider social factors also have a role to play in influencing the stances, professional or otherwise, of those working in this creative sector. The period I investigate in this book is the fifteen-year span, which opens with the election of the New Labour government in 1997, and closes in 2012 amid unprecedented levels of youth and graduate unemployment, especially in countries like Spain and Italy, so badly hit by the Eurozone crisis. This first decade from 1997 to 2007 was a period during which the *dispositifs* of UK governmentality and the new entrepreneurialism were seemingly uninterrupted by challenge and contestation coming from within the ranks of the new young creative workers. Behind the scenes of the New Labour government, great efforts were made to reduce the power and influence of the trade-union movement, and overall there was a tendency to de-politicize the realm of work. As Brown suggests, 'the New Labour branding had been specifically aimed at erasing any memories that the Party was influenced by trade unions' (Brown 2011, p. 5). In a strategy that extended the stance adopted by Mrs Thatcher when in office, New Labour shunned its historic connection with the trade unions, they were shunted aside, demonized and castigated for being old-fashioned or out of touch, or with being too closely connected with the so-called 'militancy' of the old left. During this time the 'lines of flight' came to be harnessed to the so-called talent-led economy.[7] Here we could say capture was almost effective, and the obvious question is, what were the factors that stifled critical engagement? My answers to these questions are spread across the pages that follow, predicated, for example, upon the popular sway that a widely disseminated *dispositif* of creativity could have when governments worked together so successfully with the media and popular culture, and hingeing likewise on the unlikelihood of 'organized labour' emerging from this fragmented band of new cultural entrepreneurs. During these times there was a hollowing out of radical politics from the vocabularies of art and creative economy in favour of competition and commerce, and this has had a significant effect especially in London where the celebration of talent seemed to diffuse or displace the need for consideration of working practices or for addressing questions such as low pay or poverty wages across the terrain of the new culture industries.[8] These were the Damien Hirst times.

Re-Making the Middle Class Through Creative Labour

The question of how we understand the social composition of what seems to be a relatively youthful, new middle class faction, is fraught with difficulties. One way of engaging with class in the context of the rise of the new creative economy is found in the writing of Stuart Hall, who offered an analysis of how working-class organizations were broken up and destroyed from the time of the Thatcher government onwards, while at the same time the prospect of moving upwards to join the 'property-owning democracy' was dangled as an opportunity to sections of the skilled and already affluent working class (Hall 1988, 2003, 2011). Mrs Thatcher was determined to destroy the power of the trade unions, and my argument in the pages that follow is that in some ways the sublimated spirit of these organizations lives on in the lines of flight, and in the desires for creative and rewarding work. The trade unions were about more than just the workplace; labour politics resonated across working-class families and communities and came to be embedded in distinctive cultural forms, as we know from the writing of Raymond Williams. There is a continuity between these struggles and contemporary tensions that exist within and across the space of the new culture industries, even as the 'new managerialism' works to use this as a key space for labour reform. I would propose that a familial or community ethos has a role to play in the 'refusal of work', as something that is refracted downwards through the generations, as daughters of working-class mothers dream of becoming fashion designers, or documentary film-makers, while simultaneously remembering and memorializing the experiences of their parents. In some ways this is an extension of (and more feminized version of) the argument associated with Hall's work in the mid 1970s on working-class subculture, where the class politics of the parent culture seemingly buried and dormant and co-opted by the prospect of affluence, then takes on a spectacular form through the symbolic expressions of post-war youth cultures (Hall et al. 1976). I would take this a step further now, into the age of creative economy, where subculture has become professionalized, aestheticized, and institutionalized through its formal status in the curriculum of the art school and where creativity co-opts a whole series of cultural practices previously considered informal or socially irrelevant (e.g. young people's activities in music-making or in the production of 'zines', graffiti, or in extravagant street fashion and styles). The more radical lessons learnt from cultural studies can still inflect and inform various forms of professional practice, but these are nowadays forcefully contested and undermined by recent developments in pedagogy that stress entrepreneurialism and the importance of the business plan. These perspectives, one originally from the left, the other from the right, make pedagogy, education and the curriculum key sites for the playing out of new political antagonisms.

With low pay a constant feature of this kind of work, there is the temptation to draw on the Marxist vocabulary of proletarianization, as middle-class young people are tipped downward. The term precarious labour has come to be attached to a faction of middle class, but increasingly economically marginal young people. This proletarian designation is problematic, not just because it has traditionally been linked with the old Marxist teleological notion of an eventually unified working class, now swollen with new members, advancing inexorably towards confrontation with capitalism, but also because for sizeable proportions of the ordinary and non-creative working population, most notably working-class women and migrant workers, labour has always been both precarious and low paid (e.g. seasonal factory work, or catering work). Their vulnerability and economic marginality are not lessened by the fact that freelance designers and film-makers designate themselves as precarious workers. Talking about downward mobility also overlooks the strong emphasis on enhanced status and professionalism within the ranks of the creative workforce who allocate their jobs names such as 'information architect'. In fact there is an inflation of status at the same time as there is a deflation of earning power. Middle-class young people are being pushed towards temporary work, as middle-class values more generally are being extended across the fabric of the society, and especially in the urban terrain. These new occupations carry a nebulous status, existing somewhere between the old professions, the once-secure jobs in the public sector, such as school teaching, and career pathways in the corporate world (e.g. in advertising). Often they co-exist with jobs that normally do not have high status, such as working in shops, behind the counter or waiting on tables, or being a barista or bar tender. Many young creative people pay their rent and cover their living costs through taking these jobs, which in the past would have been called day jobs and, especially when time passes and these jobs offer a reliable if modest monthly income, there is a transposition onto these normal jobs of the same more enhanced and upgraded creative values associated with the idealized career in arts or cultural worlds. The everyday life of the coffee bar, cocktail lounge or local fashion boutique begins to take on the qualities of the knowledge economy, with the workforce not just embodying the attentive values now required of service sector employees, but also acting as experts, guides and connoisseurs.[9] What occurs in these sites of seemingly temporary but often in fact longer-term work is the upgrading of the service sector. When the friendly young man behind the counter at Starbucks enters into a lengthy and animated conversation about the geographical sourcing of the beans, he is doing more than simply following the instructions in his company handbook, he is demonstrating his communicative skills, now such a key requirement in the service sector, and he is also asserting his expertise as well as his broad cultural capital. Bar work and shop work slowly undergo a change that sees the enhancement of status and skill level for those behind the counter, with the result that these jobs now exist alongside, indeed merge into, the overall creative portfolio.

Middle-class livelihoods are being scrambled and unsettled, re-arranged or re-calibrated in regard to long-term expectations. It is not just that the middle class is being squeezed, as current debate in the UK puts it, in regard to the cuts in public spending that the Coalition government have implemented. It is more that there is a major revision of certain key features of the post-war social contract, which entailed universalistic modes of 're-distribution' to the benefit of working-class and lower middle-class people alike, in the form of welfare, social security, health and education. These provisions were compensatory at that point in time when capital was keen to establish a more consensual relation with labour, and they were also to an extent re-distributionist, and thus egalitarian. As Lazzarato reminds us, this 'right to social protection' was also based on recognition of the 'asymmetry of power in the labour contract' (Lazzarato 2012). Robert Castel describes such benefits as 'social property'. In the UK context they were the outcome of sustained struggles fought by the Labour Party, the trade unions and also the second-wave feminist movement. Many of these forms of support are now being withdrawn, and this process of withdrawal takes a wide range of forms and, as I have argued elsewhere, one of the attractions for government of endorsing freelance and small-scale entrepreneurial work in the creative sector is that *tout court* there is a by-passing mechanism in place, since the burden of employment entitlements and other costs is immediately lifted from the shoulders of companies who can only gain when they take on such workers in a freelance or self-employed capacity (McRobbie 2002). Government then pleases the world of business without even having to use the words 'labour reform'. Such changes as these have ramifications across the economy, including the creative economy. If in the past employees of the institutions of the arts and culture, in whatever roles, normally had access to some form of job security as a result of those past battles fought for rights and entitlements, this is no longer the case as they too become freelance, semi-privatized or casually employed. These processes, when they are assembled and seen as a whole process, can be understood as an experimental re-making of the middle class at work where ideas of creativity and innovation compensate for and to an extent obscure the shrinking realm of protection along with welfare and various entitlements.[10]

The Florida Effect: 'Everything Is Rosy'

Richard Florida has been enormously influential in recent years for the kind of road-map he offers to international, national and local politicians across the globe in regard to the potential that culture and creativity have for urban regeneration and growth (Florida 2002).[11] For well over a decade he has been the figurehead of and cheerleader for the creative economy, advocating a business-school model comprising league tables and easily remembered catch-phrases. His success has been in playing an active role in formulating a new language for urban renewal through the role of the 'creative class', a loose journalistic term akin to sector. Florida's primary focus of attention is on cities and on how urban policy can be re-directed to attract the young talented 'creative types' whose presence in the cities is seen to be beneficial to both the local and national economy. Alongside this is his claim (first published in 2002) that growth and prosperity now depends on the activities of this expansive sector of the middle classes who can be described as creative but whose ranks also include accountants, engineers, teachers, hairdressers indeed just about everyone who does not do a manual job working on the factory floor, or a low grade service job in fast food or cleaning. This is huge cohort of people (apparently over 38 m in the United States), which Florida understands as progressive, open-minded and vital to future growth and a successful economy. Others might re-interpret this distinctly non-sociological, descriptive idea of 'creative class' as a privileged group able to push through its interests at the expense of others. Or alternately it could be argued that entrance into the ranks of this sector is now almost a necessity in order to avoid high degrees of social powerlessness. Instead of this kind of consideration, Florida emphasizes how people are able to escape the drudgery of routine and unfulfilling work. He claims that working as a hairdresser nowadays, despite low pay, opens up all sorts of career pathways for creative and talented stylists. While I share with Florida a keen interest in the desire for rewarding work, and the great efforts made to succeed in these fields, I see passionate attachment to creative work as comprising 'lines of flight', embedded familial histories of previously blocked hopes and frustrations. These then have the potential to crystallize into social criticism. Clearly, an argument like this is predicated on an historical and institutional framing, and on the possibility of certain opportunities being available.[12] These need to be looked at in connection with state-provided training and education and, in the UK especially, with those forms of facilitation and support made available during the years of social democracy and local municipal socialism. In the UK a decisive factor was the influential role of the art schools, which were later absorbed into the polytechnics and then into the new universities. Florida pays no attention to the historical conditions, infrastructure, and role of the state in providing education and training for these cohorts of young people. Instead, his frame of reference comprises loose references to focus groups, conversations with his students, personal anecdotes and quantities of empirical data turned into a run of graphs and statistics where a series of correlations presented in a snazzy fashion lends authority to the work as a whole, especially for magazines like *Fast Company*, and presumably for policy-related think tanks and civic leaders. As Peck points out, the endless range of league tables and lists, the ranking of cities according to the so-called Creativity Index and the light-hearted journalistic style of writing, provide a short-cut to winning the attention of policy-makers in need of a fast fix and a novel, upbeat and cheerful kind of approach to urban issues (Peck 2005).

Florida is also inattentive to intractable problems in the urban milieu, which in turn allows those policy people drawn to his work to relax a little, take the foot off the pedal, and concentrate on the rosy future of the creative economy, where the visibility of culture and the arts are sufficient indicators of urban revitalization. He resolutely ignores questions of housing, unemployment or poverty, words such as these are significant by their absence. Likewise by overlooking other sections of the population, the ordinary people who share the same streets and urban environment as the talented creatives, the work itself functions as a 'dividing practice', as though to suggest that cultural policy-makers need pay no attention to wider urban issues. They just need to concentrate on the winners. When seemingly forced to acknowledge the presence of working-class people, Florida says that the young talented members of the creative class can provide role models for their disadvantaged counterparts. This is in sharp contrast to the more familiar egalitarianism of past urban policies. The conservatism of Florida's thinking can best be seen in a few stray comments. He patronizingly describes the woman who cleans his house as a 'gem', who is as entrepreneurial and driven as any of her middle-class clients, and whose husband has a Porsche. No need then for organized labour among the manual workforce or for social security should they fall ill or be injured and unable to carry on cleaning. Likewise, describing the exciting atmosphere of the late-night creative city, he refers *en passant* to the fashion models along-side the 'bag ladies', as though homelessness and mental illness were simply facts of life and part of the urban scenery, contributing edginess and 'grit', rather than signs of extreme poverty and vulnerability. There is no discussion of the pressure the relatively affluent newcomers exert on local housing markets for the less well off. Alert as he is to the widening gap between rich and poor, Florida can only propose that this may be countered by the good examples set by the successful to those further down the ladder.

City leaders and urban policy people are the target for these ideas. What emerges is a new kind of urban policy aimed at pampering and protecting the privileged creative workers, in the hope that they work hard, pay their taxes and contribute to the well-being of the city by serving as role models for the under-privileged. This emphasis on the human capital model, which Florida takes from the neoliberal economist Gary Becker, combines exclusive focus on bolstering the power of the middle class, a recurrent theme in neoliberal thinking dating back to the 1930s and the ordo-liberal Roepke's aim to 'de-proletarianize' society (see Foucault 2008; Hall 2003, 2011), with a definition of both culture and creativity as assets that are to be put to work, and exchanged in the labour market as unique resources. Florida says cities need to attract these talented young people by putting in place the kinds of facilities and resources that will appeal to them, an openness and tolerance regarding gay and lesbian life-styles and a lively environment, which caters to both singles and married couples with young children. So we are left with no uncertainty as to the socially desirables in contrast to the undesirables in this world. Florida urges city policy-makers to provide the kinds of conditions that will be conducive to attracting more of the same type of people. Florida says (in the preface to the paperback edition) 'I'm not saying that gays and bohemians literally cause regions to grow. Rather, their presence in large numbers is an indicator of an underlying culture that's open-minded and diverse and thus conducive to creativity' (Florida 2002, p. xvii). However, this idea of a 'magnet effect' is also limited in terms of understanding the sociohistorical features of labour mobility. Where people go to live and/or work is a good deal more complicated than the allure of certain city environments. In most cases there are major structural reasons that mean people must stay put; one cannot just move somewhere with a portfolio to hand around prospective contacts or clients, unless one is already in possession of a good deal of capital or savings. Florida here can only be referring to a tiny percentage of already well-heeled graduates, without dependants, family commitments or other kinship ties. When faced with critics asking questions like this, Florida simply refers to yet another survey undertaken on 4,000 students, asking them their intentions and desires following graduation. What in reality underpins Florida's approach is the Silicon Valley model of hi-tech start-ups and its enrichment effect on the Bay Area, which can, he implies, be transplanted into the cultural and creative sector. In some respects it is astonishing that this 'everything is rosy' discourse (where under-performing cities can be pulled out of the doldrums if they accept Florida's diagnosis and re-invent themselves accordingly) has gained not just respectability and approval among politicians across the spectrum, but is validated as 'public policy'. In an analysis of the rise of the creative economy in Berlin, for example, Bodirsky shows just how extensively these ideas have been taken on board by policy-makers and the city government, though, as will be shown in Chapter 5 and as Bodirsky herself acknowledges, this is accompanied by waves of opposition on the part of those young designers and artists who are the subjects of the 'Florida effect' (Bodirsky 2012).[13] This confirms the wider success of business-school vocabularies and how-to type perspectives, including lists and league tables, winners and losers. A new agenda for urban policy enters into society through a mix of an upbeat, think-positive, self-consciously 'funky' fast-fix ethos, with the help of a vocabulary directly imported from marketing and public relations. The Florida effect contributes to the production of new middle-class norms, which do not include any wider social responsibilities beyond the framework of their own consumer lifestyle needs and choices. In this world there exists no discussion about hardship within and beyond this social cohort, nor is there any seeming need for institutions to support the less fortunate. The city is lifted out and transformed into a playground for cultural pursuits and pastimes, which has the effect of attracting more of the same kind of people, so as to strengthen the cultural homogeneity (albeit with a few gestures to diversity) and 'enjoyment factor' of the immediate spatial environment. This marks out the contours of the ideal neoliberal dream of the new city space where the power and presence of the middle class is bolstered at the cost of others whose 'right to the city' is now implicitly under question. In addition any historic ideals of public service or of middle-class careers devoted to ameliorating the lives of the under-privileged are swept away in a tide of self-preservation and wellbeing. This constitutes what Lazzarato refers to as a reconstitution of society wherein the new and youthful urban middle classes are able to assert themselves, and envisage themselves in a leading role, as a class in dominance by means of the seemingly innocuous realms of culture and creativity, without seeking recourse to the wider harsh political economy with which it is inextricably connected. In addition the business-school model championed by Florida supplants the long-established social-science tradition, including urban sociology and cultural studies. The light breezy tone, which is always optimistic in its reeling out lists of success stories, league tables and feel-good slogans, is also delivered in a faux-naive manner, incredulous that these truths can be considered controversial. In actuality, this mantle of liberal tolerance disguises the much more adversarial and antagonistic nature of the challenge posed by Florida. The standard emphasis on tackling urban social inequalities is replaced by images of leisure activities, which enhance the well-being of the already privileged. Many words such as poverty, welfare, benefits, social provision, local community after-school clubs and so on are simply erased from the debate. The long-established history of provision inside arts and humanities education for disadvantaged students (disability entitlements, anti-discrimination measures, etc.), which has permitted students (such as Damien Hirst and Tracey Emin) to fulfil their ambitions, is swept away as if it were not significant enough to merit a mention. Instead Florida develops a heady and exciting self-image for the new middle-class urban creatives, one which is indistinguishable from what can be found in any number of advertising campaigns seeking to target this demographic. Despite the seemingly all-inclusive embrace of the creative-class category, it is in fact reserved for high flyers only, or for those who seek to emulate this pathway. More ordinary workers whose ambitions do not coincide with this ideal are as faded out of the picture as those who are vulnerable or 'truly disadvantaged'. With this eviction from the urban landscape so also disappears ideas of equality, and of the long history of municipal socialism. Also forgotten or overlooked are those more embedded forms of radical urbanism and community activism, which did indeed bring writers and artists and other creative people together with disadvantaged populations so as to extend social provisions such as libraries, play areas, theatres, craft workshops and so on. It is this egalitarian model of urban co-operation that is jettisoned in favour of an air-brushed vision of café-society. Florida's work encapsulates the disavowal of sociological explanations, which, as Loïc Wacquant argues, is a prevailing feature of neoliberal public policy (Wacquant 2009). If the 'tough on crime' agenda of zero tolerance and high incarceration rates are the cold edge of urban neoliberalism, its soft cultural side can be seen in Florida's explicitly non-sociological vision of a cleaned up city populated by healthy, youthful-looking and self-reliant citizens.

The Politics of the Hipster Economy?

Urban hipsters can be seen as a composite of various historical and mostly male subcultural figures each associated with an 'ineffable' sense of style, a degree of aloofness and 'cool' disdain, a dandyism and a self-conscious sense of being a *flâneur*. Because they are primarily figures of fashion and lifestyle rather than say musicians or artists, they bring up to date the category of subcultural entrepreneurs whose activities I documented in the late 1980s (McRobbie 1989). Here we could see the self-employment strategies of handfuls of young people, or 'insiders' who sourced, repaired, dry-cleaned and altered selected items of second-hand clothes and fashion pieces that they deemed to be appealing to people like themselves, not just because of their cheapness, but for their uniqueness and their period authenticity. These insiders serviced the needs of youth subcultures. Their activities also corresponded with Sarah Thornton's analysis of how youth cultures were in reality less distant from the workings of commercial culture than their underground image suggested (Thornton 1996). It is this underground positioning guaranteeing a certain market value for the 'subcultural capital' that comes to be attached to the knowledge repertoire of key figures in youth cultural scenes. Not only did Sarah Thornton's study of club culture challenge the status of class and resistance as defining features of these post-war formations, as argued by Birmingham CCCS,[14] she also showed how hierarchies of taste and distinction were created within these groupings, which were a good deal more commercial and less egalitarian than the CCCS writers, myself included, had implied. In fact they produced objects and ideas that possessed a high value to mainstream companies for reasons of the insight, knowledge and expertise on emerging youth markets. This rather cold but nevertheless persuasive argument permits a contemporary understanding of today's (albeit grown-up) youth cultural 'elites' whose fine-tuned hipster knowledge is a highly significant part of their career portfolios.

Nowadays stylists, hipsters, DJs, fashion bloggers are hardly different from other young people working in marketing or in brand consultancy for the big corporations, other than the freelance terms or consultancy basis on which they deliver services and packages of cultural knowledge and expertise. This core of knowledge and taste has to be safeguarded not just because it provides the basis of livelihoods but also because large corporations can so rapidly pick up on and make mainstream this repertoire. The hipsters have to ensure they get paid for their services, even when as fashion bloggers they start off doing it for free. It is a delicate balance, which also accounts for some of the career anxieties in this field. Some hipsters can earn a living by assembling these forms of knowledge to set up a business such as a bar or shop or blog. If they want to retain high subcultural or hipster capital they also have to remain elusive and exclusive, always well in advance of mass taste while at the same time adamantly disavowing the vulgarity of the hipster label. (See also the menswear shop in Berlin Mitte *Apartment*, where clothes are hard to find in the darkness of the interior, or indeed the deliberately untidy and shabby *Comme des Garçons* outlet *Lil* on Torstrasse, where hugely expensive items are casually placed on rails next to seemingly second-hand or vintage stock.) If these hipster-shopkeepers become consultants providing insight to major client brands, they themselves have to be constantly replenishing their stock of ideas, taste and know-how for the reason that the brands will invariably translate the ideas for the mass market and then quickly need some new ideas.[15] This point extends the observation of Naomi Klein about youth stalkers being taken on in an informal capacity by large corporations to provide information and insight about how youth styles and tastes are evolving (Klein 2000). These practices have become formalized, giving rise to more clearly designated roles. Now that the idea of subculture has become entirely visible and socially understood, these formations are seen for what they can give or generate in terms of stylistic innovation. They provide a repertoire that is constantly 'translated' onto the catwalk and described as such by fashion journalists.[16] Subcultural resistance has been turned into an obvious site for 'capture'. The way in which youth styles now develop almost instantly within the orbit of mainstream consumer culture has been recognized for some years. This has come about as corporations have chased the valuable youth demographic with such dedication that barely is there a dark club space undiscovered and left off the listings magazines. If the money lies, however, in promising something unique, and as yet undiscovered, then we should not be surprised by the accelerated dynamics of proliferating hierarchies inside different urban scenes. Bars, clubs, art galleries, shops and hipster hang-outs in Dalston, London or in Prenzlauer Berg in Berlin come to be as exclusive in the atmosphere they generate, as the most upmarket fashion boutiques found on London's Bond Street. And if Sarah Thornton wrote about how some club promoters disparaged the wrong kind of customer (in both misogynist and anti-working-class tones as the 'Sharons and Traceys'), hoping to keep them off the guest list and not even in the queue outside the door, this kind of selectivity and elitism is now so normalized as to be almost taken for granted (Kosnick 2012). It is also this that gives rise to anti-hipster sentiments, as these purveyors of informal or subcultural knowledge, whose value rests on the authenticity and insider status of what they know about, come to be seen by those outside the inner circles as elitist, and embedded inside the heartland of the consumer culture, from which they hypocritically carefully distance themselves, indeed pretend to despise. The new logic of 'subcultural capital' has led to a particularly high value being attributed to the kind of street knowledge (new musics, new tastes in trainers, favoured brands of bicycles, new haircuts), which certain hipster individuals have trained themselves as experts in and purveyors of (Thornton 1996). Keeping close to the ground means these people often live in poor decaying neighbourhoods, which, in the light of this presence of middle-class newcomers, then become ripe for gentrification. In the years I am most concerned to document as pivotal to the development of the creative economy in the UK, the most visible traits of the hipsters have been ironic detachment and a seeming avoidance of political engagement, a specific lack of concern about neighbourhood and the consequences of rising rent and house prices, an aestheticism that serves as an excuse for the discounting of social and economic issues locally or globally, a lack of public-mindedness, severance from local municipal politics, and disconnection from community in regard to provision of schools, kindergartens, health centres and so on.[17] Nevertheless there is a keen interest in uncovering authentic places such as Turkish snooker halls (in Dalston, and more recently in Peckham, London) or original un-refurbished working-class pubs, and giving them new stature and significance, as if in the spirit of the urban pioneer. Despite benefiting from unexpected income, often these spaces of authenticity become ripe for takeover, buy outs or conversion into more lucrative flats or luxury apartments. In London it is only since 2012 – four years into recession – that one finds these concerns discussed in the press and social media. Widespread complacency contributed to the lack of an anti-gentrification movement across miles and miles of East London from Hoxton and Shoreditch to Bethnal Green and Homerton. Prior to the Occupy movement of 2011, such battles as have been fought have not been able to rely on these creative types, and as a result have remained largely in the hands of squatters' organizations and ageing community activists. In Berlin it is quite different, as I show in Chapter 5; the weekly listings magazines *Tip* and *Zitty*, the local daily press along with radical activist groups have challenged the deeply individualized stance of hipsters and their lack of social responsibility, often going so far as to blame their presence for the homogenization of neighbourhoods, the displacement of poorer populations and the implanting of neoliberal ideals in a city space long associated with radicalism and urban social movements.

The Digital Artisans

Two ethnographic studies of the hipster scene provide insight into the employment environment of the creative economy. Andrew Ross focuses on the 'digital artisan', while Richard Lloyd offers an analysis of a hipster neighbourhood in Chicago's Wicker Park (Ross 2003; Lloyd 2006). Through 2000 to 2002 Ross undertook eighteen months of investigation in the *Razorfish* digital media company, with the young people working there known as the *fish*. Though based in the New York Silicon Alley headquarters during the time of the study, Ross also visited and observed in the San Francisco office and also London Smithfields. Although Ross does not refer to the *fish* as hipsters, his descriptions suggest a close connection. At work they dress according to their subcultural preferences, usually with a sense of irony and quotation marks around their flagged-up style choices. They mostly all have degrees, often across the range of performing arts, anthropology, media and communications and so on. They are highly individualistic people, many able to maintain their own art work or burlesque interests after hours, despite the long hours' culture in the *Razorfish* workplace. In this case they are not freelance but enjoying what turns out to be a short stint in actual employment, where a raft of high-ranking corporate clients allows *Razorfish* to expand, and set up a string of equally informal work spaces in a range of cities. Ross's study argues that the 'irresistible' appeal of working for a new media company like *Razorfish*, with its charismatic directors and its independent style of working that allows the employees to experiment and play with ideas, as long as their work is billable to the corporate clients, is undercut by the exceptionally high level of commitment, almost cult-like, required of the staff. By the end of his period of study the company is facing closure after a series of sell-outs and take-overs and the *fish* are having to look for other opportunities, though in keeping with the optimism and motivation of this kind of worker they are not without possibilities, some returning to an original love such as music, others to academia or to set up their own business. There are two key points to be drawn from this portrayal of the buzz and excitement of this kind of hedonistic workplace, first that the hipsters here are employees and they acknowledge the high value of having their health insurance and other entitlements covered, since in the freelance world they must find the resources themselves, and secondly the principal management strategy, which is designed to extract as much in the way of ideas, creativity and commitment of time to projects, is to devise a mode of working that resembles that of the free spirit artist; this is what Ross means by the 'industrialization of bohemia'. The lifestyle of the artist comes to provide a new form of managerialism, a *dispositif* of worker-freedom, a tool for the intensification of labour, one which is endorsed by influential magazines like *Fast Company* and the *Harvard Business Review*. The ethos of the *Razorfish* office seems like a children's playground with some fish bringing in their scooters, most sporting tattoos and day-glo coloured hairstyles, amid an atmosphere reminiscent of club, pub or party.

Although Ross follows various *fish* into their leisure spaces, he does not reflect on their home base and local neighbourhoods and, given that the location of the office is in an already expensive downtown area of New York, the founders and the workforce would not stand out as unwelcome gentrifiers, since those processes took place many decades ago. The *fish* talk ironically about the pleasures of working in a 'cool sweatshop', there is no question of union organization inside the company, and they happily refer to their seventy-hour weeks. None of the respondents offers anything in the way of a critique of the work they do or of its insecurity in the longer term; in most cases Ross's interviewees are exuberant and upbeat and express themselves in the kind of enthusiastic language that any company would wish from its employees. Nor is there any visible discourse of corporate social responsibility beyond some expressions of misgivings about which kinds of clients may be ethically undesirable. The female interviewees do not raise questions of gender, or perceived inequalities in the working environment, or more generally in their capacity as digital artisans, and none seem to have children. Ross's portrait of the *fish* suggests a free-wheeling, creatively driven, socially intense but also deeply individualistic cohort. The *fish* emulate the ethos of the internet start-ups of previous decades, translating these values into a more cultural and media-led creative environment. Everyone Ross interviews appears to be a winner, or at least they present themselves as such. As far as this perhaps short moment in their creative careers is concerned, they seem unbothered by employment or social justice issues. Instead, this is an unambiguously commercial environment with the added attraction that employees can make use of their personal artistic and subcultural affiliations to enhance the workplace and add value to the services they provide.

Through most of the 1990s Richard Lloyd undertook a neighbourhood-based analysis of the hipster scene, which has gathered in the Wicker Park area in Chicago – formerly a poor, run-down area with a Latino population (Lloyd 2006). The study that emerged is indeed a highly detailed, well-executed and fine-tuned ethnographic account, following in the tradition of the Chicago School of Sociology while also influenced by contemporary theories of urban life, most notably by Sassen. But still there persists in this engaging analysis of 'neo-bohemia' a certain myopia in regard to others still living there, especially those who have not found themselves caught up in this scene. Lloyd's focus is mostly on artists and musicians, many of whom spend their time bar-tending or setting up events and parties. Some of the richest detail emerges from his conversations with people working in bars and small clubs and music venues. While there is an animated discussion of gentrification especially as the bars and restaurants become places of entertainment for well-off visitors from outside the neighbourhood, Lloyd does not consider the domestic life of the area, its schools, homes, parks or playgrounds. As a result, the hipster scene is lifted out of the neighbourly connection its members may or may not have with the locality. The economic activities include working in small digital media companies and start-ups, being in bands, working as club and dance promoters, running bookstores and cafés, working behind the bar in various pubs and serving tables in restaurants. Many of Lloyd's respondents are artists hoping to keep their own work going, while attending the opening events and parties of their friends. Overall, Lloyd argues that this flexible creative outlook corresponds with the new work requirements of post-industrial capitalism. The 'bohemian ethic' he argues 'is best adapted to the new realities' (Lloyd 2006, p. 236); at the same time it takes its toll on many of his respondents, who often have drink or drug-related health issues. This utilization of 'subcultural capital' as a means of earning some kind of living, while also enjoying the pleasures of bohemian *bonhomie*, seems to lead to a more fragile existence than the author suggests. Lloyd does not ask about how health insurance payments are covered, or about how many are supported by parents, or have access to some sort of private income. We do not find out about the turnovers of the small cafés and bars, only that some last longer than others but that there is often a relatively short shelf life for even the favourite hipster haunts. The reader cannot help but wonder about what happens at home, and this is a long-standing feature of studies that take the concept of subculture as a starting point and night-time economies as the main focus (McRobbie 1988). This is compounded by a lack of concern for the difficulties faced by hipster participants in terms of how hardship and poverty actually affect them. Nobody likes to talk about failure or disappointment or even just sheer exhaustion. The visibility of scene factors can mean an overlooking of more invisible features, such as reliance or not on welfare, age and the generational limitations of these bohemian attachments and night-time socialities.

Proletarian Nights

In his cumbersome and unwieldy attempt to offer a post-structuralist history of a selection of French nineteenth-century working-class voices drawn from a textual analysis of the letters, writing, poems and statements groups of skilled workers composed between 1830 and 1840, the philosopher Jacques Rancière, whose work was first published in the late 1970s, contests many of the accounts of working-class life that have, he argues, been impeccably tailored to fit with and exemplify the theoretical inclinations and political leanings of their authors (Rancière 2012). In this undertaking Rancière is also doing something theoretically adventurous; he is subjecting the terrain of what Stuart Hall labelled 'culturalist accounts' to a post-structuralist argument. Where the likes of E. P. Thompson found political authenticity in the voices and songs of nineteenth-century English labourers, such that their activities helped constitute the 'making' of the English working class, Rancière offers no truth of working-class association;

his collection of statements and fragments of texts and reading of them has a tapestry-like form, which suggests all kinds of unruly and fanciful yearnings and desires. His account shows these attempts at poetic writing and other similar activities to be endorsing singularity and difference and non-conformity with what the leaders of the workers' movement at the time wanted to emphasize. Winding his way through the many early labour experiments in organizations including the Fourierists and followers of Saint Simon, Rancière highlights the need for autonomy and the overarching desire for aestheticism within these early socialist groups. They do not comply with the expectations of the leaders of the working-class movement, nor do they wholly disavow it. If Marx considered factory workers and craftsmen, Rancière looks to the pre-industrial workforce of lace-makers, cabinet-makers, saddlers, scene painters, typographers, makers of musical instruments and seamstresses, many of whom endure periods of unemployment when demand drops, and who must then extend their skills and take on other jobs. Above all, they love poetry and they long for time away from the grind of their machines. Rancière is not so much portraying an ideal of 'artisanal socialism' nor is he bewailing the way in which the factory system inevitably reduced the range of skills of the pre-industrial workers. These men and women wish for some other outlets, or avenues that would allow them to pursue their ideas more fully. 'As you can see, I know how to appreciate my craft, and yet, I would have liked to have been a painter' (Rancière 2012, p. 5). Rancière says, 'What is at stake here is not the right to idleness but the dream of another kind of work' (Rancière 2012, p. 8). This is also a radical challenge to 'workerism' of the left, and the insistence that workers be disciplined at all times. The poets and singers may appear to be 'deserters' from class struggle if that entails militaristic styles of hierarchy, but they do not abandon the ideas of socialism, even as they wish to become 'Masters'. 'To dream of socialism hardly means to forget the virtues of enterprise' (Rancière 2012, p. 33). These workers seek to be independent. They also want to be able to enjoy fashion, and dress in ways that would win respect. The tailors are young and rebellious, they demand 'independence and equality with Masters they want to be able to smoke tobacco in the workshop, have time to read the newspapers and they want the Masters to 'take off their hats upon entering the workshop'(Rancière 2012, pp. 41, 42, 46, 47).

The disorganized labour that Rancière wishes to have recorded as a significant part of working-class struggles, has its counterparts in the kind of lines of flight that I argue have underpinned the desires of sections of British working-class and lower middle-class youth, to find congenial and convivial spaces of work and employment in the spheres of art and culture.[18] In effect, what I am doing is here is extending and updating the CCCS model, taking it out of the sphere of leisure into that of work.[19] In both cases, the desires and yearnings cannot be captured or contained wholly by the institutions and organizations of labour. This recalcitrance and unruliness could also be called cultural politics. The tradition of British cultural studies has recounted, in the writing of E. P. Thompson, Raymond Williams, Richard Hoggart, Stuart Hall and Paul Gilroy, how the production of cultural and subcultural forms and other genres has provided a counter-narrative to dominant social values. In this current work I endeavour to make a connection between these distinctive cultural forms and the kinds of jobs and creative careers to which they have given rise. That is to say, alongside the actual existence of the critical art work by Isaac Julien or the piece of music by Goldie, is a world of job creation and an ecology of self-employment, and my claim is that we need to understand how the works and the jobs are historically entwined. Rancière's account helps to remind us how the British cultural studies tradition embodied a kind of Marxism that understood class politics as emerging from sites other than those associated with the factory floor, organized labour and the leadership role of the party. If I now attempt to re-instate the workplace, it is on the basis of the kitchen table, the youth club or disco or street having played their own important roles in articulating the direction taken by the lines of flight. These communal, familial, collective or indeed institutional spaces permitted alternative working lives to be imagined. Cultural studies therefore anticipated a neo-Marxism open to difference and diversity, open to the equal stature of the family and the community alongside that of workplace and the sphere of formal politics.

Let me re-cap: this chapter has argued that those sectors of the newly expanded middle class in the UK who have embraced the idea of creative work, are being expected to test out the water of working life without welfare or with substantially reduced welfare. The pursuit of passionate work is both a line of flight and site of tension and 'capture' for the reason that this cultural landscape becomes a space for both labour struggle and labour reform. This is labour reform by stealth, since the objective is to re-route the young people into spheres that are unprotected in advance. Power in this terrain takes the form of 'capture', as fine-tuned instruments of state planning, training and job creation are devised to work in a seemingly co-operative fashion with young cultural entrepreneurs. Education and pedagogy, from primary schooling through secondary and tertiary sectors, become the privileged spaces for the deployment of the *dispositif* of creativity, a defining feature being the importing of vocabularies from the 'business school', which in turn become a new orthodoxy. The new urban middle class is being de-socialized, and cut off from of its earlier association with municipal socialism, public-mindedness and civic consciousness; instead it is persuaded to think and act only on its own behalf. Pedagogy is, more than before, the favoured instrument for transforming the landscape of training and learning such that the business school model is bolstered and potentially capable of supplanting the critical and analytical bodies of social science and humanities knowledge that previously were installed within the curriculum of the 'art school'.

3

The Artist as Human Capital: New Labour, Creative Economy, Art Worlds

Imagine working in the film business, moving from film to film, crew to crew, set to set, a success one month and a flop the next, a progress in which you are only as good as your last project. Work may be like that for many more of us in the next decade: at times fun and rewarding, but itinerant and punctuated by bouts of insecurity.

Leadbeater 1999, p. 64

Representing the figure of the artist as a model for contemporary capitalism flattens out the 'heterogeneity of art practice', including the persistence of what Alberto Lopez Cuenca (2012) refers to as an 'autonomous project seeking to produce non-hegemonic social practices' [see also Gillick 2010; Rosler 2011]. Artists and other cultural workers are, moreover, among the protagonists of struggles against exploitation and inequality in the neo-liberal era.

de Peuter 2014, p. 274

Creativity as Labour Reform

In this chapter, I pursue the idea that 'labour reform' is undertaken through the promotion of creative economy during the times of the New Labour government, especially in the early years starting in 1997. This proposal may seem counter-intuitive, since the very idea of work and of labour conditions within the creative sector is virtually invisible across the pages of the many reports and mapping documents. It is this absence of what might seem like an obvious topic that is in itself suggestive of a specific turn or a new agenda in this terrain. Work is not there, because in this rhetorical world it is business and entrepreneurship that now count, and so ideas of working life or labour process do not figure, since these ideas are too sociological; they are explicit reminders of what is now being superseded by an entirely different mode of activity, one that is nebulous, self-directed, taking shape with less 'interference' by the state, and not in any way connected to an industrial policy. It is self-invented work. Foucault's writing on biopolitics offers a good opening for developing an argument about labour reform and cultural policy, because of his primary emphasis on the body and on power as something that is dispersed, broken down, disaggregated and addressing itself to subjects in a corporeal way (Foucault 2008). The populations who find themselves being attended to in this way are also provided with many opportunities and incentives, there is an anticipation of reward and a series of invitations to take part, all of which go some way towards making risky jobs with uncertain outcomes nevertheless appealing and exciting. In sharp contrast to this approach to power, a good deal of British academic discussion of cultural policy is informed by a neo-Marxist political economy of media and communications approach and is arguably less able to convey the micrological processes by which power (in the form of policy) is unfolded and played out, how it is set loose, impacting on everyday activity, which might include things such as how one behaves or comports oneself, or how one makes use of one's bodily capacities. For example, in the writing of McGuigan, neoliberalism in the creative sector has something of a juggernaut momentum, tightly aligned with globalization (McGuigan 2005, 2010). This leaves unheeded how cultural policies are implemented and responded to at the level of organizations, institutions and micro-enterprises of the type so common in the sector. Such an approach is unable to consider how the rhetoric of policy has a distinctive linguistic momentum, and how these new vocabularies come to be adopted by people who are employees, as well as by those who are self-employed or who are creative entrepreneurs. Without having insight into the shape and form of such levels of reach and capture, the emphasis on transformation in regard to the prevalence of market forces and business models in the field of culture, and the rise of sponsorship of the arts, appears too general.

From 1997 for more or less a decade, there was, under the UK New Labour government, an upsurge of interest in the idea of creativity, with taskforces, teams, creative partnerships, and creative leadership programmes all assembled under this new banner for growth, which hinged around the themes of social inclusion, job creation and prosperity. The early days of the creative economy also coincided with the coming to prominence of the so-called Young British Artists, and this in turn heralded the centrality of London as a global arts city. In the pages that follow, I reflect on those cultural policy discussions that offer retrospective accounts of these years, and in section two I develop the idea of the artist as human capital. Overall I aim to show how the activity of governmentality in relation to these spheres constitutes a re-definition of arts and culture, where creativity is put to work as a vehicle for labour reform under the banner of the 'talent-led economy'. In what was once considered a relatively quiet backwater of policy, what we see is an adversarial strategy with the aim of creating lasting outcomes. There is also perhaps some degree of timeliness in this consideration, given that after all the hype of the Blair years the DCMS[1] has, in 2014, once again returned to the shadows of government, denuded of power and influence, without as much as a sign of an artist on the web pages. It has been scaled down and re-configured to engage more directly with the large broadcasting and communications sector, and the idea of the talent-led economy seems entirely forgotten or abandoned.[2] For this reason, we find articles in scholarly journals bearing titles such as 'After the Creative Economy' or 'Beyond Creative Economy'.[3]

Let me start by simply mentioning some of the initiatives and activities embarked upon when New Labour first came to office. As Hewison reminds us there was first and foremost the setting up of the Department of Culture, Media and Sport (DCMS, from what had previously been a heritage department) with Chris Smith as Minister, who in turn saw it as his role to draw the Department and thus 'culture' closer to the Treasury (Hewison 2011).[4] The Creative Industry Taskforce was established with accompanying publicity and this was followed by the rapid publication of the DCMS Mapping Documents (1998, 2001). The scale and volume of this activity is well documented and attention is drawn, for example, not just to the mapping documents, but to the reports that focused on education and skills, and to the positive role culture and creativity were to play in fostering cognitive capacities in children and young people and in promoting social cohesion. The first few years were marked by great prominence and visibility given to the potential of the creative economy highlighted by the *Cool Britannia* parties at Downing Street. The punch line was that this was a sector of industry that had hitherto not been considered as having economic value, and in addition this whole field had an egalitarian and anti-elitist dimension because 'everyone is creative'.[5] It was therefore a question of widening access and finding ways of tapping into these pools of talent.

Some genuinely egalitarian policies were introduced, such as dropping entrance charges to major museums and art galleries, and putting National Lottery funds into art and community projects. Likewise, Creative Leadership programmes were established, as were school-based Creative Partnerships. By 2006, when the hype was beginning to fade, PM Gordon Brown nevertheless gave £12m for a Skills Council to be set up (Creative and Cultural Skills) although, like most of the above programmes, by 2011 this was ended by the Coalition Government. Throughout this time NESTA[6] came to be the key independent institute for formulating ideas and policies and although re-designated by 2010 as a charity, it has retained its central position cleverly replacing creativity as the buzz word of the times, with the more technology-driven 'innovation'.

As a senior academic statesman in this terrain, partly on the basis of his own advisory roles through the leftwing London (Greater London Council, GLC) administration of the 1980s, which was subsequently closed down by Mrs Thatcher in 1986, Garnham provides a compelling account, suggesting that the ascendancy of the creative economy was predicated on assumptions being made about the wider impact of the information society, the knowledge economy and the role of copyright and IP (Garnham 2005). Garnham also describes something of his own intellectual trajectory in his analysis. His journey through both an endorsement and a critique of the Frankfurt School, its need for a stronger economic dimension, pushed him in the GLC period, to make a case for wider and more egalitarian distribution systems for cultural forms, which did not have a guaranteed success in the commercial market. With this in mind, he accuses the policies for the creative economy under New Labour of being inattentive to this same important issue in favour of an 'artist-centred' approach, which in turn disguises some of the key features such as the bringing together of arts and culture with the knowledge economy and the software sector, with the former bringing to the latter the 'moral prestige of the creative artist', while in reality the bulk of the economic hopes for the whole terrain rests on the value of the IP to the owners or licensees. Garnham claims that underpinning the buzz is an emphasis on technological innovation. Apart from this, Garnham says it was all a disorganized mishmash based on short-term goals. Despite being somewhat reductionist, this argument does indeed make sense if Charles Leadbeater's book *Living on Thin Air* is anything to go by (Leadbeater 1999). Although considered, when it was published in 1999, something of an accompaniment to the euphoria about the creative industries, the book is overwhelmingly directed towards innovation, biotechnology, the knowledge economy and the many lessons to be learnt from Silicon Valley. Only one passing comment about fashion designer Alexander McQueen brings the work into the orbit of the creative economy debate; otherwise the heroic entrepreneurs are typically from the hi-tech world of software and computing. As will be apparent later in this chapter, it is indeed this dimension of innovation that carries on when the Coalition government takes office and initiates a series of major cuts to arts and cultural funding. Garnham is also right to point to the way in which social democratic policies such as those associated with the GLC were abandoned when New Labour came to power. However it could be argued that the artist-centred approach, or what I called an 'auteur approach' (McRobbie 2002), along with the emphasis on the short-term, was more deliberately instrumental than he suggests. The focus of attention on artists permitted the development of an extensive and popular mode of address to young people as a relevant population within the education system. This worked well, since the idea of success married with creativity and with celebrity, chimed with already established themes in contemporary cultural life (such as popular TV shows like *The X Factor*). These elements could be easily translated into curriculum reform and pedagogic strategies in the form of business modules and toolkits. The focus on seemingly short-term goals conveyed unambiguously to these same subjects that uncertain futures were part of the course. This in term signals the new regime of precarity as governmentality (Lorey 2015).

David Hesmondhalgh argues that the presence of a recognizably social democratic dimension (including some elements from the GLC era) alongside the market-driven emphasis on consumer-citizens, makes the raft of policies stretching across media and communications as well as cultural policy something of a 'hybrid' (Hesmondhalgh 2005, 2010). What was retained was an anti-elitism in regard to arts and culture, and an attempt to develop a job creation infrastructure within a de-industrialized landscape. Hesmondhalgh reflects on the dilemmas for a Labour administration, and indeed for other social democratic parties in a period marked by the decline of heavy industry and the ebbing away of political support for the trade unions. In this context the so-called Third Way offers a seemingly viable pathway. Yet he neglects to consider the more aggressive dynamics of New Labour in office, which certainly retained some social democratic policies while simultaneously disavowing them, or ensuring their marginality. The hybrid is therefore more antagonistic and combative than Hesmondhalgh suggests, underscoring Stuart Hall's analysis of the distinctive form of neoliberalism created by New Labour, which begrudgingly had social democratic elements still present (to keep the old guard in the party happy) but ideally put into cold storage (Hall 2003). Indeed we could go further than this and argue that not only were previous forms of collectivism downgraded and marginalized; for example, radical film-makers' co-operatives lost their funding, as did a whole raft of community arts programmes, but that the very principle of equality was abandoned in favour of nebulous ideas of social inclusion and meritocracy. In short, a whole new political vocabulary was put in place and repeated so frequently it became a mantra of common-sense and at the same time synonymous with all that was 'new' in New Labour (Hall 2003). Hesmondhalgh et al. in their recent reflections on New Labour draw on McGuigan's analysis of neoliberalism in the field of the arts (Hesmondhalgh et al. 2014). The authors warn against a too-easy conclusion that these years were wholly devoted to fulfilling a neoliberal agenda. Pointing to the flow of money into the sector, offset by a vocabulary that prioritizes sponsorship, and public–private partnerships, Hesmondhalgh et al. are troubled by the way in which the term neoliberalism functions as a kind of umbrella under which so many different political persuasions from left to right can be assembled. Going through the facts that point to higher spends on the arts alongside a social inclusion agenda, they claim that it is too simplistic to conclude that New Labour was definitively neoliberal in its time in office in regard to matters of culture and creativity. If, conversely, we understand neoliberal governmentality as comprising a complex web of practices spanning many levels of institutions and converging on a decisive take up of key motifs such as business sponsorship in the arts and in culture, and in new vocabularies of excellence, benchmarking and of branding in this domain, then we can see that this all does add up to a significant transformation. These changes sweep across many sectors of public life, not just arts and culture and for this very reason they begin to assume the air of normality. While rightly drawing attention to the valency of the new public management discourses, with all the accompanying paraphernalia of management consultants, task forces, benchmarking, the setting up of 'internal markets', the importance of competition, and the notion of 'excellence', Hesmondhalgh et al. do not perhaps, emphasize enough the profound importance of this new era of public management discourse in the UK. It was because such a way of thinking pre-dated the rise of the creative economy, that it was relatively straightforward and logical for the same ideas to flow into the world of arts administration, where, as in higher education, ample use has been made of expensive consultancy services under the rhetoric of providing 'value for money' or as a way of 'cutting down on waste'.

The labour reform undertaken through the promotion of the self-entreprenerial ethos embedded in the creative economy was a logical extension of what had already been put in place within the more conventional world of work and employment. As we know from the work of Donzelot, and more recently from Boltanski and Chiapello, employers and managers in large corporations have for many decades sought, often through employing the services of management consultants, to find ways of enhancing job satisfaction while also encouraging self-responsibility in the workplace as a strategy designed to reduce absenteeism costs to the company, minimize worker discontent and lessen the likelihood of labour organization (Donzelot 1991; Boltanski and Chiapello 2005). The world of public-funded arts administration has in recent years been subject to privatization and the encouragement of enterprise culture, with the result that many administrators find that they too, like the artists and actors with whom they work, are also nowadays self-employed or freelance. This sector of arts workers has been encouraged to form their own companies as 'spin offs' from what was previously the public sector.

Mark Banks undertakes an extensive documenting of the various mapping documents, reports and papers published between 1998 and 2008 and pinpoints the same absence of attention that I mentioned above to the dimension of work and labour conditions within the new creative economy (Banks 2010). Instead there are frequent references to creative hubs and to the idea of flexibility and transferable skills. Even in the widely discussed *Staying Ahead* report published by the Work Foundation[7] there is little or no mention of what we might describe as an employee's or a worker's perspective, nor is there any discussion of the possible downside of short-term jobs, or of self-organized labour or indeed self-employment. This myopia to the actual labour conditions on the ground and inside flexible firms and companies confirms my argument that labour reform takes place within precisely this terrain of language, of vocabulary, of what is said where, of what is on the agenda, and what is left off. The proselytizing rhetoric of this brave new world of work achieves its objectives by removing topics and terms that would impede the momentum of the somewhat euphoric language of management studies now transplanted into the world of arts and culture under the rubric of creativity. If Garnham is right, and what was really being promoted was the knowledge economy predicated on innovation with creativity as its aesthetically appealing packaging, then the question remains, why the need for the artist to be centre-stage, what is the deeper rationale for this co-option of artistry? Banks in his account of the policy statements suggests that the strongest and most coherent policies echoing from the perspective of government or employers are for flexible, creative skills on the part of the new workforce, and this in turn justifies requirements at the level of pedagogy and curriculum. What seems like a banal outcome of so much discussion actually tells us a great deal about what is at stake. If what is needed is an entre-preneurial, self-regulated, motivated and individualized workforce, if these young people are being called on to create jobs for themselves and more or less invent new forms of work, then the seminal place in which they can be collectively addressed is that point at which they already are assembled, which is the public education system. Not surprisingly it is in the schools, colleges and universities that the 'creative and cultural skillsets' are most embedded. This same logic extends to the re-naming of university departments as Centres for Creative Economy, and to the setting up of undergraduate degrees under this new inter-disciplinary heading. Labour reform proceeds then within this space of education, for the reason that this is where new subjectivities can be addressed by means of a more strongly business-inflected curriculum. It is by these means that the arts and humanities and to an extent elements of the social sciences come to be re-configured as sites for the development of human capital. So what seems like a policy mishmash is a precise instrument targeted at a specific demographic located within the education system and now designated as potentially entrepreneurial subjects. Indeed the push by New Labour in this direction, undertaken with only a vague sense of outcomes, but with loud publicity, also served the purpose of showing Britain to be at the forefront of this move towards endors-ing risk-taking entrepreneurialism in a field that had previously been the preserve of public sector funding and conventional jobs and employment. In effect the key move here is that public relations serves the function of policy, as if it is simply enough to announce and celebrate talent, such that the very act of describing or proclaiming brings into being that which is being promoted. This then becomes a favoured mode for the creativity *dispositif*.

In a series of insightful articles on the rise of the creative economy, all of which foreground wider changes in the world of work, Kate Oakley, an insider herself, who was involved in some of the consul-tancies brought into the orbit of New Labour prior to and in the early days of office, is in a position to make clear otherwise less visible connections (Oakley 2004, 2006, 2009, 2011). This was the era of so-called 'joined-up government', and a key value was to promote social inclusion, linking with PATs (Policy Action Teams) and the Social Exclusion Unit, while also opening up a space for artists working in neighbourhood projects as well as consolidating career pathways across the sector in what in the past would have been called arts administration (as in the Cultural Leadership programme). Oakley suggests that these ideas owed at least some of their existence to cultural studies, no less, in the form of Paul Willis's thinking on working-class youth creativity,[8] even though this debt to the politics of popular and working-class culture was rarely acknowledged. She also points to the leading role of the *New Times* group with Stuart Hall at its centre (Willis 1990; Hall and Jacques 1989).[9] She traces this connection in terms of the shift described by *New Times* writers to a post-Fordist economy, giving rise to new jobs that were inherently more rewarding because of their high-skill element. For New Labour these ideas permitted a shift of attention away from the old industrial working-class terrain of 'labour'. 'De-massification', that is, a relinquishing of the idea of a working class, with its representational forms in the trade unions, in turn allowed a shift of attention to the individual and the idea of autonomy (Leadbeater 1999). Oakley does not spell out the full consequences and magnitude of what this means for the Labour Party in government, instead she describes how for a number of thinkers close to government, the idea of the network (entailing shared sets of 'social and ethical norms') comes to replace more conventional ideas of labour organization. The new era of post-Fordism somehow allows New Labour to justify directing itself to a more highly skilled and (already) individualized sector. This is indeed a significant step in the direction of labour reform, if it's the case that the new creative economy becomes a template for a move away from trade unions as the primary organizations of labour, to the nebulous notion of the network. As Oakley puts it in another article 'the network' increasingly takes over from the 'trade unions' (Oakley 2006, p. 262). Just to stress the point, the notion that networks (in effect friendship groups reliant on trust) would somehow replace the long-fought-for trade unions, and their powers of representation, is typically provocative, the dominant style of New Labour rhetoric at the time, while also testing the limits to see just how far New Labour could go in its dramatic and profound shift away from its historic connection with the unions and organized labour.[10]

It was Thompson who, according to Oakley, saw Stuart Hall as arguing that 'the left needed to recapture individual autonomy away from the right', which implies that Hall opened the door for labour reform (Thompson quoted in Oakley 2011, p. 283). In my reading, what Stuart Hall was doing at the time was attempting to come to terms with changes that were linked with the rise of post-Fordism, such as trends in consumer culture, which somehow the left had been unable to engage with. Hall's expansive ideas for how the left could forge a new popular politics were taken up and deflected in unexpected right-wing directions by Leadbeater, Mulgan and other leading figures working with think-tanks close to New Labour.[11] The will to move to a centre-left or indeed right-wing leftism under the flag of New Labour could not have been foreseen by Hall, the problem being that this New Labour conservatism coincided with views of substantial sectors of the electorate who had rallied under Thatcherism and were more easily appealed to by a New Labour, which seemed to endorse a similar vocabulary. Leadbeater, also a regular contributor to *Marxism Today*, said that with a now more individualized workforce there would be less need for the state. In other words a more individualized or networked workforce permits a reduction in the role of the state and its panoply of protective measures and entitlements. The state can shrink under such prodigious conditions. Looking back at these manoeuvres from a more conventionally Labour leftist position, MP Jon Cruddas saw that New Labour imagined a withering away of the working class so that the key remaining issue was 'access to human capital' (Cruddas 2006, quoted in Oakley 2011, p. 284). The (First World) myth of 'post-fordist socialism' was based then on the idea of an enjoyable landscape of rewarding work offset by emancipated or sovereign consumers now able to overcome old class divides through their participation in contemporary home-ownership, and an IKEA-type lifestyle. Oakley says that 'A reformed labour market was therefore believed to offer political success in a variety of areas' (Oakley 2011, p. 284). This is certainly a more seismic change than these words convey. It was because of this adversarial pathway adopted by New Labour that opportunities, for example, to consider new models for 'flexicurity' of the type endorsed by Scandinavian social democrats and trades unions were not pursued. Creativity was disconnected from any idea of labour, even as it was being promulgated as a source for growth and wealth creation. At the same time the anomalous nature of this kind of work, the 'complex overflowing of activities between the formal and the informal, the for-profit and the not-for-profit, the state and commercial actors' also constitutes a challenge for organized labour itself (Pratt 2012, p. 47). A wide and often discordant range of activities, set in a context where small firms and micro-businesses can blossom and burst within the space of just months, is indeed more than a challenge to policymakers more used to dealing with stable organizations and relatively stable workforces. What the drive for creativity has produced is not just an abnormal notion of working life, a replacement of expertise, skill and qualifications with the idea of a portfolio into which fits a whole range of wildly different capacities, but also a highly individualized outlook. From the viewpoint of New Labour, creativity seemed to have the potential for displacing and more or less doing away with the troublesome idea of 'labour' altogether.

The Artist as Human Capital

Why has the figure of the artist, who, as a worker, quickly morphs into a kind of busy creative multi-tasker, and then perhaps even a well-paid executive,[12] come to occupy a prominent place in debates about the potential of the creative industries, when the typical artist is historically associated with sporadic or minimal earnings, with a poverty-line existence, and with unpredictable 'human resources' upon which he or she must draw? This was a question I asked some years ago in some of my initial responses to the growth of the creative economy and to which I now return (McRobbie 2002). How can (fine) artists, whose working lives vary so widely from one to the next as to make any generalization seemingly impossible, have attracted the attention of policy makers and also become significant points of reference in discussions about the future of work? It is precisely this unpredictability of career outcome, its high-risk strategy as a means of earning a living along with the value that being self-employed or freelance brings to the contracting employer, who is freed from the costs entailed in normal employment, which accounts for this kind of prototype position currently occupied by the new creative workforce. This totally unpredictable pathway answers the question of how an expanded youthful population, trained in art and in the wider creative fields, and having benefited from the opportunities for higher education, which became available from the late 1980s and early 1990s, is set to enter the world of work. They will be, or are, testing out what work and occupation can look like without the benefits, protection and social security, which have been associated with employment. Artists are typically self-employed. There is still, even nowadays, a romantic ethos that surrounds their working lives. With tubes of oil paints messily laid out on a large wooden table in front of the canvas, and music playing loudly in the background, the studio is a special place. But it is exactly this paraphernalia and the romance of the scene of artistic labour that account for why the artist is someone who is, in a way, anticipating the future of work. His or her working rhythm provides a model for how various jobs and careers could shape up in the neoliberal era. The personalized pathways, individualized on the basis of possession of an original portfolio of skills, have an accumulative momentum, which in turn allows us to analyse how short-term, or project-based 'creative' careers develop. It is not so much that we can generalize, it is the uniqueness that counts. The key factor, from the point of view of governmentality, is the presumed reduction in costs to the state or employer for these so-called young creatives who must be responsible for themselves. They have to shoulder the burden of risk in regard to falling ill, or becoming pregnant without being able to access maternity leave entitlements, and this is precisely the point. Maybe they have to rely on a partner, but that too is the point. They have been propelled in such a direction without a great deal of long-term planning on the part of policy-makers, and this too is another pertinent point. These factors illustrate that the new art of governmentality is doing its work of championing risk and innovation while otherwise letting go of the reins. This cultural field offers the possibility of trying out such a welfare-free 'employment policy' in a domain that has the myth of the romantic artist or creative genius at its heart, and at the same time it is historically associated with the social good, with enjoyment, entertainment and education. What we see happening here is a kind of displacement of the antagonisms of the industrial relations that were conducted against the backdrop of the factory floor, onto an entirely different and seemingly incomparable location. This new labour force includes among their numbers the grown-up artist children of the industrial working class, those who also were somehow shunted away from political affiliation with the left to the right from the early days of Mrs Thatcher. Damien Hirst would stand as an interesting example of this inter-generational legacy, as would Tracey Emin, since both figures frequently refer to their parents and their childhood poverty, and are also known to have aligned themselves with the Conservative Party.[13]

In the late 1970s Foucault was delivering his weekly lectures at the Collège de France, most of them given just before the election of Mrs Thatcher in the UK. In the lectures he reveals the result of his investigations into the emergence of a new political style, dating back to the seventeenth through to the twentieth century, which he called the 'art of government'. More specifically he analyses the growth of a process that could be called the economization of politics, or the rise of the market as a force for re-defining the practice of government. Foucault contests the principle of laissez-faire as a defining feature of liberal government for the reason that it assumes a natural tendency for people to act spontaneously in ways conducive to the flourishing of the market. Instead behaviour and activities had to be supported in such endeavours, without however the state becoming actively involved in planning for economic growth and development.

It is this dilemma that prompts the idea of government as extending into everyday life so as to encourage the kind of activities that will enhance the place of the market in society ('a state under the supervision of the market' Foucault 2008, p. 116). Of key importance for the advancement of liberalism in the twentieth centrury is the thinking of the Freiburg School at work in Germany from the 1930s to the 1950s, otherwise known as the Ordoliberals. Foucault provides a detailed account of the writing associated with the journal titled *Ordo*, which also allows him to extemporize on the distinctive features of contemporary neoliberalism and to make some fine-tuned connections with this art of governmentality, its emphasis on a state which will 'accompany the market economy from start to finish' (Foucault 2008, p. 121), its focus on overseeing the 'conduct of conduct' so as to be propitious to prevailing market conditions, and the way these come to be taken up by Western governments at the time he was delivering his lectures (e.g. in France under the leadership of Giscard d'Estaing).

The reflections of a group of German economists, including Euken (who, as Foucault cryptically points out, 'went silent' during the Nazi years) and Roepke, may seem far removed from my attempt in this book to understand the significance of a population (a term favoured by Foucault) of new creative workers, or cultural producers. In fact we can glean a good deal from this historical work by Foucault and by his subsequent considerations, in the same volume, of the take-up of many of these ideas by the later Chicago School led by Thomas Shultz and Gary Becker. What is crucial about the Ordoliberals is the way in which they expressed their antagonism to the state, indeed Roepke likened Beveridge's welfare state and the 'English socialists' to German Nazism. He also wrote that the newly devised welfare state leads to 'an even more centralized action of proletarianization and state control that destroys the middle class' (quoted in Foucault 2008, p. 189). While we can account for their allergic reaction against a planned economic strategy on the grounds of their hostility to Communism (Foucault does not quite spell this out), what the Freiburg scholars were doing was inventing a new and more palatable right-wing political philosophy, which was demonstrably different from fascism, a key feature of which was a profound belligerence to organized labour and the trade unions as well as to state ownership and centralized planning. Equally important to this line of thinking was their hostility to social policy and to any forms of welfare beyond a bare minimum. The value of Foucault's account is its pertinence to the moment it records in France in the mid-1970s in the context of ongoing industrial militancy (*La Grande Menace industrielle*), but also by extension in the UK, where the oil crisis and organized labour brought about the 'fiscal crisis of the state', which Stuart Hall was also, at the same time, documenting in his book *Policing the Crisis* (Foucault 2008, p. 194; Hall et al. 1987). It is important to draw attention to the strikes and labour struggles of that period as having a lasting impact on the new governmentality of arts and culture. This is a connection Lazzarato has pursued in his accounts of the struggles in France of *Les Intermittentes du Spectacle* to seek recognition by the unions and government, thus ensuring access to benefits and welfare payments. If, in the UK, the defeat of the working-class struggle was a decisive feature of the Thatcher years, we can see the seeds of this being spelt out in the writings of the Ordoliberals, and we can pinpoint the centrality of the mid 1970s as the turning point in the transition to a more full-blown neoliberal economy. New Labour's creative economy can be partly understood in terms of this marginalization of old labour in favour of New Labour.

In regard to the question of unemployment, always a key issue for Western governments as well as for organized labour from the late 1970s onwards, Roepke re-defines such a category of person as in transition, and as moving out of one unprofitable activity to another more profitable one. Here again we see significant changes of vocabulary as the worker is now an actor or agent engaged in specific forms of 'conduct' based on strategic choices. He or she is an 'abilities machine' who 'can do' this or that particular thing (Foucault 2008, p. 224). Alongside all of this anti-state invective from the Freiburg School, accompanied as it was by a view that welfare was a cornerstone of the proletarian movement and thus antipathetic to middle-class interests, we also see the emphasis that runs through this thinking on supporting 'fresh, non-proletarian' industries (Roepke makes this point strongly, looking to craft as an example; Foucault 2008, p. 157) and with this the absolute centrality of the figure of the entrepreneur. The important thing is that this kind of person is also understood as a life force, someone who according to Rustow (another of the Ordos) embodies a kind of politics of life, a *Vitalpolitik*, and who is able to multiply his wide range of activities, thereby spreading the risk. It is this kind of person who can use the market and its competitive mechanisms to entrepreneurialize wherever he sees fit, at every available opportunity. Rustow's *Vitalpolitik* embeds the new entrepreneur deep down into the rich fabric of everyday life, where she or he is provided with emotional ties and spiritual reward in what might otherwise be a sphere of 'cold, calculating, rational and mechanical' activity (Foucault 2008, p. 242). The importance of finding enjoyment and reward in work itself is an important counter to the Marxist idea of 'alienation'; this new kind of workforce will have no reason to find common cause in the monotony or boredom of labour. Pleasure at work is thus an instrument to help ward off the dangers of worker dissatisfaction and thus 'combination'. By turning more people into small entrepreneurs, capitalism will be renewed and will be able to deflect all threats from socialist movements. And the 'birth of a new art of government' will ensure that through constant vigilance, activity and innovation, the right kinds of economic institutions develop (Foucault 2008, pp. 168, 176). Of course this is an ideal, the reality of which may never have been fully reached; nevertheless it has shaped and continues to shape the culture of everyday life in the US, and in western Europe and especially in the UK where it was heralded by governments from Mrs Thatcher onwards as the key to economic success, the alternative to the old post-war social order dominated by the trade unions and public sector institutions, and issuing forth a programme of actions through which a competitive ethos would wash away the residues of 'the social'.

This entrepreneurial spirit is to become so enmeshed in everyday life that the lines between work and life will be dissolved. This is also the ethos of the small businessman or woman who has an entrepreneurial vision of his own life as it is lived, such that this brings new kinds of rewards, not just financial but emotional, on the grounds that there is widespread approval for such persons. The *Vitalpolitik* emphasizes the commendable risk-taking personality. If we translate this into the contemporary scene of creative economy we can make more sense of what I have called the ethos of 'passionate work', which envelops the identity of the cultural entrepreneur and which decorates his or her publicity material as a kind of statement of intent and declaration of suitability for participation in this sector. When we talk then about subject formation we might say that passion becomes a normative requirement, indeed a cliché, in the outlook and presentation of self in this milieu. Norms such as those governing conduct also have profound implications for personhood, narrowing and prescribing the range of individual styles and modes of conduct that are deemed appropriate and likewise punishing those that depart from such straitjackets of the self. The cheerful, upbeat, passionate, entrepreneurial person who is constantly vigilant in regard to opportunities for projects or contracts must display a persona that mobilizes the need to be at all times one's own press and publicity agent. This accounts for a flattening and homogenization of personhood or, as Sennett would put it, a 'corrosion of character' (Sennett 1995).

A final feature of this set of discourses to which Foucault draws attention and which is relevant to this current undertaking is that of human capital, a concept most closely associated with Gary Becker of the Chicago School. Michel Feher also finds occasion to expand on Foucault's writing on the Ordoliberals, the Chicago School and human capital as a mode of 'self appreciation' (Feher 2005). This new subject is one who is constantly calculating the best way to enhance, preserve, maintain and exploit those capacities constituting the basis of his or her own treasure trove of value, the human assets that have somehow accrued to him or her. Little is said however of the manner or mode of acquisition of such capital. Foucault looks to those accounts in psychology that stress 'innate elements' or hereditary factors or a good family environment. Bourdieu of course provides a much more sociologically rigorous account of 'cultural capital', one that is, however, as Feher reminds us, tied up with a model of social reproduction, and thus with how power confirms existing social hierarchies rather than with how it proceeds through the more enticing possibility of change, mobility, transformation and even, as Lazzarato sees it, revolution (Bourdieu 1984; Lazzarato 2012). In effect, human capital has the ability to revolutionize capitalism, and I would add, ironically for Bourdieu, on the strength of the potential of cultural or subcultural capital (Thornton 1996). Shultz in particular emphasizes education as the key site for investment in the self. In the US this translates into going to a 'good school', a rather banal point, as Feher indicates; but indeed borne out if attention is turned, in the UK context, to the new emphasis on branding and ranking educational institutions, thus introducing new status and competitive factors in a terrain that hitherto had been relatively anti-elitist in its overall self-image. This permits new gradations of human capital to be measured more acutely on the basis of which course is undertaken in which college. Not only does the business studies module become a key component of the 'art school' provision, but fierce competition among individual students figures more prominently as a pedagogic strategy, even if as Michael Craig-Martin has put it, this is competition 'in the best possible way'.[14] By these means human capital is brought to life in the classroom, seminar room or drawing studio. So again to stress the point, while seemingly transparent as a concept from the Nobel prize-winning economist Gary Becker, it is just this quality that has given the idea such traction and applicability across the social domain, valued for its capacity to mobilize social change and to garner public support and engagement as something participatory, predicated on 'healthy' competition. Human capital as personal potential then becomes an instrument of pedagogy; it defines how a population such as art school or creative media graduates are nowadays trained; for instance to develop and then to exploit or maximize as a uniqueness and a singularity something that cannot be duplicated and is therefore a personal signature, a style, a 'portfolio'. The meaning of professionalism for art students is also now understood in terms of entrepreneurialism. This is seen as an accompaniment to imagination or inspiration. It also marks out the economization of imagination, the marketization of creativity. It does not just supplement the already existing capacities of the subject but drives them, steering the artistic subject in particular directions that are conducive to commercial success. Human capital functions then as a technology of the self; it is a key aspect of the *dispositif* of creativity. And the artistic career designed according to this kind of template becomes a symbol for the high-risk career pathways that are also normalized across the new cultural industries. Since the artist has also historically embodied a kind of free spirit, an unbridled freedom of movement as he or she roams about in search of the ideas that will inform the next piece of work, then here too is the secret to the prominent place now occupied by the artist in the policy worlds of the creative economy. As Foucault says, the 'motto' is to 'live dangerously' (Foucault 2008, p. 168).

The 'Type' of Artist Subject

> While the history, structure and modes of exploitation specific to neo-liberalism have been well documented…the type of subject that is both constituted by this regime and tasked with upholding it has been rather less studied. (Feher 2005, p. 25)

> It doesn't seem like work to me. It's like an artist. An artist just does whatever he wants to, and can just sit around all day and paint when you feel like it. (Fashion student interview, 29 May 2003, quoted in Bill 2012, p. 54)

But does the creative workforce live as dangerously as Foucault imagines? In addition, how can we begin to undertake a study of subject formation in the manner indicated by Feher when the idea of a self-expressive subject is so forcefully disintegrated in contemporary social theory? While fully aware of the dangers of assuming a fully formed artist-subject, whose testimony renders a set of transparent and self-evident views or opinions or narrative accounts, there is nevertheless something of value in surveying how self-defined artists and creative personnel do indeed talk about their working lives. This means considering how they actually experience their own labour process. And in fact the 'type' of artist or creative subject has been a question that has exercised the interest of various contributors to cultural economy debate in recent years. For instance Amanda Bill, in her study of fashion students, wonders how 'these girls are made "subject to" or "prone to" take up the goals of a creative economy' (Bill 2012, p. 51). There is another problem that arises if we seek to develop Feher's wish to consider the type of artist-subject formed under the logic of human capital. When and where are the various toolkits, pedagogies and instruments actually implemented? In what kind of educational packages are they delivered? How might it be possible to judge the impact of this business studies approach? Without the resources for such an undertaking, I must here rely, instead, on some more general observations. For instance the media, especially the UK press and television, have been privileged conduits for the dissemination of and popularization of many of those modes and styles that have transformed how we think about higher education and post-formal education and training. There has been extensive debate about how to engineer a more business-like outlook among the nation's young people and often this is made interesting or even exciting through formats of entertainment that rely on stories of personal ambition, dreams of achievement, available mentoring by high profile business leaders and of course competition. The toolkits approach, the need for internships, work experience and for courses in business and entreprise, are therefore subject to such extensive public debate across the media, as to have become entirely unremarkable and thus normalized.

Those authors who have investigated creative subjectivity have generally done so from a sociological perspective, with a focus on semi-structured interviews with people working in or training for this creative sector. For example, Hesmondhalgh and Baker are concerned with how their respondents across three sectors (television, magazine publishing and music) explain and justify their massive investment of time and energy in fields characterized by short-term contracts, by high rates of casualization and by a proliferation of freelance jobs (Hesmondhalgh and Baker 2011). The authors are perplexed by the seeming willingness with which their interviewees commit themselves to twelve-hour days (camera-operators) and also report on the awareness of the respondents that union membership can mean losing the job or pricing themselves out of the market. The people working in television describe the pleasures and rhythms of seeing a good job done. Like the other professionals interviewed, they each have clear ideas about what constitutes a good outcome, a high quality of work achieved and this is another factor contributing to the justification of long hours and low or unreliable income. Hesmondhalgh and Baker enter into a highly relevant discussion about what constitutes good work in this field; indeed this is one of the distinctive and original features of their study. They point out that such a topic has been missing from debates on creative labour. They say 'post-structuralists' (i.e. Foucauldians) refuse the challenge of producing guidelines or being prescriptive about what may constitute a good or a bad job, while others such as Boltanksi and Chiapello simply shy away from addressing the pressing problem of thinking through how a social justice model could apply to the modern work economy. Hesmond-halgh and Baker argue that on the one hand 'self-exploitation is a misnomer' since there are harsh structural factors that produce an illusion of self-determined autonomous freelance work in the creative sector (in effect echoing what I have argued elsewhere, which is that structural features are devolved down to be absorbed and shouldered by individuals); on the other hand these authors also recognize that many creative workers have little or no inclination to get involved in forming or joining a trade union. But is this so surprising? As we will see in the chapter that follows, the UK lurched during and after the Thatcher period to a service economy, the cost of which was the substitution of old secure jobs for a plethora of part-time or flexitime positions. In this kind of economic environment, organized resistance at almost all levels fades as a realistic strategy, unions are weakened and, in the 'property-owning democracy', mortgages have to be paid. In such a context notions of (creative) workplace politics need to be re-imagined entirely.

One difficulty in *Creative Labour* is that the authors do not fully take into account the distinct professional occupational cultures that define each of these fields of work, cultures that are known of in advance of entering the terrain, and that also give rise to distinctive pathways in the longer term within each sector, with this kind of knowledge becoming widely available and part of the normal working environment. For example, someone may have barely completed one year at *Red* magazine before quickly looking for a move to *Style* magazine. In short, there is a lot of labour mobility in the world of magazines and a sizeable amount of working time is given over to keeping an eye open for new posts coming up. *Creative Labour* is not a longer-term study of media occupational pathways; instead the research takes place over the course of a specific period of time, so the professional routines of job changing and mobility, which also provide something of a cushion or even ironically a kind of security, are less apparent. Entering into worlds such as these is akin to embarking on a career as an actor or theatre manager; the long hours and uncertain futures are known risks, these are unconventional workplaces by definition, but the personal or subjective rewards are palpable. If we were to ask someone recently graduated, whose love of theatre has propelled her to take a job in the box office with a view to working her way up to be a stage manager, about what she might expect on the longer term, she would be sure to reply along the lines of long hours, nights working until late, getting home after the show has ended and after wind-down time with the cast, sleeping until about lunch time and then starting all over again.[15] The same may be true for so many people working in television and radio, not to mention the music business. This is so engrained, so much common knowledge, that the workforce usually adapts informal as well as formal ways of navigating pathways. Although the authors refer to the atmosphere behind the scenes in TV production, which can be 'exhilarating in its intensity' with 'camaraderie and fun' and although they comment that this can be a positive aspect of otherwise irregular work, they downplay this intensity and the remarkable resilience about moving onto the next project displayed by the interviewees.[16] Hesmondhalgh and Baker gloss over the high degree of self-reflexivity of the respondents. The ways in which they speak, including a low level of complaining and grumpiness, are also part of the occupational culture. It is also perhaps too easy to overlook the energy young people have, and the ways in which they invest this when working in a field which corresponds with their childhood dreams. Indeed, across most of the existing studies of subject formation in the creative sector we find countless references to childhood, to a love of drawing from a very young age, to the influence of growing up in a creative family, or to the experience of going to an exhibition that had a lifelong impact and so on. Amanda Bill quotes one young woman student as saying, 'Yeah well I was never academic, and I'm not sporty, at all! So I've always just taken creativity as just my thing' (Bill 2012, p. 57). In effect many of these jobs are 'dream jobs', there is a tremendous appeal to work that involves putting on a show because of the adrenalin and the euphoria and excitement when it all goes right, and the emotional outpourings when it goes less well. This apparently obvious point may also be a key to the paradox of 'knowing self-exploitation'. For any thorough analysis of the politics of creative labour this degree of 'capture' by the idea of a dream job has to be fully considered. Various factors account for this 'love for the job'. The well-established occupational cultures, known to young people well in advance are part of the attraction. This enthusiasm is also informed by awareness of not just other dull, routine or unrewarding jobs, but also by the possible shadow of unemployment, which makes a leap into fashion, art or the theatre even more appealing if there is 'nothing to lose'.

Socially Engaged Artists

Various issues confront the sociologist investigating the idea of artist-types, from the viewpoint of human capital and contemporary neo-liberal regimes of self-entrepreneurship. In what follows I suggest three ideal types, with many artists, inevitably, falling into more than one of these ideal types. The first is the 'socially engaged artist', the second is the 'global artist' and the third is the 'artist-précariat'. In each case I draw from existing scholarship and from the ongoing work I have been doing with visual artists in London and Berlin over a period of several years (McRobbie 2004). So, who are the professional socially engaged artists? There are various available definitions of socially engaged art, each of which emphasizes that this is art that foregrounds relationships between artists, communities and organizations, or art that has specific community-directed aims and outcomes, which favours collaboration and partnership, which fosters deep and lasting relationships with audiences and the public. These artists show a high degree of self-reflexivity and awareness of the realities and difficulties of pursuing such a career, offset by a sense of purpose, determination and belief in the socially valuable role played by the professional artist (see also Oakley 2009). They are deeply aware of the circumstances of their own artistic labour. Taylor and Littleton's anonymized interviews with fine artists several years after graduation throws light on this category of person (Taylor and Littleton 2013). One, for example, tells how her degree show was purchased in its entirety by Charles Saatchi but, as she ruefully describes, since then very little has happened. The artists interviewed by Taylor and Littleton tend to look for teaching jobs or for work in community settings or in publicly funded organizations. As one respondent says '...you have to accept that as a fine artist you gonna get paid peanuts' (Taylor and Littleton 2013).[17] It is hard to plan for a future in such circumstances and these respondents (reflecting the interviews in my own previous short study) emphasize the need for a second, if not third 'day job'. As another respondent said 'I'm an artist or I'm unemployed or I'm a mother. So take your pick' (Taylor and Littleton 2013). What was revealed in the small-scale survey I myself undertook with a group of artists who also fitted this category was a recognition of the exhausting schedules of part-time jobs with which they set themselves up in order to ensure they remained identifiable as professional artists, even when this meant they only got to their studios on a Sunday afternoon (McRobbie 2004). They too gravitated towards jobs that had a social use value rather than a commercial or entrepreneurial focus. Some got paid to teach photography to socially disadvantaged or socially excluded youth. Others had part-time jobs in arts therapy. Often those with the strongest socially engaged agenda were part of a flow-through process, using London to gain valuable experience and social contacts in order to return a few years later, to set up artist-led community initiatives and even youth clubs, in their country of origin (e.g. Brazil, Peru, Greece). Taylor and Littleton stress the strong professional ethos of the artists they interview and a sense of grievance that it should be so hard to earn a living in this way. This is offset by an awareness that being an artist is not a normal job and that this is part of its attraction. Instead of an overtly entrepreneurial ethos, what is seen is an understanding of the material circumstances of artists' working lives, and what needs to be done to manage such an unpredictable lifestyle. More generally, with this category of artist there is a concern in the work itself with matters of socio-political import, such as the environment, sexuality and gender, with popular culture rather than high culture, and with the interminable question of how art, which evades the clutches of the market, can be viable. These artists seek to be part of a wider dialogue about cultural politics and they tend to emphasize co-operation and solidarity rather than competition. Interestingly, almost all the artists interviewed by Sarah Lowndes in her book about Glasgow-based and Glasgow trained artists endorse this kind of stance, even though several also could be described as 'global artists' on the basis of prizes won and prestigious shows across the world (Lowndes 2003).

The Conduct of the 'Global Artist'

I use the category of 'global artist' to refer to an artist *persona* equated with international success and recognition across the art world. There have indeed been various studies undertaken of this category of artist, including Howard Becker's well-known work, several studies by Bourdieu, the more recent account of the rise of sponsorship in the arts by Wu, and two works by Sarah Thornton (Becker 1982; Wu 2003; Thornton 2008, 2014). Thornton's most recent book, which is based on a series of interviews and encounters with a selection of the world's best-known artists, provides the most useful context for the present discussion. On the one hand Becker's account of the art-work itself as being the final outcome of the labour of legions of assistants and technicians and cultural producers, is highly relevant here, since these artists are indeed seemingly surrounded by press agents, dealers, collectors, gallerists, curators, directors of art spaces and so on; on the other hand what also emerges is a model of subjectivity that adheres most closely to the artist as heroic individual, able to command the attention of so many with charm, charisma, stamina and in some cases a ruthlessly entrepreneurial outlook. Among Thornton's interviewees, Damien Hirst for example knowingly mocks his own vulgarity on the topic of money. Jeff Koons likewise plays a kind of cartoon character, the artist as wealthy showman, while Ai Wei Wei, politically committed, nevertheless orchestrates a kind of bravura artist-performance with himself, body and soul, as the art work, one that seems effortlessly to exude greatness. These are figures who can command the attention of audiences across the world; they are written about extensively and are the subject of films, documentaries and TV and radio programmes. Thus the question of conduct and of self-positioning within the art market is an important business strategy. It is in this domain that both the artist and the art work speak together as one voice as it were, and across the range of artists interviewed by Thornton distinct positions emerge in relation to precisely the nature of the art market and its workings. So, on the one hand Thornton's interviewees are acutely aware of how to play the game and how to position themselves in the context of this kind of interview for this kind of book; on the other hand they also reveal the social and political value systems to which they subscribe. Martha Rosler, for instance, is emblematic of second-wave feminist art, and her critique of 'market-driven' art and contemporary neoliberalism is vociferous; Isaac Julien refers to how his most recent work, *Playtime*, tackles this very subject of money and art world commercialism, while Tammy Rae Carland, whose work also serves as the book jacket, talks about having grown up in a 'welfare-class neighbourhood', the kind that 'art students visited to do their 'street photography' assignment'(Thornton 2014, p. 71). Thus we could say that even for the type of highly successful artist existing within this world of dealers and wealthy collectors, where the imperative to self-entrepreneurialize is tantamount, nevertheless there is a sense that artists constantly reflect critically on these very processes and the expectations that surround their own activities and that seem to dictate their behaviour and conduct of the self. They subject the institutions within which they make a living to constant scrutiny.

Then, stepping away from Thornton's account, but remaining focused on the realm of the global artist, in particular considering some of the black and Asian British artists,[18] we can see directly that this neoliberal mode of subjectification is both normalized to the extent that its requirements to constantly self-entrepreneurialize become routine and habitual (in much the same way that academics nowadays have constantly to update their CVs and engage in a wide range of self-promotional activities), so also is there deep awareness of the damaging effect that this endless activity has on daily life and health, while also reducing the time for the work itself.[19] The 'thinking time' is curtailed. Most of these artists too would prefer to live less 'dangerously', but are nevertheless reconciled to the demands of the job. What success means is that commissions and invitations to do shows across the world, come to them and allow them to make the work they want to. As a counter to neoliberal subjectification process, the concept of line of flight applies very well to these British but also 'global' black and Asian artists, since what can be seen across their work is some strong and undeniable presence or trace of inter-generational memory, one that rests on the experience of racial injustice, suffering, poverty or inequality. Drawing directly or indirectly from the writing of figures such as Stuart Hall, Homi Bhabha, Gayatri Spivak, Paul Gilroy and Frantz Fanon, and so in a sense indebted to post-colonial theory, these artists are deeply engaged with questions of colonial history, with miscarriages of justice and with the racialized politics of policing. Foremost too in a good deal of this work is familial memory as line of flight. This is vividly present in, for example, the *Ice Cream Project* (2004) by Chila Burman, where she recalls the daily labour of her father, an immigrant to England who made a living by first hiring then buying his own van, from which he sold ice creams and ice lollies on the beaches of the Wirral in Merseyside.[20] Similar tropes of memory of parental labour (in this case home dressmaking) can also be found in Yinka Shonibare's extensive use of batik textiles in his sculptural pieces.[21] This entire body of work asks questions about the experience of racism and it explores the strategies adopted by post-colonial people, which allow them to contest social domination, often in a subterfuge way. In Isaac Julien's *Vagabondia* these lines of flight come together in the section when he lets his mother speak directly to camera: 'my mother's text is in creole and was meant to be purposefully untranslated, positioning the spectator in relation to the original function,... it was not meant to be understood by the "colonial master"...It was an example of difference not always being available for translation, as such...its power is within its ability to withhold knowledge. That was the point of "hearing" creole as opposed to it being debated upon in Anglophone circles.'[22] Clearly this is an example of how post-colonial artists become, to use a Gramscian phrase, organic intellectuals, while also working in a global context, in effect they are transnational artist-intellectuals whose mode of address is forcefully directed towards diasporic and dispersed global populations.

The Artist-Précariat

The artist-précariat is a type of artist subject associated with the new global radicalisms and protests of the banking crisis and the post-2008 period of austerity, but emerging originally with the EuroMay-Day Movement of the early 2000s. Avowedly disenchanted with existing leftist groups, parties and platforms, these artists are profoundly shaped by the possibilities of digital media, open source, and peer-to-peer software (Terranova 2004). The shape and form of these new radicalisms often owes a great deal to a combination of new social media modes of instant communication and gathering, along with street theatre and performance art. The political *persona* of this artist-subject is also connected to developments in social and cultural theory, including both the focus on the potential politics of 'becoming' associated with Deleuze and Guattari, the various debates on post-Fordism, and the overall impact of the work of the neo Marxists or autonomist Marxists Hardt and Negri (see Raunig 2012). We could indeed pin this down to that point when mostly European 'socially engaged' artists encounter more sociological debates about post-Fordism, this in turn often connected with specific influential figures of an earlier generation. For example an artist like the Berlin based Marion von Osten, now in her fifties, describes how her own practice was heavily indebted to both punk DIY cultural politics and the writing of the Birmingham CCCS, including the work of Stuart Hall.[23] In teaching but also through informal self-organized events, conferences and activities as well as in the world of galleries and museums von Osten went on to interact intensively with this younger generation who looked to Deleuze and Guattari for a re-definition of creativity and inventiveness, and for whom the idea of what bodies can do to produce new worlds, provides both a further radicalization, and a direct challenge to the preferred artist subject *persona* of the new creative economy. The rhizomatic tactics and strategies of such creative activities are totally incommensurate with the vocabularies of the toolkits and business studies modules, and thus can be seen as a direct challenge to the 'entrepreneurial university'. In the field of precarious politics there is a multiplicity of points of engagement, against austerity and youth unemployment, in favour of 'occupation', against the increasing polarities of wealth and poverty, against short-term working without protection and security, against zero hours contracts and so on. In this space of activism there are squats, teach-ins, camps and assemblies. Artists and their fellow-protesters, engage in social research, investigating for example their own conditions of precarity and undertaking surveys among similarly positioned young people in different cities across the world (see Lorey 2015). As de Peuter says 'Artists and other cultural workers are, moreover, among the protagonists of struggles against exploitation and inequality in the neoliberal era' (de Peuter 2014, p. 274). This movement of the precarious seeks to create an 'emerging commons' (de Peuter 2014, p. 276). Likewise Rogoff has described the 'exceptionally creative modes of dissent 'developed by artists, curators and museum direc-tors frustrated by the kind of policy drift towards the marketization of everything' (Rogoff 2010, p. 10). It is within this sphere that the most innovative and dynamic forms of radicalism are being invented, since the lines of connection move freely from quite seemingly basic on-the-ground debates about creative labour and enforced precari-zation, with for example the growth of internships, to more philo-sophical considerations of precariousness based on concepts such as modulation, striation, de-territorialization, re-territorialization, exit and exodus (Raunig 2013; Lorey 2015). Precariousness is 'trans-formed in neoliberalism into a normalized political and economic strategy for securing domination' (Lorey 2015, p. 56).

Artists are hardly subdued populations, and from all three catego-ries there are many who enter into a disputatious dialogue with the very form of subjectivization that acts to ensure a quietened and market-oriented population of creatives. As de Peuter points out (see the opening quote for this chapter), artists have also actively objected to the role they have been expected to perform, as pioneers of the new economy. This is not to say the regime of biopolitics with its focus on artistic human capital is ineffective, overturned or subverted. The premise of capillary power is that it sets things in motion, it unleashes certain words and phrases and it sees them enter everyday vocabularies, it moves over and through so many organizations and institutions, and it also moves over and through the individuated body of the artist population, seeking to implant modes of conduct, all the while anticipating opposition and even revolt, which can, in turn, if interesting enough, be cynically plundered for insight and innovation for use by corporate culture. These new discursive regimes also comprise stable and decisive points of intervention, for example in education with its toolkits, new business pedagogies and modes of fiscal reform, giving rise to populations of creative workers formed in indebtedness and embarking into a labour market characterized by short-term work and projects without the protection of the now almost dismantled welfare state. The population within these new estates of pedagogy is, however, unruly and resentful of this mode of control, even when it has a superficial appeal. They are aware that they are being trained up and then left to their own devices to create a living for themselves. This new force of critique can be seen across the pages of the New York based online magazine *e-flux* (see http://www.e-flux.com/). The artist subject is intended to be a symbol of labour reform, someone willing to 'live on thin air'. It is an ironic re-working of Joseph Beuys to say that today 'everyone is an artist'. And yet the logic of the *précarité* movement is to take up this challenge and reclaim this slogan from the policy-makers into something more in keeping with Beuys' egalitarian intent. We can conclude then with the argument that the point where toolkits, instruments and new entrepreneurial pedagogies find their institutional (and non-institutional) home, those spaces in which they are introduced and become embedded as new orthodoxies, also become sites of antagonism and tension. Ideally the entrepreneurial university would see something of an erosion of the old intellectual 'freedoms' of the university and art-school system, and its replacement by what we might call the 'business-school model'. It may even be that the actual outcome of policy, such as the formulation of instruments and toolkits, is less important to contemporary power than the push to expel from the academy and to expunge from popular memory, the traces of lines of flight that memorialize previous moments such as those characterized by a radical social democratic agenda for arts, which made culture a public good and which supported free education, across all three sectors, primary, secondary and university level. This would be to argue that the creativity *dispositif* is charged also with the task of de-historicizing those institutions whose existence was at least partly due to decades of post-1945 political struggle waged across a range of sites including the trade unions, school teachers and academics, the UK Labour Party prior to New Labour, the women's movement, anti-racist organizations, as well as the educational departments of the art galleries and museums sector.

4

The Gender of Post-Fordism: 'Passionate Work', 'Risk Class' and 'A Life of One's Own'

Risk Class and Mobility of Gender

In this chapter I make partial use of two of the concepts from my previous feminist writing. One is the assemblage of forces that together construct a 'post-feminist masquerade' as a way of revoking on putative equality by inscribing young women within a series of elaborate body rituals defined by the fashion-beauty-complex. This suggests, with a 'post-feminist' ironic touch, a femininity that defers, in the end and somewhat reluctantly, to male privilege and hence to the status quo (following Joan Rivière),[1] and thus serves ultimately if ambivalently to uphold existing gender hierarchies despite the suggestion otherwise (Rivière 1928/1986; McRobbie 2008). The second concept is that of 'working girl' (McRobbie 2008). This helped refine an analysis of what happened or rather what would ideally happen when these new (active but docile) subjects of post-feminist times entered the labour market with their good qualifications (thanks to the meritocratic efforts of New Labour). What would happen, I hypothesized, was that, having abandoned the idea of a new feminist politics, on the urging of powers that be, these young women, at that point at which they became mothers, while also wanting to maintain a career, would adhere to the principles of the 'work–life' balance, which shared some elements in common with the post-feminist masquerade insofar as it assumed a kind of 'sexual compromise' or settlement; that is, a way of reneging on ideas of gender equality in both home and workplace, and thus foregoing any feminists' demand for equality in favour of a strategy that entailed conventionally feminine practices of self-management and planning. By and large women would compromise in their careers, by stepping back from so-called normal career progression, so as to fit in the demands of busy motherhood, and they would relinquish the need to request full participation of their male partners in domestic duties, thus avoiding conflict, the danger of becoming a stereotypical 'nagging' or complaining wife, or else a confrontational angry feminist. In searching for ways of dealing with such obvious inequalities, women could turn to the feminine media and popular culture and the quality press and TV, which would provide an endless supply of household and workplace 'solutions' and managerial strategies for dealing with these post-feminist crises. Most important, in this regard, across these channels of media, is the attention paid to maintaining a vibrant and sexually attractive appearance. At no point in time can the busy young working woman afford to 'let herself go'. For New Labour this agenda of self-management provided an alternative to the feminist debates from previous times within the Labour Party, which challenged male partners and husbands to share household duties. It also meant that male careers were not to be forestalled by domestic duties beyond tokenistic periods of paternal leave. Bearing these concerns in mind, in this chapter I focus on both working girls and working mothers through the lens of post-Fordism and the modern work society. In keeping with the thematics explored in previous chapters I try to decipher the fine lines between acquiescence and accommodation to the various forms of regulation and control that shape the new world of work, in this case creative work, and those openings to opposition or 'lines of flight'. For women, new forms of feminism connected with the politics of precariousness provide such a space for antagonism to the new work regime, but as I shall show this is countered by the prevailing and powerful ideology of 'passionate work', which, although it has a long legacy in the history of feminine popular culture, comes now to stand as the female version of the more macho Steve Jobs (of Apple) ethos of 'love your work', which in turn reduces the potential for new forms of labour organization and even justifies wage stagnation and regression (Gregg 2011; Adkins and Devers 2014).

With these counterposing forces of passionate versus precarious work, I propose in this chapter that the gender of post-Fordism is female and that, at least in the UK, since the shift to a post-industrial, service-sector led economy, women have participated in work (albeit often in a part-time capacity) across the boundaries of social class and ethnicity, to the point that this wage-earning capacity marks both the 'sense of equality' and some of the limits of liberal feminist gains in the struggles for equality. In a real sense, such battles came to be fought with the idea of gaining economic independence from a husband or partner as an objective, and this providentially fitted with some of the concessionary gestures that could, from the late 1970s, be made to the rising tide of feminist demands. Work marks the spot. Young women are addressed as enthusiastic 'career girls'. This 'settlement to women' then stands as a backdrop against which many major socio-economic changes are played out. Such a notion of settlement has certain national characteristics, with the result that what pertains in the UK does not necessarily exist similarly in seemingly comparable western European countries such as Germany or Italy, or indeed in the rest of the Western world, and comes consequently to act as a marker of cultural differences. Alongside this consideration of women as a driving force for the UK work-society I also, in this chapter, go against the grain of a good deal of sociological thinking in regard to questions of gender, class, work and ideas of social mobility. There is much current sociological writing that dispels the myth of social mobility and points to the widening gap of wealth and poverty in the UK, and which also shows that there are greater chances for decreasing social mobility than politicians across the party spectrum wish to acknowledge (Savage et al. 2013). My emphasis here is that, under the impact of two decisive forces, those younger women who would typically have been seen as working class, come to be symbolically severed from the socio-economic and cultural context of working-class life. These forces are the expansion of further and higher education, in particular the new universities and art schools, and the shift to a service economy, with post-Fordism changing the modern work economy, so that it now is at least partly organized around 'immaterial labour', 'emotional labour' or, in my own parlance, 'passionate work'. So, social inequality undoubtedly increases under the conditions of contemporary neoliberal society, but at the same time there is an expansion of the middle classes, especially the lower middle classes, with the illusion (or sense, or affective condition) of mobility being key to the achievement of successful femininity. Perhaps this paradox is actually the point. Women remain disadvantaged in comparison to their male counterparts in the labour force (e.g. they have low pay, wage gap, glass ceiling, part-time work), but despite their actual income or material life circumstances, young women are now propelled by strong ideological forces in media and popular culture, into a more nebulous social terrain that can be described as 'aspirational' and so they feel themselves to be 'on the move', to be overcoming past obstacles, which held them back. They are lifted out of the entanglements of race, ethnicity and class, and addressed simply as a population of women. These young (formerly working-class) women do not disavow their class or ethnicity of belonging; instead, they simply see the potential for a more exciting life, or as Ulrich Beck puts it a 'life of one's own' (Beck 2000). Beverley Skeggs' writing on respectability most accurately captures one important dynamic in this seeming de-classification process (Skeggs 1997). She shows how normative femininity comes to be attached to the need to dis-identify with traditional female working-class values and lifestyle. This becomes more sharply marked within the politics of neoliberalism pursued from 1997 under the New Labour government. There is an unmooring from working-class identity, as young women increasingly orient themselves towards those jobs that bear some of the trimmings of the service sector, especially those focusing on self-presentation, on being well groomed, on body-work and on the media and culture industries, even if at the lower reaches of these hierarchies, such as fashion retail or hairdressing. Such jobs do not mark out a decisive improvement in life chances; nevertheless, they rely on an understanding of the attractive, well-groomed body as being a key part of the job, and this in turn becomes a mark of pride, a sign of self-responsibility and a way of 'feeling good' about the self. Self-perception, in an individualized society, is directed towards a less class-defined existence. These young women want to 'uproot' themselves and go somewhere. Entrance into a new swollen middle class does not, however, come with any promises of economic security or stability, even with the possession of a degree qualification. Indeed as the process of expansion occurs so also does the idea of 'middle-classness' come to be equated with increasing insecurity.

For this reason I find the term 'risk class' recently proposed by Ulrich Beck to be a valuable tool to think through this process of movement or 'social mobility' (Beck 2014). I want to retain the idea of social mobility, using it against the grain to suggest something other than the projected movement upwards with which it is typically associated. This is mobility, which does not quite know where it is going. Social mobility as a result of women taking up the kinds of jobs that have recently become available in the new service sector may be notional, but symbolically it means a lot, because the alternative is equated with individual failure. Nowadays young women's feminine status depends on having an interesting, possibly creative and ideally glamorous job. As Sabine Hark has also argued, it is as though the path forged by feminism in this respect has been more profound, perhaps unintentionally so, in that it opened up a structure of opportunity, a world of possibilities, even if it remained unpopular and unpalatable to the women who gained some of these opportunities as a result (Hark 2014). Of course, this does not mean there were not also new hierarchies created, new forms of degraded labour in the service sector occupied by women who were not able to benefit from aspirational jobs. The care sector, the call centres, the cleaning jobs and the supermarket check-out jobs have all seen huge growth in the last twenty or so years. They too are dominated by women. But if we focus on younger women only it is possible to see a 'refusal of work' taking the form of an escape from drudgery and monotonous work in favour of self-directed, and more autonomous activity. One way of understanding this is to suggest that the idea of 'romance' has been deflected away from the sphere of love and intimacy and instead projected into the idea of a fulfilling career. No longer looking for a husband as a sole breadwinner, young women romanticize the idea of career. They want to find work about which they can feel passionate. Passionate work in turn becomes a further mark of feminine intelligibility and success. This desire transcends the boundaries of both class and ethnicity, while simultaneously retaining and even reinforcing hierarchical characteristics along these lines of demarcation and difference. In the pages that follow I seek to give an account of this new romance of feminine work. Of course, it is not so totally new. Girls' popular literature through the twentieth century produced many narratives that celebrated the idea of an exciting job, from becoming a ballerina, to being a show-jumper and working with ponies, to training as a journalist or 'roving reporter'. These kinds of dreams are no longer the prerogative of the middle classes and have become much more widely circulated. The words 'dream job' have emphatically entered the terrain of everyday life, especially for young women.[2]

Feminist scholarship on work and employment, especially in the UK, emerged from the mid 1970s onwards within the paradigm of industrial society and was, as a result, directed towards working-class women's experience, usually on the factory floor. It was a terrain defined and investigated by socialist-feminist sociologists (see Pollert 1981, 1988; Phizacklea 1990; Westwood 1985). Books with titles such as *Girls, Wives, Factory Lives* conveyed an interest in everyday life for women on the shop-floor, and indeed one question was that of resistance and opposition and how working-class women countered the reality of repetitive low-paid and low-status work. Often it was the dual role they had as wives and mothers (with pictures of weddings and babies decorating each woman's cramped work spaces) that provided an escape from unrewarding employment. Despite the occasional visibility of working-class women as active trade unionists (e.g. the Dagenham car factory walk-outs of 1968 and the Grunwick strike of 1976) it was more often the case that women were seen as supportive of their husband's militancy (such as the organizing of miner's wives during the miner's strike of 1984). The time needed for labour organization beyond working hours was seen as conflicting with the dual role they had as mothers and home-makers. Annie Phizacklea's important study of fashion manufacturing in the West and East Midlands drew attention to the inaugural moment of post-industrialization for Asian women whose husbands had been laid off from the car factories (Phizacklea 1990). With small pay-offs, these men were able to set up as small-scale fashion and clothing suppliers with their wives sewing for long hours, sometimes on a home-working basis, or else in small production units comprising just a handful of machinists, pressers and others involved in assembling cheap ready-to-wear items for market stalls and low-cost fashion retailers. Anna Pollert also moved to considering the emergence of post-Fordism through her important essay on the 'Third Italy', at that point seen as the exemplar of the shift to short runs, just in time systems of production, EPOS retailing and the use of highly skilled (female) producers scattered about the small towns and villages of the Emilia Romagna area of northeast Italy, with the *Benetton* company best exemplifying all the features of post-Fordist fashion (Pollert 1988). The question is, what happens to the younger generation of this female workforce whose lives were spent on the factory floor or at a sewing machine or knitting machine at home? Young women take flight. Updating the debate on the Third Italy, Hadjimichalis has recently made the point that the children of this Italian workforce adamantly do not want to carry on alongside their parents (or mothers) doing the same kind of job; instead they would rather be fashion models (Hadjimichalis 2006; see also www.businessoffashion.com). Old ways of working and producing (such as hand-working) are downgraded and fashion is the site for this kind of creative aspiration process. Today the daughters of the mothers look for other opportunities with higher status. This desire is then seen as accounting for the loss of skill in the fashion production sector, a loud refrain across the fashion sector. Young people do not want to work in a gloomy and possibly dirty factory environment, they prefer to work in a 'studio space'.[3] We could say then that the development of post-Fordism finds symbolic expression through generation and the desires of working-class youth and their flight from unrewarding, mundane work. They take hold of this opportunity to do something different, giving rise to what the auto-nomist Marxists call 'the refusal of work'. The argument I make in this book is that this refusal is more of a desire and a yearning for rewarding work, something that is within sight and perhaps within reach through access to further and higher education. This 'flight' also acquires gendered characteristics. The impact of 1970s feminism made the idea of a career for young women something completely acceptable. Unlike the autonomist Marxists I do not make such fulsome claims for a new radical politics emerging from the 'social factory', instead I see a field of ambivalence and tension, where lines of flight connect past parental struggles with the day-to-day experi-ences of their children in the modern work economy. Labour anxieties are refracted through ideas of creativity and the demands of self-organized work. What we see is a new arena for individualized con-testation and questioning within the landscape of contemporary labour reform and the modern work economy. Overall in this chapter I aim to offer some new theoretical insight in relation to gender and the politics of creativity through a critique of the work of the autono-mist Marxists.

Birmingham v Bologna: *Operaismo* and the Successes (or Failures) of Class Struggle?

The strand of radicalism associated with the Italian autonomist tradi-tion was relatively dormant during the 1980s and early 1990s but sprang to the attention of readers with the edited collection by Hardt and Virno (1996) along with *Empire* (Hardt and Negri 2000) fol-lowed by *Multitude* (Hardt and Negri 2006). In the many articles and books written in recent years on the topics of precarious labour, immaterial and affective labour, all of which are understood within the over-arching frame of post-Fordist regimes of production, there is a failure to foreground gender, or to knit gender and ethnicity into prevailing concerns with class and class struggle. While theoretically capable of endorsing the difference and autonomy of various groups including the category of 'woman' and the politics of feminism, the concept of multitude is developed with an implicit focus on the male worker, with the result that questions of gender and feminism, con-sidered alongside and within the idea of affective labour, nevertheless

appear as an afterthought. Despite the prolific use of Deleuzian concepts of pre-subjective processes of becoming without becoming fully
formed, the earlier masculinist class politics of the shop-floor in
which Negri and others were engaged through the 1960s in fact
remains a template for this work and for recent responses to it,
without, for example, the kinds of conceptual framings of Stuart
Hall's notion of articulation (Hall 1988, 1992). Taking up the idea
of disarticulation to show how gender comes to be severed from
questions of class, I rally Stuart Hall's thinking to develop a feminist
politics of cultural and creative work without the 'hang-over' of
'shop-floor workerism'. I make the claim that the gender of post-
Fordism is female. By prioritizing gender I am also critiquing its
invisibility in this current field of new radical political discourse
associated with writers like Hardt, Virno, Lazzarato and Negri.[4]
I challenge these writers for their insistence on class, as the defining
meta-concept for understanding contemporary work and for imagin-
ing a radical political future. Fundamentally this is a 'labour-society'
model where the 'decline of labour' and the shift of the centre
of gravity to the non-work sphere, is blamed for a wide range of
contemporary pathologies including the 'opacity of groups', widespread de-politicization, and the 'ruin of the self ' (Virno 2005,
p. 20). These writers take their lead from the shop-floor and are
then disposed, because of significant social changes, to consider
'life itself', that is the non-work sphere, the sites of everyday life, or
indeed the field of culture and community. In contrast to this the
Birmingham Centre for Contemporary Cultural Studies writing
started with the scenarios of everyday life and developed a *Marxisant*
approach which allowed proliferating struggles to be understood in
articulation with, and sometimes against each other. Class was, from
the start, a cultural as well as an economic category and, as Stuart
Hall argued, it always existed in articulation with other determining
forces[5]. Of course for decades it has been the intention of governments to attempt to disarticulate class society by ideological means,
to reduce its salience and to downplay the central antagonism between
capital and labour. These have been successful strategies pursued now
over a period of forty years (e.g. in the UK since the time of the
Thatcher government) and this fading out of class has to be taken
into account in any cogent sociological analysis. The defeat of
working-class politics, and the vilification of organized labour has
had lasting repercussions for young women, is what I am suggesting.
These changes are coterminous with the rise of individualization,
with the various attendant technologies of the self which are designed
to work in a highly seductive manner with various enticements. Class

is displaced and relegated to a twilight zone, at just that point at which women are moving decisively into the labour-market, so much so that these processes need to be seen together. The 'older men' of labour are being replaced by the younger women, for whom the trade union is less of a focal point in their working lives. The antagonistic relations formed in the struggle between capital and labour, or between the state and subordinated social groupings whose subjugation entails a distinctive relation to labour (for instance the unemployed, and those people who are left in poverty because of an inability to work because of illness or disability), continue to provide the key structuring mechanisms for class formation, but this formation does not exist in isolation from the equally influential factors of gender and ethnicity. And in the time of post-Fordism and of post-industrial society in general the experience of being a 'worker' is but one element in a more complex configuration of personhood. Despite the Deleuzian moves introduced around notions of difference and becoming, as well as the use of the more capacious concept of the multitude, Hardt and Negri are locked within a class model which permits no space for reflecting on the centrality of gender and sexuality in the post-Fordist era, with the result that there is a failure to consider the meaning of what is often referred to as the feminization of work.

Hardt, Negri et al. urge a return to Marx's *Grundrisse* and to the abstract knowledge concretized in machinery (and now in the computational codes) of production. This affects the relations of the workforce in the light of the increasing significance of this abstract knowledge or General Intellect. Where machines or computers do most of the productive work, the standard measure of value for the work carried out by the actual workforce is lost. Marx predicts this leads to widespread social disruption and class struggle. Virno and the others instead see new forms of cynicism and opportunism develop not from within the workplace, but from outside, in everyday life, or in the street which becomes a site for 'urban training' (Virno 2005, p. 14). It is the shallowness and superficiality of these states of mind which lead Virno, for example, to envisage such discontent eventually transmogrifying, through a politics of disenchantment, into new political subjectivities. But, I argue, without a concept of 'culture', the idea of 'the street' can only connote a weaker space which is not the shop-floor and hence not primarily an expected location for class politics. In this thinking the idea of the factory-floor still takes precedence even when the workforce is in flight from it. Gender questions, when they are taken up, instead of being considered through the idea of feminization of work, emerge through a focus on the family wage and how this kind of pay settlement historically made to the male worker, meant that care work and the domestic labour of reproduction carried out by women came to be relegated outside the field of value and hence unpaid. It is to this 'old' dilemma that the Hardt and Negri-influenced feminists return, to my mind as though twenty or thirty years of scholarship on sexuality, difference, and on gender, culture and ideology did not exist. There is, then, a reductionism based on a hierarchy of abstractions at play here which configures the 'classic' antagonism between capitalist production and its subjugated workforce as the primary force for understanding contemporary sociality. In contrast a cultural studies approach, starting with Hoggart and Williams, and especially through the writing of Stuart Hall and Paul Gilroy, de-centred the significance of the factory and looked to the social and urban environment, to women, to youth, to immigrant communities, to the fields of leisure and sport, to popular culture and entertainment.

Arguably the 'culturalism' found in much of the early CCCS work led to an over-stating of the capacity of working-class populations for resistance and perhaps to an over-emphasis on the power of the symbolic meaning attached to the items (such as hairstyles, fashion, motor-bikes etc.) with which such groupings chose to identify themselves (Hall and Jefferson 1976). Young black and white, male and female, working-class people were able to take hold of these cultural resources, often with spectacular effects. But as various critics of the CCCS work showed, these were often short-lived rebellions or else they were quickly channelled into the commercial machineries of media production, as discussed in previous chapters of this book (Thornton 1996). Nevertheless, one reason why this work, most of it carried out in the mid to late 1970s, remains significant is that the concept of culture which underpinned it was historically and politically rooted. It shaped everyday life and leisure, the workings of the various social institutions, and the wider urban environment. Thanks to the writing of E. P. Thompson, Raymond Williams and Richard Hoggart, the idea of popular culture as a landscape for resistance and protest had a legitimate place in social understanding. The *Operaismo* work is notable for the way it brings back ideas of agency (but this time without a subject) to the forefront of political thinking, which in turn permits a different idea of resistance to power to emerge. By abandoning the teleology in Marx, and combining the Deleuzian notion of desire with the concept of *potenza*, Hardt and Negri writing in *Empire* see the possibility of 'decentralized or mass conceptions of force and strength' (Hardt and Negri 2000). Three innovative elements are brought into play: *first*, a decisive attempt to project forwards in the context of the defeats of the Left in Italy and to imagine and envisage new potentialities for radicalism through dissecting what Virno calls the 'emotional situation' characteristic of contemporary subjectivity; *second*, this possibility for radicalism is based on a subject-less form of class politics, now configured as flows, as waves of action, as lines of flight, and as events; and *third* while fully confronting the scale of defeat through the 1980s, years that, according to Virno, saw the growth of a celebratory postmodern lifestyle, there is in this work a deliberate attempt to reinstate a sense of victory over the capitalist machine. The authors see post-Fordism as a response on the part of capital to these *potenza* struggles of the working class through the 1960s and 1970s. They repeatedly cite the 'refusal of work' on the part of the young factory workers (in Italy and France) who would not conform to labour discipline, and who exited the factory. More specifically they see capital as having to make concessions (or give some ground) such that, with better wages in their pockets the working class expresses new desires, new dreams of lifestyle. Likewise young working-class people declare their wishes for a different and better life. Yet lacking a strong concept of working-class culture these authors can only rest their case on the refusal of work, and on better wages to allow a disposable income. In contrast the Birmingham CCCS writers envisage resistance now displaced away from the parent culture and the various factory shop-floors, which were also the sites of worker defeats during those years, to the scenes of youth culture; that is, to where their children find opportunities to express the dilemmas of powerlessness of their parents through symbolic means by virtue of their engagement with the objects and styles of consumer culture that can be subverted and played back in the form of subcultural politics of meaning. While it is never quite clear where the refusal of work from the viewpoint of the Italian authors leads to, (i.e. where do those who refuse actually go?) its significance lies in its ability to take capitalism by surprise, and force some concessions. In contrast the Birmingham School (drawing on Gramsci's notion of the 'national-popular') had a more historical definition of culture as common or popular resource, which could potentially remain in the hands of its owners. My own contribution to the CCCS work argued that working-class young women were able to appropriate aspects of feminine popular culture to register their own disenchantment with the societal norms of decorous young womanhood, and with the limited options available to themselves in contrast (McRobbie 1976). For example working-class, low-achieving girls at school would defy rules about hair, make-up and nail varnish, while punk girls wore garish 'vulgar' make-up and borrowed from the wardrobe of so-called unrespectable women, 'tarts' or prostitutes. As Hebdige and others pointed out, all of these expressions including those by girls drew on a repertoire of forgotten or somehow lost elements of past working-class lives (Hebdige 1979). In retrieving this tradition now I am also re-inflecting it, with young women nowadays bringing to their creative or cultural workplaces something of the politics of the 'parent culture', not a specific class politics, more a desire to overcome the limits imposed on their parents (or mothers') lives through their subordinated position in the labour market. In this context culture plays the role of social glue for the intergenerational recording of past struggles, for the history of domination to be archived and not forgotten. It is these histories that inform the lines of flight that I argue are a characteristic of contemporary 'hairline politics' and that have a particular resonance in regard to younger women and the micro-political tensions around feminism, which come to be played out in the field of creative labour.

Where my argument connects productively with the *Operaismo* writers is in the idea of mobility, and the desire to escape a lifetime of repetitive, low-status, unrewarding work. (This could also be seen in Dick Hebdige's seminal account of British mods; see Hebdige 1979.) The autonomist authors offer an original analysis of post-Fordist's need for brain-power (mass intellect). One of the concessions granted was that work could become more meaningful, and that the workforce could be allowed to act more autonomously in the workplace and have a greater decision-making capacity. This coincides with or even triggers the development of new technology and new forms of communications and information-based production. The combination of this brain-power along with new communications technology means that capitalism is able to deliver high degrees of customization and design in its commodities to increasingly diverse and lifestyle-conscious groups of consumers including the now more mobile working class. Overall the successes of the class struggle result in higher wages and a more participatory and intelligent role in the workplace. Capitalism, according to these autonomist writers, was forced to concede to the workers' struggles of the 1970s. In contrast to the more usual account of the rise of post-Fordism (such as Lash and Urry 1994) the *Operaismo* writers offer a perspective that foregrounds the agency of the labour force and the changing nature of work itself. These factors are indisputably important, as is the focus they provide on the ways in which young people expressed a desire to 'exit the factories'. In Italy capital was forced onto the defensive, as fewer younger people were willing to subject themselves to labour discipline. Jobs had to become more attractive to workers, for them to be willing to perform these tasks. Post-Fordism is then an incorporative strategy and capital is weakened because having given way, in certain respects, it finds itself reliant on the mental capacities of the work-force in an unprecedented way. And because the workers are able to exercise their brains, thereby achieving a kind of autonomous space for critical thought and reflection, they are in a profound sense less captured by the dogma and dictates of contemporary power, and capital lags behind them, increasingly dependent on their ideas and initiatives.

These mental capacities, it is then argued, produce a disposition towards co-operation and collectivity, qualities that are also required in the new workshops or studios of cognitive capitalism. 'Today the production of wealth requires cooperation and interactivity' (Hardt and Negri 2000, p. 48). The workers now need to talk to each other and make joint decisions; they can argue and express their opinions as to how a commodity needs to be produced or a service provided. With this quality of interaction, the workforce is therefore now better able to re-imagine solidaristic forms of mutual support and co-operation. Hence the strand of optimism. Lazzarato points out that the workers can now also become entrepreneurs themselves, no longer must they be seen only as employees and as mere wage labour-ers and of course this chimes well with the growth in the last three decades, of freelance or precarious self-employment among young people or with new forms of micro-entrepreneurialism associated with the growing cultural and creative and media sectors of advanced capitalism. It also permits that a labour politics no longer be seen as dependent only on the role of 'worker'. But there are fine lines of difference between the *Operaismo* writers as to how far this *potenza* can be stretched to envisage such possible forms of communality or 'commons'. There is a discrepancy between the contributions of Hardt and Negri and Lazzarato, and the darker comments from Virno and Berardi (Virno 2005; Berardi 2009). Joyful ideas of com-munality and even communistic sentiments are countered by a power-ful regime that inculcates cynicism and opportunism. This cultural milieu of small talk and parties exasperates Virno pushing him, and then Berardi also, to refer to the psycho-pathologies of contemporary subjectivity. With the tight lines between work and leisure dissolved, with spare time taking on the urgency of working time, they see this party culture and its subjective states as being transferred into the workplace, infecting it. We might stop here for a moment and reflect on this interesting observation. Are these psycho-pathologies also gendered? How do young men and women experience distress differently in their attempts to make an independent living in these new informal fields of work? How would such affective states be analysed? There are paradoxical dynamics, a 'healthy' potential for mobilization against oppressive work offset by a toxic brew of life-threatening psycho-pathologies, including depression, panic attacks, alcoholism and drug addiction. There are also some significant absences in these accounts, do young women get the same chances for brain power and communality as their male counterparts? Or, are the new spaces of cognitive capitalism superficially egalitarian but in reality still gender-segregated labour markets? Rosalind Gill's account of new media cyber-workers is relatively mild in its critique of a culture norm in these workplaces that re-instates male privilege and celebrates a return to sexism, albeit with a pervasive irony predicated on some gestural but dismissive awareness of feminism (Gill 2007).

Hardt and Negri in *Empire* rely on an expanded concept of working class that becomes 'multitudinous' and no longer tied to specific nation states, thus including migrants and refugees moving across continents in search of a better life. While the women's movement is fleetingly referred to for the role it played in disrupting the nuclear family and thus interrupting the reliable supply of youthful labour (presumably by encouraging women to have fewer children), this emphasis on women's prime responsibility for reproduction is not updated. This is a class-dominated and gender-essentialist account of the changing world of work. Despite possible openings to gender within the multitude, gender is subsumed into class, as is race and ethnicity, and feminists may well experience a kind of flashback to moments where women could only legitimately be considered if cast in the language of either domestic labour or reproduction. As Gayle Rubin reminded us, Marxism (even Marxist-feminism) was simply not able to understand and critically engage with the wider questions of sexuality that at the time resonated across the many spheres of everyday life including work (Rubin 1984). The centrality of Deleuzian desires, corporeality and libidinal flows, does not solve this problem. The idea of multitude may well be broader and more capacious than class. Indeed the use of Deleuze disguises the inattention to gender and ethnicity. The sites of most of the struggles referred to are traditionally male sectors such as car assembly lines and the related activities associated with the automobile industry. The industrial militancy, which, the writers argue, created the crisis for capitalism, took place once again in largely male-dominated sectors. Even when the authors refer to the black struggles in the US in the 1960s they focus on the car assembly lines again and not on the community, which was the nodal point for Civil Rights (Gilroy 1987). The refusal of work and the exit from the factories was a primarily white male activity.

How then can we talk about the gender of post-Fordism? The women's movement reached a peak in the years that coincided with the crisis in profitability for many major companies across the world. And since the structure of patriarchal society at that time had produced gender-segregated labour markets with men occupying the better paid and more highly skilled industrial jobs, the shift to a post-industrial economy adversely affected the employment prospects for working-class men while having the opposite effect for women. The nature of work in a post-Fordist economy favoured the large skill-pool and the flexibility of the female workforce. In the UK, women flowed into work from the mid 1980s and have continued to do so ever since. The UK has seen the growth of post-Fordist techniques of production in various sectors, for example, retail, fashion and clothing, furniture and household goods, DIY, and a huge service sector, which booms especially in London and the southeast as London became a global city and centre for the finance industry through the 1980s. As women are more present in the workplace, new goods and commodities become available, catering for the needs of the working woman rather than the mother at home. Sean Nixon showed how the fashion retail chain *Next* set up in the early 1980s offered a perfect example of fashion with high-design content targeted towards the new style-conscious and aspirational white-collar worker (Nixon 1993). What seems to start with *Next* in the UK, expands across many products and goods, leading twenty years later to a global rise in spectacular consumption, for which women serve as the main market. The flow of women into work goes hand-in-hand with the expansion of further and higher education and the flooding into the universities of young women in increasingly high volume through the 1980s and onwards to the current moment. Where in the mid 1970s only a tiny trickle of middle-class young women went to university, thirty years later girls outnumber boys in their take up of university places and in some universities there are twice as many females as

males. Across Europe and the US and other affluent countries it
has become normal for women in their thirties and forties today to
have much higher qualifications than their mothers. Young women
from working-class backgrounds have taken up the opportunity to
train and consequently make their way up through the ranks of
various administrative and institutional sectors, including the public
sector, health, education, welfare, as well as in the new financial
services such as insurance. Young black and Asian women across
different socio-economic backgrounds seek higher qualifications
and better-paid work. With all of this activity inevitably there is a
corrosion of the old core of working-class people, as the young
men (of the Hardt and Negri argument) who started off in the factories in the late 1970s, thirty years later, face early retirement or
redundancy. During these years in the UK and elsewhere (e.g.
Germany, Italy, France, the US) there have been processes of class
de-alignment, class fragmentation and new forms of social divide
based on more acute polarities of poverty and unemployment on
the one hand, and relative affluence on the other hand. Women
come to embody processes of mobility and transition. Some take
on extra work because their husbands are made redundant,
some black women, mothers and daughters alike, are the main
breadwinners because racism more widely and labour market conditions in particular discriminate against their fathers and brothers
in specifically gendered ways. Gender is made to articulate with
wider female individualization processes so as to seemingly diminish
the significance of class, so that its new political meaning for women
rests on this faded-out status (Bauman 1990). If working-class
young women, through media and lifestyle are exhorted to dis-
identify with a working-class position, if in the jobs they do such as
retail manager in fashion shops like *Karen Millen* or *Warehouse*,
there is no tradition of trade unionization, but there are possibilities
for further education and 'lifelong learning', is it not the case that
by and large capital and the state have succeeded in producing
an aspirational female workforce in this respect, so that the envisag-
ing of labour organization and the optimism of Hardt and Negri
are over-stated? How do the politics of the General Intellect or the
dimensions of cognitive capitalism play out, for example, in the
expanding fashion industry? The answer to this question is more
ordinary than the autonomist writers would envisage, there is
indeed an in-flow of higher qualified people across this sector but
this is no guarantee of a political consciousness emerging, instead it
can simply mean that the capitalist machinery works more efficiently
than before.

Affective Labour

When we shift registers away from the antagonisms of capital and labour brought about by the ascendance of the general intellect, downwards to the actual field of struggle, examples are relatively few and far between. Lazzarato follows the actions of *Les Intermittents Du Spectacle* in France, but we would find it hard to locate comparable struggles by women in the creative sectors fighting for either union recognition and hence better social security, or indeed for entitlements for freelance workers or for the self-employed, let us say in regard to maternity leave or for childcare provision such as access to employer-run creches. And, as I suggested above, there have been few recent labour campaigns within the fashion retail sector, where women predominate, for the right to union recognition. In the context of campaigns such as UK Uncut and Occupy, these have been orchestrated largely by people, such as students, working outside the sector not inside. A further difficulty appears when some of the abstract concepts from Hardt and Negri that envisage moments of liberatory joy or communistic impulses within the communicative communities that come together within the new fields of work, are taken rather too literally, resulting in a celebratory account of agency in unlikely locations, as in the case of upscale fashion modelling (Wissinger 2007, 2009). With the exception of writing emerging directly from a theoretical dialogue with figures like Hardt and Negri such as that by Lorey (see also Raunig 2013) who makes a direct connection between the *potenza* of the General Intellect and the uprisings dating back to the EuroMayDay 2000 rallies by precarious workers in western Europe, the possible politics of affective labour can indeed be misconstrued, yielding to an untenable notion of radicalism, even taking into account the emphasis on spontaneous actions and deliberately short-lived events (Lorey 2015; Raunig 2013). For this reason my own focus for the remainder of this chapter and in its conclusion will be on the management of female affect as a requirement for 'pleasure in work' such that not to find and express such enjoyment becomes a mark of personal failure or of being the wrong person for the job. The tool for achieving this contemporary affect is 'passionate work'.

Discussing the concept of affective labour, Michael Hardt maintains the *potenza* emphasis of the autonomist Marxist tradition, by seeing possibilities for subversion and for the creation of new forms of sociality, in effect glimpsing an alternative to capitalist rationality, through this kind of work (Hardt 1999). He acknowledges the fact that affective labour is, and has been, significantly gendered and associated with women's activities. Hardt defines the idea of immaterial labour as part of the 'production of services that result in no material and durable good', but instead 'immaterial goods such as knowledge or communication' (Hardt 1999, p. 10). While he uses immaterial labour interchangeably with affective labour, it is the latter that leads him to consider the realm of 'maternal activities'. Hardt comments that increasingly forms of labour entail elements of care, or emotion, and that these labour practices have the capacity to produce 'collective subjectivities' that could contest the formidable power of contemporary capitalism. In effect this is where Hardt extends the General Intellect to the kind of work usually performed by women. Hardt is here pinpointing features within the now expansive service economy (where even manufacturing is envisaged as a service) that rely on such high degrees of communication as well as informatics, that this has the possibility for an overflow of sociality and a force for transformation. Because affective labour is now in a 'dominant position in the contemporary informational economy', so also is this possibility all the more significant. There is the rise of a communications and information led economy, with the consequences that brings for labour, now in effect disaggregated, dispersed beyond the factory gates into the field of everyday life, and disorganized. Despite this, there is a potential for new forms of autonomist collective action, often emerging from unpaid or low-paid domestic work. In this regard Hardt looks at the biopolitics of female agricultural workers in India, mostly female, and the whole realm of care work and domestic labour in advanced capitalism, which under the influence of feminism acquired a political significance. On the one hand capitalism has never before made such extensive use of the 'manipulation of affects', which entails 'human contact' and proximity, a kind of tactility and corporeality in everyday working situations, while on the other hand this kind of labour traditionally associated with women has the possibility of producing what he calls (inverting Foucault) a 'biopolitics from below'. Capitalism is now organized so as to produce experiences that offer a sense of 'well-being' and that promise states of 'excitement, passion and even community'.

But the joyful-excitement factor, generated through the manipulation of affects, for which the mostly female workforce is trained, can too easily be seen as embryonic of some new radical politics of affect. Hardt restricts his references to feminism to family work or the care sector, there is no sense of what a new feminist analysis of 'emotional capitalism' might look like. This has led to some writers taking up the vitality of the new capitalism with its inherent capacity for 'communism' as a reason for celebrating aspects of immaterial labour with a degree of naivety and with little concern for the way in which subjectivities get shaped up to perform these tasks within a framework of individualization, extreme competition and self-reliance. The *Operaismo* writers envisage a new politics of immanence where the cracks within this informational capitalism are the moments or events of becoming. I take these cracks to constitute a kind of hairline politics, which can just about be retrieved or reached for, when, for example, the lines of flight remain faithful to a family narrative of memorialized exploitation or past labour injustices. Capitalism makes a seductive offer to young women with the promise of pleasure in work, while at the same time this work is nowadays bound to be precarious and insecure and lacking the protection of conventional employment. The kind of peer-to-peer gifting and the development of open-source software that is developed within online activist communities offers possibilities for new radicalisms to extend themselves with speed across many territories, but these activities of the self-reflexive precarious workers have to be set alongside the less politically aware part-time retail assistants folding the jumpers in *Uniqlo* or *Benetton* (Terranova 2004). Hardt and Negri unintentionally license a seemingly de-politicized account of forms of affective labour in the fashion and beauty industries. Debates about vitality within the terrain marked out by immaterial labour, alongside the sociality of the mass intellect harbouring the possibility for the 'communism of capitalism' and also extending the reach of these excitations into the ranks of the newly entrepreneurialized workforce, can lead to the idea of affective labour justifying and re-habilitating elite careers in the celebrity-dominated media and entertainment industries. Wissinger for instance, in a special issue of the journal *Ephemera*, remarking that the fashion modelling she is investigating is usually extremely well paid, sees this labour as part of the new landscape of precarious work. Such models as those signed to top agencies like Storm in New York 'create community' as they perform 'emotional labour' with 'feelings of vitality and aliveness'. In another co-authored article Wissinger sees New York 'high-end' models as positively contributing to urban regeneration (*pace* Florida) while also being 'less mannequins than they are CEOs of their own corporation' (Neff, Wissinger and Zukin 2005). This kind of perspective demonstrates how loosely writers can make use of affective labour when feminism is cast aside (this author acknowledges that 'gender' was 'outside the scope' of her work). The danger then lies in the newly capacious concept of the precarious proletariat of post-Fordism that permits fashion models who command vast daily fees for their labour being seen as part of this expanded class (or multitude) for the reason that their work is often casual and insecure. Reflecting the all-comers style of Florida's 'creative class' this puts models like Kate Moss in the same bracket as low-paid, female care workers who also perform emotional labour in their daily duties with elderly people suffering dementia. In short the renewed current of Marxist autonomist thought, when directed to normatively gendered work such as fashion modelling, without the presence of a strong feminist perspective, can lead to a confusingly celebratory account that is unable to differentiate among the harshly hierarchical divisions within the expansive field of immaterial labour.

Emma Dowling redresses this weak reading of affective labour through an auto-ethnography of her own time spent working both full-time and part-time in an expensive restaurant where staff were trained to adjust their smiles according to the exactly measured space between themselves and the customers (Dowling 2007). This viewpoint foregrounds the management of emotions and the cultivation of their specific tonality according to the training manuals and handbooks provided by the employer. It recounts the specific techniques deployed such as the 'mystery diner' to test the staff on their adherence at all times to the elaborate protocols of welcoming and charming the customers with light conversation. Dowling is sceptical about the claims made by Hardt and Negri and others regarding the possibilities for resistance among immaterial labourers. In her years on the restaurant floor or at front of house she sees little scope for labour organization, and resistance hardly goes beyond the kind of micro-strategies that de Certeau labelled 'poaching', in this case a chef illicitly cooking restaurant food for a fellow worker. This is a classic example of new managerialism requiring staff to bring their own intelligence and their personalities to the job, creating a relaxed and enjoyable 'dining experience'. Dowling was encouraged to entertain the guests as though they were personal friends, taking care to order a taxi home should someone become the worse for wear from drinking too much. Affect is therefore something required of staff, a fundamental condition of the job; it is also, as Hochschild argued in her study of cabin crew, something that must be sincere, the waitress has to be able to convey her genuine enjoyment in what she is doing, she has to demonstrate 'pleasure in work' (Hochschild

1984). This deployment of affect is also, contrary to Hardt and Negri, something that can be measured in the calculation of value, since wages can be kept low if service charges and tips are high enough to compensate the restaurant staff for more minimal take-home pay. Dowling also points to rigid hierarchies among the paid staff with the more elegant and educated staff mingling with the guests as waiting staff and the kitchen workers, often from migrant backgrounds, more likely to be out of sight and not entitled to the benefits of the tips and service charges. A more extended feminist analysis would have paid attention also to the recruitment policies in restaurants like these, which seek out slim and beautiful and immaculately groomed young women for this kind of role, such that they reflect the quality of the goods on offer in much the same way as the sales assistants in luxury *haute-couture* fashion boutiques are required to embody the brands in their personal style and body image. Here, too, where so many assistants work on commission, personal charm, intelligence and *savoir faire* work to maximize the profit margin and depress wages in favour of individualized competition among the workforce in the bid to sell. The need for a feminist analysis is not reduced simply because in jobs such as these it is nowadays just as likely that handsome and well-dressed young men will also be appointed to the sales floor or restaurant space. On the contrary, a feminist account would fully investigate the specific deployments of gender attributes and the extent to which sexual hierarchies are thereby maintained.[6]

Gender Performativity at Work

'Passionate work' can be understood within the terms used by Donzelot in his account of pleasure in work as a force that acts to reduce the likelihood of labour organization, in this case specifically for young female subjects in post-feminist times who are expected, or normatively required to participate in waged labour (Donzelot 1996). A desirable job becomes part of the panoply of attributes by which cultural intelligibility is acquired. In a context where creativity is a *dispositif* for instigating a new labour regime marked by self-enterprise, the idea of work corresponding to one's inner dreams or childhood fantasies also banishes, to some separate realm entirely, the idea of organized labour (despite the unionization of white-collar work in the last decades). Passionate work is then inherently individualistic and conservative. It is identifiably 'girlish' and enthusiastic, a trait or mode of behaviour and demeanour associated with the heroines of Jane Austen whose 'opinions are all romantic' (Austen quoted in Campbell 1987, p. 54). Colin Campbell has considered the shift away from Max Weber's Protestant Ethic, which, with the rise of consumerism, is transformed into a 'romantic ethic'. I offer a further transposition in the direction of a (feminized) romantic ethic of production, rather than consumption. The Romantics, Campbell reminds us, glorified individualism as uniqueness and creative genius, and the passionate disposition with which romanticism was associated elevated imagination and 'other-worldliness'. When translated into the context of the current discussion, these traits can be understood as indicating a disregard for matters of the monthly salary in favour of a bohemian anti-economy, which in turn can have the effect of permitting low pay or wage stagnation to prevail (Bourdieu 1993; Adkins and Devers 2014). Young women have been compelled to succeed in school and in further or higher education in the last fifteen years or so, within a political vocabulary dominated by the values of neoliberal thinking. The post-feminist masquerade instructs its subjects on how female bodies are expected to appear in the office-space or design studio (such as the 'fashionable' London publishing house where the fictional character Bridget Jones is employed) (Fielding 1996; McRobbie 2008). The professional field of work most closely aligned with this passionate *dispositif* is the fashion industry. The naive enthusiasm of the intern character named Andrea Sachs in the film titled *The Devil Wears Prada* shows both the meaning of passionate work as a young woman's romantic quest for job satisfaction, and the process by which, through emulating her colleagues, she learns how to make up and dress in the required style of post-feminist masquerade. (Expressions of almost ecstatic enthusiasm for internships in the fashion sector are familiar to many academics whose students are often eager to find work, despite awareness of long hours and almost no pay. Internships can represent the summation of dreams for young women, even when they are counselled against willing self-exploitation.)[7] Three recent studies reflect the 'intimate' relationship that young women have with fashion; in each case there is a similarly intense attachment to the creative work I first encountered when studying the working lives of young London-based fashion designers in the mid 1990s (Arvidsson et al. 2009: Bill 2012; Larner and Molloy 2009; McRobbie 1998). Bill's study of fashion students points to exceptionally high levels of investment in the fashion labour process. Like the designers I interviewed in the mid 1990s, Bill's respondents happily work through the night in preparation for a show (McRobbie 1998). As they say, 'we were working crazy hours'. In a similar vein, the Milan survey undertaken by Arvidsson et al. focuses explicitly on labour conditions in Italian fashion, with 67 per cent of the respondents being female, 60 per cent being degree-holders, and with an average age of thirty-three. Arvidsson et al. show how, despite low earnings (with those under twenty-five barely taking home 500 euros a month), and with a long hours culture built into the jobs, still the young women expressed love for the jobs and for the opportunity to learn new skills and to take part in some of the 'buzz' of the glamorous fashion world in Milan, including parties and events. As the authors suggest, 'Passion it appears has become a means of production, systematically promoted and put to work as part of the institutional framework within which brand values are produced' (Arvidsson et al. 2009, p. 18). Larner and Molloy offer a persuasive feminist analysis of established women designers in the emerging New Zealand fashion sector where there has been government support for this home-grown creative industry, which in turn provides the wardrobes for 'other busy working women' now active as wage earners in the New Zealand economy. These designers struggle to keep their enterprises afloat, and to some extent their excessive enthusiasm also functions to justify the sheer effort needed to keep going. The question confronting these feminist authors is: what does it mean for women to become entrepreneurial actors? They are torn between previous feminist scholarship, with its emphasis on female employees rather than on small-scale employers, and the new questions thrown up for feminist social science when the work landscape is now littered with self-entrepreneurial practices. Where are these to be located in the divide between capital and labour? Must we consider these women to be hard-driven would-be capitalists, prepared to exploit their own employees and interns? Or ought feminist scholarship now to be more receptive to women's need to self-entrepreneurialize? The authors seem ambivalent, seeing some expression of anxiety on the part of these designers manifest in their collections, which reflect the angst and tensions of 'gendered neoliberal subjectivity'. One way of resolving this problem as to how one approaches, sociologically, the category of the newly self-employed, is to take into account those factors to which I have referred throughout the book so far, an expanded new middle class propelled into entrepreneurial activity through their training and within the wide remit of the creativity *dispositif*, many of whose subjects may otherwise be working within the long post-industrial shadow of unemployment or else of under-employment. Alongside this is the point made by Lazzarato, which is that those who in the past may have been 'workers' are frequently nowadays entrepreneurs.

I pose the idea of passionate work being a distinctive mode of gender re-traditionalization (as defined by Adkins) whereby the conservatism of post-feminism re-instates young women's aspirations for success within designated zones of activity such as creative labour markets, which then becomes spaces for the deployment of highly normative femininity such as 'girlish enthusiasm', which can be construed as a willingness to work all hours for very little pay in the hope of gaining a foothold in the field of work (Adkins 2002). This would imply that the idea of passionate work requires a more forceful feminist critique than has been available so far. One location from which a critique emerges, is from the *précarité* movement, which has creative labour as a central platform for new modes and styles of political activity and campaigning. As already argued in the previous chapter, this debate in turn hinges on the idea of post-Fordism as it touches upon the lives and work expectations of arts, humanities and creative graduates. Adding a feminist perspective means seeing that female labour market participation in the post-Fordist economy marks both the summation of changes brought about by feminism, and its limits. This movement into work is overseen or managed by a regime of femininity, which addresses its subjects as aspirational and relatively unanchored by ideas of class, particularly of being, or having been working class. Work for women, even in a call centre, has come to stand for equality achieved. Adhering to ideals of normative femininity within a framework of paid work, ensures a kind of delivery into a world less tainted by the social realities of class and inequality. By in effect marrying her work, having devoted so much romantic energy into finding the right job, rather than the right man, the woman can uplift herself into a relatively undesignated middle-class social category. Landing in such a space, let us say as a visual merchandiser, she is confronted with changes being wrought upon the middle classes, the scale of which pitches it into a risk class status. Isabell Lorey makes the argument that precarization is now a dominant mode of biopolitical governmentality, one that affects not just the already marginal or low qualified workforce, but everyone (Lorey 2015). For Lorey, contemporary post-Fordism is synonymous with precarization. In contrast, my focus in this book is on the active production of a young middle-class stratum of people, by means of decisive governmental interventions exercised within the apparatuses of education and training, for whom creativity is both a passport into desirable or even passionate work, and an instrument of capture, the cost of which is the removal of historic forms of protection and security. In undertaking such an expansion of the middle classes and by providing training for this new creative occupational grouping, governmentality is pre-empting discord and social unrest. By these means there is an extension of the new (self-) managerialism already for decades established inside employment, outwards into the realm of self-employment. This way creativity comes to serve as a precise instrument for labour reform. For young women, achieving a degree and finding a job in the media, or in an art gallery, is a guarantor of middle-class status, if not comfortable middle-class existence and economic security. Bearing in mind what the ordo-liberals said about the aim to de-proletarianize society we could see creative young women today as exemplars of this process. However, economic insecurity and having to learn to live on freelance contracts does not eradicate significant differences between the middle-class precarious young women artists and creatives and those women who have much less possibility for mobility and for whom aspiring to a dream job is a hopeless endeavour. While for the working-class young women who are childless and thus have the option of working in clubs in Ibiza as dancers or as bar staff, and thus are able to become mobile in this particular kind of way, their counterparts who are single mothers at home and trapped on a housing estate, have no such opportunities.[7] If reliant on benefits, such young women are stuck and shamed for this incapacity to become mobile through various media-led moral panics.

Lorey, in the spirit of Hardt and Negri's understanding of communistic impulses, and taking their remarkably prescient ideas about new political formations based on events and on non-homogeneous singularities into account, understands the general condition of precariousness as a starting point for struggle. Following the earlier account provided by Rodriguez (2008, p. 390)[8] on the Spanish feminist Precarias a la Deriva group, Lorey describes the solidaristic activities of these young Spanish women, mostly students, unemployed graduates and artists, who set about trying to forge connections with other low-paid precarious female workers across the city, while also gathering extensive knowledge about what it means to be a precarious female worker today. Like others influenced by the autonomist writing, Lorey embraces the idea of flight or exodus as a practice of struggle. I also have signalled the lines of flight, and the possibilities for movement on the part of young women as something more than individualization process and entrepreneurship of the self. My account of flight stresses not so much full-blown modes of political organization such as those developed by the

European *précarité* movement, but more a matter of hairline politics often reflected through processes of inter-generational relations and memory. Lorey sees the *potenza* of going away and starting something new, echoing Virno through the idea of exodus. This seems to suggest exploring and inventing ways of living within a new political imaginary. It could mean, for example, leaving the parental home and moving into a squat as a way of avoiding the 'rent gap' economy of contemporary urban housing. Nevertheless, if we stick with the image of the single mother of young children, who is also a subject legally bound to keep her children in school and provide for them accordingly, even if in poverty, this model of flight (to a squat or to a new location hundreds of miles away) finds its limits where care responsibilities, legally as well as ethically, restrict the options for movement. Such a woman would find it hard to organize a move out of (or flight from) the tower block to a nicer, healthier location for her children, and in addition she would immediately lose all her welfare payments or her workfare job. Lorey challenges Robert Castel's critique of the reduction of welfare and benefits and the dismantling of welfare on the grounds that this was always a selective and protective system that only offered the male worker a family wage of benefits on condition that the wife and children remained reliant on him as the breadwinner. Where Castel looks to the re-constitution of welfare as a tool for social integration and a guard against chaos, Lorey rightly points to the exclusions embedded within these programmes based on protection for national populations only, making the point that new measures for protection would need to be for everyone. Following the lead from the various articles collected together by Gržinić and Reitsamer (2008), Lorey's work reflects a shift in recent debates on creative economy so that they connect more directly with the anti-capitalist protests and the Occupy movement. Exemplifying what has been labelled 'theoretical activism', Lorey writes as an activist who, having charted the precariousness of creative labour, then reflects on the new political movements that have emerged from the recognition of the shared states of insecurity heightened as a result of the austerity measures adopted by governments in response to the banking crisis, national debt and the dramatic loss of value of the euro. This linking of young graduate populations faced with unemployment across Europe with the emergence of self-directed creative and entrepreneurial work, with this folding into new forms of political organization, is persuasive. The new waves of feminism, which have also taken root within this wide constellation of precarious activism, mark out alliances between queer, transgender and feminist politics, with an emphasis on the care work that women, including mothers, nannies and sex workers, find themselves expected to perform. This wide umbrella also extends to the global fashion industry and there has been a much more vocal critique of the new sweatshops as well as the exploitation of unpaid interns inside some of the world-famous design labels. This has in turn given rise to an awareness of the anomalies of passionate work leading to willing self-exploitation, especially where, in a sector-like fashion, those looking for a job in the industry are predominantly female. But understanding of this reputation for exploitation in fashion does not stop the flow of enthusiastic young designers and design-related personnel into the sector and, once inside the fashion world, even on a freelance contract, the corporate machine stifles dissent and takes steps to ensure a docile workforce, which is all the easier to do when contracts are temporary and much sought after.

I have argued that the creativity *dispositif* gains a particular momentum from the gendered practice of 'passionate work', which, particularly during the period of New Labour's neoliberal turn, comes to be amplified and enhanced by the 'post-feminist masquerade'. These together become a powerful force for engendering female conformity with the new work regime. If young women describe themselves as passionate about their work, this is often a youthful declaration announced at that point at which they are entering the labour market; however it promises with maturity something akin to the right kind of business disposition characterized by Sheryl Sandberg (COO of Facebook) in her best-selling *Lean In* (2013), where she encourages young women to remember at all times to 'smile', such that smiling (i.e. performing heteronormative femininity) becomes, once again, a prescribed way of progressing on the career track for women (Sandberg 2012). We are reminded here of Hochschild's ethnographic analysis of US cabin crew staff training, where the young women were told to 'work' their smiles (Hochschild 1984). By these means the subjects of post-Fordist work, employment and self-employment, are required to be normatively feminine, with passionate work expressing the way in which this is exuded as a bodily style, an exuberant enthusiasm. That this kind of conduct has become so routine in upscale restaurants, in art galleries, on the flight deck, in the department store, and even, as Tatjana Turanskyj's film *Eine Flexible Frau* (as referred to in the Introduction) shows, the call centre, makes it all the more surprising that Hardt and Negri and the other theorists of post-Fordism and affective labour so overlook the dominance of women's work and the attempts in these labour markets to re-traditionalize gender as a de-politicizing containment strategy. In these circumstances being a career girl is something young women are both congratulated for and required to express gratitude for. Despite the decades of feminist struggles for workplace equality, young women entering the now precarious world of work are nonetheless expected to be beholden.

5

Fashion Matters Berlin:
City-Spaces, Women's Working Lives,
New Social Enterprise?

Introduction

> It must be clearly stated that an assessment of nationwide development
> trends shows that the cultural and creative industries are not going to
> be a driving force for the creation of 'traditional jobs.
>
> *Creative Industries in Berlin*, Wowereit 2008[1]

In this chapter I introduce the results of research into the scene of
small-scale fashion designers in Berlin (using qualitative methodologies including semi-structured interviews, observational visits and
specially arranged research events) and I also take this as an occasion
to reflect further on those points at which the forms of address of the
creativity *dispositif* come into contact with living subjects. In Berlin
we find both a stronger, more vocal antipathy to the business regime
of fast fashion, so-called luxury fashion and the big brands, on the
part of producers, in favour of an *auteurist* outlook and we also see
that the programmes emerging from the ideas of new creative economy
as overseen by the Berlin Senate (and also at national level), though
increasingly driven by a neoliberal agenda, remain strongly inflected
by social democratic thinking. The reality of the need for public
sector support at key points in creative careers is recognized and
acknowledged on the pages of the various official reports. The vocabulary of the business school is less apparent in the everyday debates
among those who administer and oversee the creative sector in the
city, and this means that, while constantly under pressure to become
both more commercial and less reliant on subsidy of any type, the

designers are envisaged, especially at early points in their careers, as 'worthy of support'. Not just for this reason, this current chapter swerves away from attending to the dominant neoliberalism of the creative sector and takes the form, instead, of a case study of fashion design micro-entrepreneurs (mostly, but not exclusively female) in the city of Berlin. This analysis serves as an alternative to many of the threads of argument presented in the previous chapters, and it points to the possibilities for, as well as the difficulties in, setting up and sustaining, different models for fashion as part of the cultural economy. In some ways it suggests a new fashion imagination within a framework of job creation. In the case of Berlin, the emphasis on self-entrepreneurialism is less embedded within a governmental strategy for labour reform *by other means* and is more part of a history of 'alternative culture' within the city. In this context 'passionate work' is less spectacularly visible and performative. As will become clear in the course of the pages that follow, an emphasis on the details of production and process from design through all of its stages (including a craft dimension) makes for a less euphoric designer-subjectivity. There is a more direct relation with sewing and pattern-cutting than is the case for their UK counterparts, and overall a stronger commitment to city and neighbourhood.

The specific nature of this Berlin culture of production needs to be set, however, within a wider context. In the light of the prominence of debate on new creative economy, studies of fashion cultures of production, have tended in recent years, to migrate away from sociology and cultural studies to cultural and economic geography (see Larner and Molloy 2009). Here is found a lively discussion about how fashion plays a role in place marketing, in urban branding, in tourism, and in the growth of both local and global culture industries, while the historical city *tableau* is also constantly (and sometimes ruthlessly) deployed to produce difference and distinction within competitive fashion worlds (Florida 2002; Breward and Gilbert 2006; Gilbert 2011; Rantisi 2004; Jakob 2009). My own earlier research on London-based designers and their livelihoods drew on the 'cultures of production' work; this was influenced by both Bourdieu and Foucault (Bourdieu 1993; Foucault 1988, Du Gay et al. 1997; Braham 1997; McRobbie 1998). This current chapter retains an interest in small-scale fashion enterprises, and asks how young women (and a handful of men) designers and producers in Berlin navigate their way through the spaces and the pathways available to them partly as a result of proactive forms of urban governance seeking to promote local economies, while also encouraging job creation through entrepreneurship. To chart these kinds of careers it is necessary to offer

some reflections on important shifts within the global fashion industry, as well as to pay attention to fashion practices in different cities.
No one would suggest that Berlin could compete with fashion's recognized global cities, Paris, Milan, London and New York, so the
question is raised as to how cities that have a strong and distinctive
urban style (such as Copenhagen, Stockholm, Barcelona, but why not
also Glasgow, Dublin, Warsaw, Budapest?) strive to translate participation in fashion design cultures, into sustainable livelihoods. The
designers themselves, often battling to stay in business, give the city
the possibility of a unique fashion identity. Indeed it is on the basis
of not being a competitor with Milan, New York or London that
Berlin's capacity to re-imagine fashion cultures of production along
more egalitarian lines becomes realizable.

The last ten years in Berlin have seen the appearance of a proliferation of fashion activities. These include (a) the visibility of a remarkable number of small companies, indeed micro-enterprises of just one,
two or three people,[2] (b) designer-owned fashion shops (or boutiques)
with rails of clothes for sale in the front, and, within sight, an atelier-
production space in the backroom, where there are bales of cloth,
sewing machines, pressers, and patterns hanging from the ceiling,
creating a neo-artisanal image while also drawing attention to the
importance of space and environment, (c) fashion, sewing and production projects, which also function as co-working spaces (such as
NEMONA, Common-Works, NadelWald) dotted about the recently
regenerated Kreuzberg and NeuKoelln neighbourhoods of the city,
(d) a lively programme of bi-annual Berlin Fashion Weeks, (e) the
arrival of major fashion retailers in the Mitte neighbourhood including *Acne, Cos, Comptoir des Cotonniers,* and *Comme des Garçons,*
(f) a strong interest in distinctively Berlin fashion scenes on the part
of the press, media and listings magazines, and finally (g) access to
an array of forms of support and subsidy from various offices for
local urban renewal, as well as neighbourhood job centres.[3] These
Berlin enterprises are located in well-positioned and affordable spaces;
they are mostly run by young women on a freelance or self-employed
basis. In the cases that I investigate, there has been a conscious effort
to draw on local skills from a pool of (what is referred to as) migrant
female labour, including knitting, sewing, tailoring, pattern cutting
and crocheting and this is seen as having some impact on the wage-
earning capacity of women who would otherwise have been at home.[4]
This is a not uncontentious issue, as it typically reflects aspects of the
prevailing discourses of German multi-culturalism and the politics of
integration as they are played out at national, regional and city level.
In a context where applications can be made by designers for support

for new enterprises, the chances of winning support are enhanced when reference is made to strategies for social inclusion through training and upskilling of economically disadvantaged and usually ethnic minority women. This kind of initiative wins favour with local, national and EU-funding bodies, since it utilizes the favoured language of job creation strategies along with that which emphasizes the social integration of migrant women, as well as environmental factors in regard to fabrics, textiles, re-cycling and so on.[5] In Berlin there has been a long-established tradition of social projects, usually operating under the umbrella of not-for-profit, third-sector organizations and NGOs, and co-funded and supported by various EU schemes and federal programmes, as well as by the Berlin Senate (city government). These have tended to provide training, social work and political education for women and disadvantaged groups.[6] By taking fashion production into this terrain of social projects and providing on-the-spot training for low-qualified women and girls, the identity of fashion culture undergoes a change, while at the same time exposing itself to questions of instrumentalization of ethnicity, and to racializing assumptions about the talents or skills of Turkish–German women for so-called traditional handicrafts. Overall, this approach is in sharp contrast to that in London where, from the early 2000s, the prevailing creative industry policy vocabulary has been to develop more elite-level professional careers. The Berlin fashion social enterprises (I am defining these small organizations quite loosely; they all demonstrate a commitment to wider community, ecological and social issues) can tell us something about how, despite the economic recession, meaningful and rewarding jobs can be created.[7] The actual returns may not be high, but the support from government in the form of small grants and subsidies for space, has wider benefits, as I will go on to argue in the conclusion.

The aim in this chapter will be to interrogate the processes underpinning this new urban creative industry suggesting the wider social value of the support from the city council (e.g. embedding of women's employment) and other agencies, while also pointing to some intractable problems. These arise from the tensions connected with a combination of a fine-art fashion ethos, with a neo-artisanal or craft/ design approach, which must inevitably compete with the speeded-up and corporate rhythms of the global fashion system. Although the Berlin fashion milieu has indeed developed a distinctive urban niche, most designers want to operate at a more international level, and of course Berlin fashion enterprises are by no means unaffected by trends in global fashion production and consumption. The last fifteen years have seen the impact of fast-production techniques, which allow high street retailers like *Zara* to bring clothes similar to those seen on the catwalk onto their rails within two weeks.[8] In Berlin the main high street competition comes from *H&M, Zara, Mango, Esprit, Marco Polo* and most recently from *Primark*. The Swedish-owned *Cos* has had the greatest impact, for the reason that its design-signature borrows directly from a kind of urban style already associated with Berlin's indigenous fashion designers. This sharp, slightly chilly aesthetic challenges hyper-sexualized and glamorized styles, and for this reason the *Cos* image directly encroaches on the visual terrain marked out by more independent Berlin designers (such as Mongrels in Common, Majaco or Signorzia), who are often struggling to stay in business. If we take this high level of competition into account, and also remind ourselves of the power of brands in contemporary fashion and the more recent reliance on celebrity endorsements, then we could say that the very fact of the existence of this lively independent scene of designers and producers in Berlin has to be set against the global forces that present formidable competition to micro-enterprises such as these. There are two ways of looking at this. Either we see the tiny outfits comprising two or three designers as inevitably under strain, and destined not to survive, or we can make a strong case for fashion to play an active role in developing possibilities for local urban employment and for contributing to a conversation about meaningful work. This would mean recognizing the different kinds of practice co-existing within the industry as a whole, such that a craft as well as a design ethos, and an environmentally aware fashion sector, which plays a key role in urban regeneration and in keeping neighbourhoods alive, all have an important place in the fashion system. Policy-makers and campaigners would also have to encourage a stronger push within consumer culture for buying local fashion.

Berlin: Not a Shopping City?

While there is a good deal of discussion in the quality press and in a range of management journals about fashion as a global industry and about the rapid rise recently and in recession times of 'fast fashion', the fine details of this new political economy of fashion have not been subjected to extensive analysis. Any investigation of small-scale designers in Berlin must be informed by this bigger picture and also by the specificities of the German clothing industry and the place of fashion design within the sector. Lane and Probert provide good insight into the clothing industry in Germany (alongside the US and the UK) and this timely study, though it makes no mention of small-scale design activity, would make it reasonable to claim that there is a wide gap in Germany and hence in Berlin between the major economic players, including both manufacturers and retailers, and the micro-economies of the Berlin-based designers (Lane and Probert 2009). There is very little in the way of connection, never mind collaboration, of the type that has become a defining feature of designer activity in London. In Germany, where, like most other developed countries, there has been a decline in manufacturing and the textile industries, this has been less marked and less conflict-ridden than in the UK; indeed trade unions and other bodies have been involved in negotiations around what have been 'gradual' closures, made easier by the German workforce (presumably male-dominated) also showing less interest in these usually low-skilled and low-paid jobs. What remains of the industry carries higher skill levels requiring more extensive training and there has also been a move into 'smart' textiles. Overall, this means that clothes produced in Germany especially for the multiples and large department stores still carry some of the signature of the producer and supplier where there is an emphasis on quality and cost and, as Lane and Probert put it, less concern even for 'fit', not to say design and fashion trends that are overwhelmingly associated with the youth market and the appearance of fast fashion stores such as *H&M* (Lane and Probert 2009, p. 73). The hangover of historic anti-competition restrictions dating back to the post-war years (mid 1950s) means that there is a limit to the number of stores that can be opened, and also on the possible sites for fashion newcomers into city-centre areas. There is also a restriction on sales and discounting as well as on shop opening hours. In addition the bunching together of 'self-organized independents into purchasing associations', which gives rise to mass or bulk buying from manufacturers, works to diminish unique or distinctive designer signatures in favour of seeming functionality and relative uniformity. As the authors suggest, this creates a 'restrained, low-profile retail sector abjuring hedonism'; indeed they claim that 'spending on clothes and shoes has shown continual relative decline since 1988' (Lane and Probert 2009, p. 74), putting Germany eleventh in European tables for *per capita* spending on fashion and clothing items.

Several factors account for the disparity, indeed disconnect, between the mainstream fashion and clothing industry in Germany and the design-led micro-enterprises found dotted across the city from Mitte and Prenzlauer Berg to Kreuzberg and NeuKoelln. As Lane and Probert explain, the protectionist environment, which means that even non-unionized workers can expect higher wages than their counterparts in the UK, lessens the possibility for informal and (unfortunately) low-paid production and assembly work, which in turn raises costs for newcomers or 'independents'. This means that the small fashion enterprises are indeed one-person businesses or two self-employed people working alongside each other as a team or partnership. There are also barriers (including migration restrictions) against informal economies, which in the UK would be led by people from ethnic minorities, for example the small-scale production facilities first described by Phizacklea as led by 'ethnic entrepreneurs' able to enter the market with low labour costs and low capital investment (Phizacklea 1990). It is these kinds of local units that have, for two decades, serviced the growth of independent or own-label fashion design in London, with relatively low costs on both sides. Again it is quite different in Germany, where there are strict rules about qualifications and what in the UK would have been called 'registered trades' (*Handwerksrolle*) in this case relating to craft-work and artisanal activity such as tailoring and sewing (Lane and Probert 2009). The tiny start-ups are therefore forced to work in such a way as to be almost wholly separate from the mainstream of fashion design and retail (including the big internationally owned luxury brands) in Germany. This means that the fashion media, especially the magazines, from German *Vogue* to *InStyle* and *Grazia*, give a lot less coverage to up and coming Berlin designers than might be expected, and instead they follow the lead from London and elsewhere, profiling 'emerging talent' as defined by US and UK *Vogue*. This also has consequences for sales by Berlin designers, one of whom said in interview 'a key problem is that German buyers do not place orders for Berlin-based or for German designers. They do not have loyalty in this way.'[9] Most significantly it means that there is limited access to the kind of collaborations with and support provided by British retailers such as *Topshop* for young UK designers. This then is the tough environment in which the fledgling design sector must establish itself according to its own priorities and agenda. What is gained by virtue of access to grants and subsidy for space is lost by this weak to non-existent contact with large companies. It also accounts for the orientation towards an avant-garde or subcultural identity among the city's designers.

Zwischennutzung (Temporary Use) Spaces

> Artists and creatives at the beginning of their careers are obliged to be able to present their work to the public, without there necessarily being a profitable marketing situation. (*Creative Industries in Berlin*, Wowereit 2008, p. 81)

What kind of space can fashion micro-enterprises occupy within the bigger fashion world? The spread of small independent fashion shops exists within a relatively new tourist map of Berlin. These are not high streets like those in New York or London, nor are they chic upmarket fashion neighbourhoods as found in Milan or Paris. They are located in the Mitte area, which, after the fall of the Wall, became a centre of gravity for young people, and which has also been re-generated to become an important cultural and social space for the city since re-unification. Prenzlauer Berg, which was also in the eastern sector, close to the wall and home at that point to dissidents and artists, likewise underwent waves of modernization and gentrification since 1990 (Mayer 2004; Cochrane and Jonas 1999; Bernt and Holm 2005, 2009; Kalandides 2007). Crumbling blackened tenements, which were found to have old coal-fire heating, and shared toilets have been transformed into magnificent upmarket apartments and those that were demolished have been replaced by the kinds of anonymous if colourful condominiums found in most cities of the world today. This has given rise to tides of opposition and resistance such that the anti-gentrification movement is a powerful force in Berlin political culture (Ahlfeldt 2010). The terms gentrification and anti-gentrification are contentious, abbreviating the complexities of urban change, rising land values and the role of international property speculation in times of neoliberal governmentality, where local powers and politicians are under pressure to sell off valuable land in order to bring in revenue, especially in a city with high unemployment and a decisively post-industrial economy. Many people who may be regarded as gentrifiers are also anti-gentrifiers. They may have moved in to the neighbourhood in recent years and then become involved in campaigns to hinder the incursion of the kinds of businesses or people who have no reservations about displacing poor or disadvantaged residents or tenants. These same local activists themselves will often be working in fields such as the creative arts and media, which in turn rely, to an extent, on the new tourism in the city, including the art market people and the tourists and audiences for the many events and festivals which take place on a year-round basis (Pul 2011). The term gentrification itself needs to give way to an extended debate about the political economy of the city, including the threat posed by speculative capital, and the danger of losing historical spaces (such as the Tempelhof Airport) and buildings to avaricious and predatory property developers (Springer 2006; Pasquinelli 2010).

It is in these same areas undergoing rapid processes of change that we find numerous little fashion shops operating from the ground floors of blocks of apartments. The main new fashion streets in Berlin coincide exactly with the streets and neighbourhoods in which young 'creative' people now congregate, to live and socialize, as well as take their children to school.[10] More recently, there has been a flowering of a fashion neighbourhood in the working-class and Turkish–German district of NeuKoelln, especially around the streets running off the busy area around Hermannsplatz. Within the last seven years this has gone from being a very quiet run-down neighbourhood with many empty properties, to become a lively, indeed bustling with energy, location for international students, artists, writers, fashion designers, film-makers and others, all drawn to the area because of its cheapness, available spaces, and the sudden appearance of DIY bars and clubs as well as art venues. Again, there are high levels of opposition and anger about the appearance of a party scene and its offshoots, such as the profitable hostels for backpackers and young visitors, and more recently the short-let small apartments or *Ferienwohnungen*, which are attractive to landlords, not just for the high profit margin, but also because these developments are exempt from rent control.[11] This political consciousness, which stretches across sectors of the population, young and old, middle class and working class, means that there is resistance to aggressively pursued property development, and the destruction of the original urban environment.[12] Unlike in London, there is mobilization in the form of demonstrations, there are campaigns, and these issues are widely publicized in the press and on television.

The world-renowned success of Berlin-based techno music, one of the biggest sources of income for the city, lies at the heart of these discussions (Bader and Scharenberg 2010; Lange 2012a). It spawns various other activities that also create jobs for people across the city, mostly in the service sector connected with hostels, hotels, bars and restaurants, media, marketing and the creative economy. There is no doubt that the fashion start-ups and small shops also benefit from the visitors who come to the city for this vibrant music scene. Within urban creative economies there are inter-dependencies between music and fashion (Hauge and Hracs 2010). It would be a mistake, however, to over-emphasize this connection. There is a thriving street fashion and club wear presence in Berlin, especially for menswear, but fashion exists within a different sphere of space-time relations from the music scenes (Lange 2012a). Club cultures carry many restrictions and exclusions according to age, status and subcultural capital (Thornton 1996). Fashion has its own hierarchies, of course, but its rhythms are more intensely connected with everyday life, and not contained by the temporality of the night-time economy. Many young fashion

designers in Berlin are making clothes for children, and there is also
a thriving vintage sector. Nevertheless, both the fashion and music
activities depend on low rent space, often available on a temporary
use basis known as *Zwischennutzung*. These temporary or vacant
spaces and their informal or DIY use by various groups of people in
Berlin, from artists and 'queer community living projects' to 'inter-
cultural gardeners', have been extensively considered by Colomb
(2012), who makes the connection between these activities and
that of 'open source urbanism' (Misselwitz, Oswalt and Overmeyer
2007, cited in Colomb 2012). Later in this chapter I will propose
fashion social enterprises as a female 'post-Fordist place making'
(Colomb 2012).

Zwischennutzung in Berlin emerges from the historical situation
that existed following the end of the GDR and the Communist regime
in 1989. Despite the uniqueness of this heritage this does not make
it so exceptional as to be irrelevant in regard to other post-industrial
urban environments, especially in times of severe economic recession,
where shops lie empty and business premises are also abandoned.
The Berlin temporary use system is not so much direct subsidy, as a
way of allowing use of both city-owned properties and spaces owned
by private landlords by not-for-profit enterprises deemed 'worthy of
support'. Sometimes the applicants need only pay for utilities such as
heating and electricity (*Betriebskosten*). Since 2005 *Zwischennutzung*
has been handed over to an agency (*Co-opolis*) which also provides
urban development consultancy services for use of space in neighbourhoods designated for regeneration. Potential users of space can
submit a 'well-written plan' and the agency will then help with negotiations with potential landlords. The Berlin Senate (city government), burdened with huge debts, is constantly seeking to reduce
subsidy, and meanwhile more and more young people, often new
graduates, are trying to enter these creative fields and are looking for
reduced cost work spaces.[13] In effect work-space and job creation
have to be considered alongside each other. There are numerous
schemes for job-seekers to become self-employed, all of which entail
complicated case-by-case applications, which can nevertheless allow
monthly unemployment payments to be supplemented by earnings of
not more than 50 per cent of the rate of benefits. This system of
Einstiegsgeld, along with various other (*Aufstocken*) schemes that
allow low wage earners to receive top-up benefits overseen by the
Job Centres, and which also include the controversial mini-job system
(paying 400 euros per month), attract criticism for in effect institu-
tionalizing low wages. Likewise, beneficiaries for both the more gen-
erous *Grundungszuschuss* and for *Einstiegsgeld* complain about the

time constraints linked with this provision, on the basis that starting-up a fashion business requires more than a one or two-year plan. As is the case with all project working, the emphasis on grant application is relentless because the time-lines and duration of grants is always limited, usually to a two or three-year period. Still, because the creative industry policies for the city specify an explicit commitment to women's employment (in itself a unique provision within creative industry discourse) we can explain the volume and visibility of small fashion workshops in neighbourhoods like NeuKoelln on the basis of these initiatives being deemed worthy of support.[14] City governance supports both urban regeneration and the need for jobs for women. This has led to a higher level of female entrepreneurial activity, including fashion production, than can be seen in comparable cities. These small-scale enterprises feed into a creative industry agenda, which aims at being socially inclusive and egalitarian, rather than simply talent-led.

Fashion Production after Post-Fordism

We have already seen how far apart the mainstream German fashion and clothing sector is from the activities of small-scale Berlin designers, but other factors relating to changes in the global fashion system also impact on their chances for survival and their modus operandi. Global cities are able to exert an enormous influence on how the fashion industry operates locally and globally. Auspicious economic circumstances such as those found in the handful of global fashion cities bring mutual benefit to the large established companies and fashion houses as well as to the numerous small players, including the culture intermediaries, who are able to find niche roles and multi-tasking possibilities for themselves within the orbit of the organizations and institutions such as galleries and museums, now strongly interested in contemporary fashion design as well as its history. These young people are also looking increasingly to the emerging fields such as fashion forecasting and intelligence as sources of employment and self-employment. This is clearly the case in New York where, alongside the large US fashion companies, there is such a concentration of art institutes, design schools, forecasting agencies, textile workshops and small manufacturing units, and of course a major presence of fashion media, all within the space of a few blocks of fashion district. Hence, there are jobs to be found and livelihoods to be created for individuals who are able to diversify their skills in the avenues that open up often in quite unpredictable ways. Rantisi (2004) describes the specific feature or special ingredient of the New York fashion formula, which is its strong orientation towards merchandising, and this, along with a well-established system of internships and work placement schemes, accounts for the high success rate on the part of graduates from the Fashion Institute of Technology and of course from Parsons School of Art and Design (Rantisi 2004).[15] Dense social networks, processes of agglomeration, and tight integration between key organizations benefit the young people trained in these specific schools. Rantisi also points to the knowledge economy, including the trade press, and how it shapes the commercial strategies of the big fashion companies, to the extent that design is relegated to a lesser role, in favour of keeping a grip on future trends as a way of planning in an unpredictable customer environment.

Rantisi's New York-focused account has proved to be prescient; she points to the huge expansion in retail, with design-sensitive companies like *J Crew* occupying a substantial place in the market, she notes the value attached to celebrity endorsement, the desire for alternatives to this unapologetic and bombastic commercialism but the struggle for affordable space, and finally the diminishing role of the designer him or herself as source of originality, imagination, talent and skill. He or she now seems to exist lower down the fashion hierarchy unless the name is already so established that it can be utilized as a brand strategy. The submerging of the designer and the requirement that he or she develops a wider portfolio of skills and expertise particularly in the direction of marketing and fashion knowledge has become a defining feature of the directions taken by leaders in the field. Where innovation and competition are driving forces, these players are looking for employees who can work in large multidisciplinary teams and who can comfortably defer to speeded-up commercial imperatives as well as show themselves willing to learn new techniques and master incoming information technologies. In a recent analysis of fashion companies we can see how the sector most associated with the successes of the Third Italy model of production, where companies (most famously *Benetton*) adapted with such ease to the emphasis on style, quality, short runs, EPOS and JIT systems of production, now negotiates a pathway in even more intensely competitive environments. These authors argue that fashion producers nowadays need to have access to advanced systems of fashion forecasting so that they can be constantly scanning for trends (Aage and Belussi 2008). This particular post-industrial fashion ecology can rapidly incorporate (and drop) Fordist principles in off-shore sites such as Vietnam and Cambodia and combine these with local, highly skilled producers, who in turn adjust their work practices according to the dictates of the incoming knowledge flows (in classic post-Fordist fashion). Fashion designers working for the large global players are now more likely to be constantly travelling, visiting factories across the world, overseeing quality control, forming strong relationships with local contractors, to ensure reliable deadlines, as well as developing a familiarity with the fine details of complex industrial processes. These kinds of companies, mostly the big brands, can simultaneously draw on the latest development in information technologies and also on the most basic and mundane skills of seamstresses and hand-workers. The extensive factory system spread across many developing countries and regions from Bangladesh to Vietnam reminds us that regardless of the balance between Fordist and post-Fordist processes of production, this is a sector that relies largely on a long hours and low-wage off-shore workforce often labouring in dangerous and unhealthy conditions.

Across the global fashion cities there is a significant gap between the kinds of companies like *Zara*, which now operate with a precision control mode to minimize mark-downs in this most unpredictable sphere of consumer culture, and the small start-ups for whom markdowns in price because of poor weather or because a rail of stock simply does not correspond to customer demands, can spell disaster (Gilbert 2011). The steps taken to deal with this situation, by fashion policy-makers and fashion academics who are listened to by city government, have generally relied on setting up collaborative relationships with larger companies. But these partnerships can also be seen as drops in the ocean. Nowadays through social media, companies are able to get up close to their consumers, in some ways cutting out the role of buyer for the reason that buyers can always make the wrong choices, resulting in poor sales. Social media provide an effective instrument because they are able to invite young consumers into the heart of the production process, making them pro-sumers or co-creators (Arvidsson and Malossi 2011). The presence of the consumer inside this post-industrial and social media-led system also permits the gathering of data and information on an unprecedented scale, such that new designs can be checked and double checked against the market segment. No wonder then that a different communications-oriented skill-set is needed at all of those points at which companies seek to ensure their position and profits. With these marketing-led processes so dominant, the importance of the designer him or herself begins to fade (Arvidsson and Malossi 2010). Other strategies are constantly being developed, such as the new emphasis on sales assistants as point of contact (McCarthy 2011). Store managers and sales assistants are rewarded for providing the kind of constant feedback that depends on fine-tuned communication skills, as well as powers of observation and insight. This coincides with retailers now preferring to employ graduates working on a casual, short-term or part-time basis. Attention has also been drawn to the way in which large companies can take steps to avoid losses by endless checking and filtering of particular styles and looks and items. These firms rely on both in-house designers and external experts brought in as freelance consultants to firm up ideas so that they fit with evolving trends (Aage and Belussi 2008). Not only can *Zara* have catwalk-influenced styles on the rails in a record time of two to three weeks, the company has also pioneered sophisticated ways of cutting losses, such as the buying in of cheap bulk grey fabric (from a supplier owned by the same parent company), which is then dyed only at the last minute according to customer preferences; these are monitored from one day to the next. Teresa McCarthy describes how an industrial system model means that *Zara* is able not only to sell a remarkable 85 per cent of its stock at full price, but it also has a stock turnover period of just thirty-six days, in comparison to the sector norm of ninety days (McCarthy 2011). The company is more centralized than its competitors and, according to McCarthy, there are seamstresses at hand in the headquarters able to produce samples more or less on the spot. The main manufacturing is also done within Spain as well as in Portugal and Morocco, in what are described as 'sewing workshops'. The intensity of this process and the various devices installed to minimize losses demonstrates what it means to be a global producer in contemporary fashion with more than 1,830 shops in seventy-nine countries, making Inditex (the *Zara* owner) Spain's most successful company. This is a post-industrial knowledge-led system where the distinct skills and imagination of the designer are offset by fashion forecasters, by market intelligence, by innovation in production processes, by cheaply sourced textiles, and by an emphasis on direction, 'look-books' and on making use of young consumers and their own input and taste trends, now so easily available through social media.

'The Work Is Done for Its Own Sake'

In many respects Berlin fashion, operating within the dual logic of urban creative economy and the global fashion system, has no option other than to present itself as a localized niche. But this in itself offers interesting scope for analysis. Could one see it for example as a counter-capitalist fashion sector, informed and sustained by a residue of both radical and social democratic elements? Could one assess its value in terms of uniqueness, for its ethical, environmental, craft-oriented, socially engaged and thus more serious design 'signature'? Or is it the case that the (albeit decreasing) buffer of welfare provision in the successful German economy and its polity protects creative workers from the absolute hard edge of poverty, eviction and social marginalization (e.g. one does not see the food-banks in Germany that have become a common sight in the US and the UK). Welfare provides a bridge into work, by means of self-employment schemes and, once in work, it also is there, should the business fall apart, at least in terms of there being health provision, schools and kindergarten for children, and more job-creation schemes to fall back on. This infrastructure is important because the fashion micro-enterprises find themselves up against the power and might of the so-called retail giants. How can small fashion producers create sustainable livelihoods when the presence of these retailers breathes down their necks, even hoping to absorb and profit from some of the unique and sometimes dubbed 'anti-commercial' ethos that pervades fashion and the wider cultural scene in Berlin? This is a formidable challenge. With some irony, the micro-enterprises are somehow expected to donate the magic ingredients of their counter-cultural atmosphere, to allow the bigger companies to expand their market share. This seemingly anti-capitalist spirit finds itself looked to because it can provide the kind of 'edginess' or innovation that will help retailers finesse their appeal to young people (Boltanksi and Chiapello 2005). *Nike* and *Comme des Garçons* have developed ways of buying into or emulating the anti-commercial ambience, but currently *Acne* and *Cos* are the most dedicated and successful in this strategy.[16] Indeed, rather than direct copying or infringements of IP and copyright by the larger companies, what we could say is that the entire milieu and ambience of the 'Berlin city scene' is drawn upon to develop innovative, or 'cutting edge', commercial strategies. These retailers have stores in the key locations in Mitte, where passers-by include the widest and most relevant demographic mix. A critical, counter-cultural, 'hipster' ethos is looked to for its ability to provide an elusive subcultural capital, thereby helping large companies in their search for insight, knowledge, trends and innovation (Thornton 1996).[17] The further paradox lies in the need, on the part of the city government to attract inward investment and especially those companies and retailers who will create jobs in the city. There is a shift away from support to the tiny enterprises, to a more forceful business-led agenda. In the highly contested space of city politics the Mayor grapples to find a way to translate this counter-cultural ethos into something attractive to investors.[18] This in turn gives rise to further rounds of debate in popular media such as listings magazines and also in academic milieus about the ways in which subcultures are crudely instrumentalized as city assets in urban branding processes (Bader and Scharenberg 2010; Pasquinelli 2010; Colomb 2012).

Berlin has a population of 3.4 million people. It is highly visible of course, because of its historical significance as one of the key cities of European modernity, for its significance during the Nazi regime, and then, following the end of the Second World War, its pivotal role in the Cold War. With little industrial, post-industrial or finance infrastructure, it has, for more than fifty years, been reliant on various forms of subsidy from the federal government and, since the wall has come down, this has been diminished and replaced with an agenda based on privatization and de-regulation, and an expectation of returns in the form of rising land values, office spaces and rental incomes from the kinds of companies who would see new opportunities brought about by re-unification. Various authors have described the mistakes of excessive borrowing and investment-driven over-building and the exaggerated expectations that companies would re-locate to the city and create substantial numbers of new jobs (Ward 2004; Mayer 2004; Cochrane and Jonas 1999). It is these factors, along with some population shifts following re-unification, that account for Berlin having the most available office space of any comparable European city (Ward 2004). Along with this, and despite the success of the German economy, the city has retained a high rate of almost 12 per cent unemployment. (Even in my own quiet residential neighbourhood of Schoenberg, there are countless empty shop spaces on the ground floors of apartment blocks with the sign *zu Vermieten* posted on the windows.) This is a city of renters, where almost 90 % of people are tenants rather than home-owners. There are also in place, despite opposition from landlords, rent controls, which continue to provide some protection against rising rents, and the pressure to move out to make way for new populations willing to pay more. Rents (though rising) are as a result not exorbitant, and although wages for those in the creative and cultural sectors are low, or irregular, it is nevertheless possible to make ends meet, while struggling to get a business or small fashion start-up off the ground. One is less likely to risk home and all security as one would in London, however the reality, acknowledged in the *Creative Industries in Berlin* report, is low and very modest, often minimal level incomes across the full stretch of the post-Fordist media, culture and arts economy. In the concluding section I will interrogate in more depth this idea of low returns in the context of a 'meaningful and liveable life'.

I entered this Berlin fashion sphere at exactly those points that seemed to suggest self-employment for predominantly female young graduates as a kind of grounded, bottom-up activity. For three years, though in an interrupted way, I have been observing these activities as well as interviewing and talking with participants.[19] Many of the younger designers work exceptionally long hours and, despite good reviews and publicity in the Berlin press, find they do not have the resources or capital investment to employ others to carry out the tasks that need to be done. One designer from a well-known label said in interview how she did not have the resources to pay someone to keep track of actual sales in those shops that had placed orders (while also maintaining the friendly social relation with the shop-owners to ensure they continue to place orders) and likewise she needed someone to undertake web design and the whole business of moving to online sales.[20] There is often a high degree of anxiety and a constant need to adjust to changing circumstances; this can entail sudden reductions of the level of local government support or it can mean a key person in the enterprise leaving, getting ill or having to reduce working hours following the birth of a child. Failure can occur at every point in the fashion process (bad weather, successful clothes copied by the high street, less successful clothes remaining unsold, fabrics fade in the wash etc.) and for this reason designers often need to have in place various strategies that comprise additional part-time jobs such as bar work, or making clothes for friends on a one-off, cash in hand, basis. This reminds us of the proximity mini-enterprises have to the hidden or informal economy. Despite the various agencies available to advise start-ups on business support, on finance including tax returns and on entitlements for the self-employed, almost inevitably there will be some margin for doing some work 'on the side' especially when the businesses are in the earliest stages. The work culture in Berlin shows enthusiasm tempered by sober and well-informed realism, a pattern found in almost every interview we have carried out over the period of three years. The designers have been forthcoming about the difficulties they face applying for bank loans, the escalation of rents for business premises, and the perceived turn towards a city branding policy on the part of the city government, rather than on finding mechanisms to support the designers themselves. Overall, these creative activities appear to be embarked upon without a strong business plan. Indeed, they correspond to what Bourdieu called the anti-economy of artists (Bourdieu 1993). And this seeming naivety perhaps performs an important role as a justification for the long hours worked and the minimal returns. In an interview with one of Berlin's best-known designers we were told that, to begin with, he did not even think about selling the work, he had no idea about costing pieces or a collection. All his efforts were invested in producing the work itself, like making art.[21] There is, alongside this fine-art ethos, the longstanding German focus on high levels of training and professional skills, as well as craftsmanship, which transform the job into a source of pride and self-reward, and this too compensates for small take-home pay. The shop, or the line of clothing are worth a good deal more to the owner or designer than the balance sheet. 'The work is done for its own sake.'[22] The young woman at her sewing machine within the view of customers is saying, 'This is my workplace, this is what I do.' The design and lay-out of these small shops, the construction of a specific 'chic' atmosphere inside the shops, the choice of music, the clothes themselves, all of these contribute to an ethos that challenges the homogeneity of the 'high street'. These are independent, often female-led undertakings (Jakob 2009). Where there is a shortage of jobs and high rates of unemployment these shops demonstrate effort and determination to self-organize and transform the urban landscape. The bales of fabric and sewing machines are there to tell the customer something about the narratives of production. The paper patterns and the pressing machines also in sight of passers-by make the point about this being a neo-artisanal craft-oriented approach. Femininity is deployed in an independent and expressive way, quite at odds with the dominant ('work that smile') styles of the affective economy (Hochschild 1984). Various factors shape these female-led fashion activities, first, the new artisanal or craft mode that intersects more broadly with the recent post-recession self-organized economies; second, the influence of the *Mittelstand* craft tradition in Germany, which offers a sense of pride and reward in work even if the returns are modest; then there is also a new inflection of the Berlin radical scene, including those that from the mid 1970s had a more explicitly political agenda, such as the feminist not-for-profit organizations specializing in training and vocational education for disadvantaged girls and women, including those from ethnic minorities; and finally there is the post-Wall subcultural economy, which incorporated a 'dissident' attitude most evident in the music and club sector. These currents come together to produce two distinct modes of production, one of which is 'fashion-art', the other a neighbourhood 'fashion-craft'; in the section which follows there will be a discussion of the potential here for urban counter-cultural economies based largely on 'female post-Fordist place-making strategies' as an alternative to the prevailing accounts of hipster lifestyle and gentrification (Colomb 2012).

Fashion Art

> Even trying to borrow 5,000 euros from the bank can be difficult.
> (Derya Issever, interviewed 6 November 2013)
>
> We have been brought up on the ideas of punk and the avant garde.
> (Marte Henschel, *Common-Works*, 28 June 2012)

Arguably, the population of Berlin is more politically invested in the vexed issues of city-space and planning than elsewhere.[23] This strong sense of attachment and belonging extends into the various sites used for Berlin Fashion Week shows (Exner 2011). The evocative city spaces are much more actively drawn upon by designers showing their work and they are used as promotional devices that contribute meaning, value and atmosphere. This outward look to the city itself, a kind of place-making activity, means that fashion designers (who are mostly female) are more involved in and knowledgeable about the politics of space than would normally be the case. The establishment of a biannual Berlin Fashion Week (sponsored by Mercedes Benz) has provided young Berlin designers with the kind of institutional frame needed for them to achieve visibility nationally and internationally (Exner 2011). The event itself, as well as all the promotional activity surrounding it, creates a narrative that allows the designers to show their work and to make connections with key contacts from across the world. This represents a major source of Berlin city investment for its fashion sector. The guides and publicity material produce a map of activities for business visitors and also for the general public. The Summer 2012 Calendar, for example, lists 104 events hosted in showrooms, shops, galleries, backyards, pop-up stores, hotels and other locations including U-Bahn stations. The abbreviated Event Check section draws attention to one exhibition titled 'Going Green' and another simply called the 'Ethical Fashion Show'. The role of key retailers is also apparent, with all the main shops being listed as hosting parties and receptions. However, from this high volume of activities only about twenty designers and labels appear to aspire to an independent *haute-couture* or 'high-fashion' status. These are the designers who regularly feature in blogs as well as in the quality press and fashion media in Berlin.

Five of these 'high-end' or fine-art oriented Berlin fashion designers were interviewed as part of this current investigation. They are Michael Sontag, Majaco, Issever Bahri and Esther Perbandt. Alongside them is Rita in Palma, who makes *couture* pieces such as lace collars, crochet undergarments and 'evening dress gloves', and for this reason I include her in the *couture* category. It has also been possible to draw on comments and discussions (including those by the *couture* designer duo Augustin Teboul) that took place in the context of a number of special 'research events' hosted in both London and Berlin.[24] In the course of nearly three years we have also spoken to and interviewed various experts including Marte Henschel, a trained designer, now director of a well-known producer services company *Common-Works*, one member of the Senate,[25] other policy-makers and academics, as well as two fashion lawyers, with these meetings and interviews all taking place from June 2012 on. What has become evident is that art-oriented fashion (or fashion art) in Berlin has to struggle to assert this identity, for the reason that fashion in Germany and also in Berlin has existed as the elite luxury end of the clothing industry and is associated with status, power and wealthy consumers, or else it has been considered part of popular or even the debased 'mass culture' of Adorno's analysis, and associated with the uniformity of post-war consumer capitalism (Adorno 1991). Any idea of fashion as art has to be imported from some other international cultural spaces and institutions such as the art schools of the UK or the US. Fashion designers in the city have had to contest this low status through emphasizing the academic value bestowed on fashion design through the degree-awarding processes at the prestigious universities,[26] and they have also had to look to the importance of 'subcultures' in the city for their expressive value and the social role they play in giving voice to young people, in relation to style and leisure identity, ethnicity, queerness and so on. Where in London both of these factors have long been recognized and indeed exploited by major companies eager to reap the rewards with lucrative collaborations, this has been almost non-existent in Berlin. It is also less popular as an option for struggling designers, who are torn between recognizing the need for commercial partners and feeling the need to protect the purity or authenticity of the label as part of the overall non-commercial identity of fashion design in the city. These are all designers who win prizes and are in the public eye through favourable press reviews and blogs, especially during Berlin Fashion Week. They have a high visibility in the city and are part of the Berlin branding exercise overseen by the city government. The websites of Michael Sontag, Esther Perbandt, Issever Bahri and Augustin Teboul are testimony to intensive work over a period of years since graduation. These designers have carefully developed distinctive *haute-couture* oriented, art-directed collections. Their work functions as 'pieces' and the statements found on the websites or Facebook pages suggest the influence of contemporary art theory, philosophy, architecture and (sub)cultural studies. Michael Sontag for example is interested in flow and in interrupting the usual temporality of fashion, and this becomes an aim that is formally inscribed in his fashion, as he plays with shape, fabric, and movement around the body. Augustin Teboul (with stockists in France, Italy and Asia) pushes the boundaries of sexuality, working entirely in black with intricate lace crochet-work, and questioning and re-configuring the female body. Esther Perbandt aims at melting down the boundaries between fashion and performance art; she also explores the subcultural avant-garde with androgyny, she has worked with the well-known Italian artist Marco Pho Grassi applying his painting technique directly on to her clothes, and she has formed her own band, performing as a singer and musician. Her most recent collection was titled GROTESQUE.

Designers like these face various problems including (a) low customer sales or problems to 'access the markets' (Kalandides 2014) (b) difficulties in securing loans or capital investment especially after three or four successful collections (c) the high cost of employing staff (d) the question of export and of getting known outside Germany and outside Berlin. The first of these is the most intractable. Ideally, they want to manage their own sales rather than losing track of what happens to collections once they are on the rails of unknown stockists who often fail to report back on what has been sold and what will be marked down or discounted. Having a shop connected to a work space or live-work unit in a good location is therefore optimal. One designer[27] regretted earlier strategies that entailed trying to do everything – including collections, fashion fairs and keeping on top of production. She said that had she concentrated only on the shop and work space she would by now have two shops rather than one. Meanwhile, she has now learnt to produce what her customers in the neighbourhood of Prenzlauer Berg, along with the passing trade of tourists, seem to like from her work. As it is, she is still paying off debts accrued through the earlier stage. In contrast, Perbandt[28] has adopted a more avant-garde approach to business, seeing herself now as an art director and using her shop simply as a front window 'for the image'. Mining German film and theatre history through the image and style of the actor Valeska Gert (who worked with Brecht), Perbandt has staged events at Rotersalon, which is part of the world-famous Volksbuehne Theatre at Rosa Luxemburg Platz. Perbandt offers a professional art-oriented perspective on the specifics of Berlin fashion; she is, as she said, 'inventing how fashion can be sold and marketed'. Michael Sontag who, like Perbandt, has been supported by the Berlin Senate (through the showrooms set up in New York and Paris during the big fashion weeks)[29] sees this problem of sales as uppermost, and for him the possibility of gaining more control over his sales lies in having his own shop open in late summer 2014. Low capital investment and distrust on the part of banks means that, as was the case with London designers in the mid 1990s, these are jobs without capital (inverting Beck's idea of capital without jobs) (McRobbie 1998; Beck 2000). Several designers explain that they have to look to friends or family for interim or indeed start-up support, this is an issue across the art-directed and also the craft-based design sector (Kalandides 2014). They urgently need injections of cash to be able to keep moving and to have access to specialized equipment and to the new media technology required of all small businesses today. Slowly there is a sense that collaborations with bigger partners may go some way in solving this problem. But these are only entered into with caution. Sontag has recently worked with a shoe company and one of the other designers expressed a wish to work with a German *Mittelstand* glove company. As Berlin fashion academic and consultant Oliver MacConnell said in discussion, 'To survive, the designers need more than a few thousand euros, some could be major figures in the fashion world, but they need millions.'[30] This point is most evident in staff costs, the use of interns, the higher awareness in the sector of exploitation, the panoply of schemes to encourage employment in the form of mini-jobs and the reality of self-employment and cash-in-hand working.

All of these factors, along with the final question of how to work with overseas markets, represent the full gamut of commercial factors that weigh down heavily on fashion designers, who declare themselves to be artists, partly out of self-belief and partly because such a stance, as Bourdieu reminds us, justifies to an extent the reality of low earnings. The irony here is that fashion does not fall under the same category for state funding as the fine arts, opera, ballet, or theatre (as is the case in the UK with the Arts Council of England and Wales). It is therefore forced to find some middle way, testing the ground of carefully planned collaborations, which benefit both parties without risking loss of 'authenticity' and overall reputation. Are designers, then, in reality more like DJs and independent music producers in the city? (see Lange 2012b). Or can the avant-garde art direction being pursued by Perbandt mark out a decisive step towards bringing fashion closer to performance art or architecture, indeed blurring the boundaries of these categories, by means of looking for one-off gigs, commissions, and art-based installations? These attempts to evade or avoid the marketplace of fashion raise a key question. Can such endeavours be seen as inherently radical, as designers seek alternative ways of working? There is also the question of the work itself and the values it endorses. What then can anti-capitalist fashion be? How can designers have a critical stance on the fashion system while still remaining players within it? Perhaps the important thing for now is that this stands out as a marked, indeed defining feature of Berlin fashion, something perhaps remarkable and bold in such an otherwise uncritical and conservative creative industry. In the section that follows, this argument is pursued by looking at fashion activities, which have a more explicitly social agenda, that is, where fashion is undertaken as a social enterprise. What role does this kind of work play in creating an alternative and not-for-profit urban economy?

Salons of Job Creation? Social Start-Ups in Berlin

A good deal has been written about the sudden visibility of the area of NeuKoelln as a rundown multi-cultural neighbourhood now finding itself subject to property speculation, rising rents, and the encroachment of a new middle-class population, with the consumer culture to match their tastes. Discussing these issues is fraught with the danger of the glib exoticism of cultural difference, a common feature of lifestyle journalism or of colluding with some of the terms of reference that are part of the policy-led language advocating integration and reflecting comments by Angela Merkel that multiculturalism has failed. Taking the lead from Onur Komurcu we must be aware of how racializing processes in this Berlin context work to establish and control the parameters of what is required of or expected of the Turkish–German subject who is still considered somehow a migrant or a part of migrant culture (Komurcu 2015). It is important then to avoid repeating the stereotypes of Turkish–German women as 'local' and in possession of hand-work skills, with the graduate designers or social entrepreneurs implicitly white and German. Certainly, this kind of typecasting is frequently deployed in the process of writing grant applications, indeed it is almost a requirement to deploy such a vocabulary. Sociologists, myself included, succumb, even if knowingly, to what Komurcu describes as the 'lure of cultural diversity'. This occurs for instance when for the sake of providing a summary description of the neighbourhoods in which these social enterprises are located, the researcher produces a kind of sketch of people and their activities. How not to be part of the 'lure'? How to avoid a colonizing gaze?[31]

It is the various streets off Hermannsplatz in NeuKoelln that have become the centre for fashion activity. The small workshops are set alongside an array of shops of the type often found in poor and so-called migrant neighbourhoods across the world, what Simone calls 'popular economies' (Simone 2010). In NeuKoelln these comprise flower shops, funeral parlours, an old-fashioned 'damen-moden' shop with blouses and tops ('nimm 3 zahlen 2') in the windows. There are also any number of internet cafes, mobile-phone repair shops, betting shops, amusement arcades, cocktail bars, hair-dressers, wedding-dress boutiques, washing-machine repair shops, driving schools and bakeries. These kinds of shops are also familiar spots in working-class neighbourhoods in most Western cities, and in this case a far cry from the elegant and sedate streets of Prenzlauer Berg. (It was an antipathy to bourgeois life in Berlin that pushed Walter Benjamin to 'explore' the excitement and the sexual possibilities of working-class Berlin in the early years of the twentieth century, see Benjamin 2009.) On more than one occasion the point was made in discussion with designers that this NeuKoelln location worked for their businesses because the Turkish–German Muslim women who took part in the training programmes or else who were already employed as pattern cutters or as knitters and crocheters did not travel far outside the neighbourhood and did not feel comfortable in Prenzlauer Berg. Some of the designers we inter-viewed simply deployed these stereotypes (in a friendly and empa-thetic way), saying that many of these women are quiet and quite shy. At such moments as these there is a flicker of tension in the research process, since at least one of the *haute-couture* designers in the study is herself Turkish–German, as are several well-known designers in the city.[32] In using this kind of language what is perpetu-ated is the idea of Turkish–German woman as low skilled and unqualified, rather than as, more accurately, increasingly likely to be graduates looking for the same kind of work as their white German counterparts.

The streets in which this fashion and craft activity is most visible are on turnings off Hermannsplatz and past the large Karstadt depart-ment store. It is easy to spot workshops where during weekdays a couple of young women make up clothes (as well as '*Kunst und Handwerk*') in a shop-front studio space looking directly onto the street, and they then sell the goods at the weekend market stall just a few minutes away by the canal (www.neukoellner-stoff.de). In another street a young Chinese–German woman whose shop is ironically titled *Fu Manchu Flagship Store* sits at her sewing machine, with the products, dresses, tops and skirts on display on rails and in the window. There are three fashion social enterprises located in this group of streets in NeuKoelln, they are *NEMONA*, *Common-Works* and *Nadelwald*. I describe these as social enterprises because they emphasize a teaching and learning dimension, an egalitarian management style, a commitment to ethical issues in fashion and textile production, a strong focus on contributing to the neighbourhood and forging connections with local women and girls who may have an interest in sewing, making and more generally in fashion. All three enterprises have a kind of open-door policy. In the times I have visited or been a passer-by I have seen women of different ages knock the door and request information about the activities. In the case of *Common-Works* and *NEMONA* the field of ideas that informed the setting up of these businesses is clearly within a recognizably social democratic framework. *NEMONA* has won support from the EU Social Fund and all three have secured local grants in the form of help with rent, space and equipment, so they have been deemed 'worthy of support'. In addition, despite having trained in fashion, their founders have not set themselves up as fashion designers but rather as fashion producers, as managers, or in the case of *Nadelwald* as director of a co-sewing space. The overall style, self-image, presentation of work and social media visibility suggest an attachment to the values of a kind of post-punk DIY/DIT sensibility (itself a loose signifier of radicalism), and to working in a more collective and cooperative way than is normally associated with people trained in fashion.

One of the questions raised right at the beginning of this chapter was the relationship between the tools of current governmentality in the form of the creativity *dispositif* and the subjects for whom they are developed through the existence of various instruments and toolkits and technologies of 'support'. In the German and specifically the Berlin context these instruments take two forms mirroring the different styles of fashion production already outlined above. For the fashion artists there are carefully modulated programmes overseen by the Senate and designed to extend their impact on the market of possible consumers. This recently has taken the form of the Berlin Showrooms in New York and Paris during the official fashion weeks in those cities. For the fashion-craft producers the programmes and forms of subsidy are more social in nature and entail a double layer of training and skill enhancement. In effect these fashion social enterprises act as offices (or salons) of job creation for the cultural economy. The women who run these small organizations are all relatively fluent with the language of the social enterprise. What is novel about this vocabulary is that it marries social objectives of neighbourhood improvement through local employment with the idea of self-expression through fashion and craft work. These are all relatively young enterprises, just three or four years old, and what unites them in terms of ethos is the commitment to providing training and support (or coaching) for newcomers entering the field, whether at the level of learning, manufacturing and production skills, or working as an independent designer. The hard language of business plans and cash flow is muted in favour of earning a living and keeping the enterprise afloat.

Bearing the letters DIY on its promotional material (available in German and English) *Nadelwald: 'What You Sew Is What You Get'*, is located over five large, high-ceiling rooms, with rough frescoes across the walls, and decorated in a kind of shabby version of *haute-couture* salon elegance. A series of oil paintings hangs across two walls, in one room ('the store') there is a rail of clothes for sale, including scarves and accessories; elsewhere there is the paraphernalia of sewing including wracks with paper patterns, magazines; one room is full of industrial-standard equipment and machines, there are rolls of fabric as well as haberdashery items including ribbons, threads, scissors and all that is needed for what the owner and founder Swantje describes as 'self-making'(*selbst machen*). This is a space for learning how to design and make clothes, as well to understand about all stages in fashion production, from sewing and knitting to pattern cutting and so on ('*Schnitt und Stricken und Haekeln und Naehen und Ziechnen und Mappencurse und vieles mehr*', 'you only need to bring your material and you can get going…and you can sell the items in the store'). There are opportunities at low cost (and reduced rates) to take short courses in designing a whole collection as well as in making dresses, blouses and other items. Trained in fashion design in Darmstadt, Swantje moved in 2010 to Berlin to set up her own business, with the wider agenda of developing a co-sewing movement ('we are part of the co-working movement, we offer flexible times to work, whether you are a designer, or just do it as a hobby or if you have a creative spirit, you can make and sell'). So far the open-door policy has worked well at neighbourhood level, attracting the interest and participation of local women of different ages. Almost all the Berlin newspapers and listing magazines have carried articles about *Nadelwald* and this in turn has drawn the attention of those involved in the larger co-working spaces in the city, especially *Betahaus*. The idea of co-working has also attracted, in the last year, the interest of the Berlin Senate for the reason that it has a more dynamic profile, one that comes from the worldwide success stories of Silicon Valley. Consequently *Nadelwald* benefits from bringing together traditional women's skills, which can be tapped into and developed, with a contemporary flexible, self-organized, micro-organizational set-up that also has the advantages of overcoming the isolation of freelance home-based working as well as encouraging the collective development of new ideas. Thus *Nadelwald* straddles two frameworks, one led by the idea of local female skill-enhancement for future labour market participation, the other belonging to the more decisively middle-class world of co-working spaces for young creative professionals. The same pattern can be seen in each of the other social enterprises and emerges then as a model for double job-creation strategies adopted by the policy-makers and rolled out in the form of these fashion-craft workshops. These are fashion social enterprises and start-ups rolled into one, 'social start-ups'.

Common-Works describes itself as a fashion production agency. Its founder saw the need for the city's fashion designers to have better access to well-organized and technically competent producer services. 'There was no well-functioning infrastructure in the Berlin fashion scene. There were people producing high quality products; however they lacked the ability to network and find the right producers.' The function of *Common-Works* is now to play an agency-type function or 'Zwischenmeister' role in bringing together design practitioners with the manufacturers, textile suppliers, producers and engineers needed to bring a collection into fruition. There is a community ethos among the members of *Common-Works* who come from different skill backgrounds, for example, graphic design, 'hand crafting' and industrial engineering. This expertise allows the team to be able to 'support with the development of products as well as entire collections throughout the value chain of production'. In addition *Common-Works* provides coaching and workshops for newcomers into the fashion scene, it does outreach work with local schools and it is a strong advocate of ethical practices in textile production and across all parts of the industry. We could say this enterprise functions as a good example of female 'post-Fordist place-making' insofar as it produces by bringing together a constellation of mostly female-led economic activities within a specific neighbourhood of the city in a style that departs from the louder 'hipster' pronouncements of creative economy, harking back instead to earlier feminist traditions for supporting women's employment and economic independence (Colomb 2012).

NEMONA is also based in NeuKoelln and its parent company *Inpolis* was founded by urban geographer Ares Kalandides, who wanted to set up a company that would do what he had seen working well in the 1990s in Greece, where fashion companies had sought to develop a more egalitarian production process to bring together designers with producers and with a local workforce of highly skilled women. Kalandides himself plays an active role in creative industry policy-making in the city and explicitly argues for greater attention to be paid to those who work as sewers, pattern-cutters etc. in the orbit of the so-called creatives and providing many practical and technical as well as creative services but who are often overlooked. *NEMONA* plays a co-ordinating and events management role, which connects into a network more than forty local NeuKoelln designers and approximately sixty producers (i.e. knitters, sewers, tailors etc.). Winning an EU Social Fund grant has allowed the co-ordinating role of *NEMONA* to develop, and this has involved a good deal of 'out-reach' work in local Turkish community centres and with women's groups. In this case, informed by up-to date social science vocabular-ies, this outreach approach is informed by wider understanding of the problems of the 'lure of cultural diversity' (Komurcu 2015). The two women involved in running the projects took great care to build trust between themselves as project leaders and the women from the Turkish–German community. They asked permission to attend women's groups and community centres to establish the kind of skill-pool in the area and to assess the interest to be involved. By finding ways to update these skills as well as making use of social media including Facebook to advertise jobs coming up, it has been possible for women, previously unwaged, to begin to earn some income, while also remaining in the neighbourhood, working flexible hours to meet the needs of their children and families. This in turn has also pointed to new lines of work and involvement for *NEMONA* particularly working with local Job Centres, which, as is also the case in the UK, are not at all adapted to dealing with the desire for occasional and casual work for women as a first step into the labour market. These women want to work but cannot jeopardize some of the tax credits or benefits for childcare for low income families, which are calculated on the basis of the applicant being either in formal part-time or full-time work. In effect *NEMONA* moves to incorporate in its activities the role of enhancing employability and providing training for women who are interested in fashion and clothing, but who have few formal qualifications. This part of the work of the company brings it closer to the older more established third sector and not-for-profit organiza-tions especially those that came out of feminism and also had exper-tise in attracting EU Social Funds. Once again there are female 'post-Fordist place-making' strategies here in evidence through a feminist interest in impregnating female skills and expertise in the local neighbourhood identity, so that NeuKoelln comes to be associated with women's fashion-crafting competences and expertise (Colomb 2012). This has been partly achieved by taking over otherwise empty shop window space as a display cabinet for such activity (as part of the *24 Hour NeuKoelln Fashion Weekend*).

Conclusion

In this chapter I have made some efforts to portray a model of creative economy that differs from those prevalent in the UK by virtue of the resilience of a social democratic vocabulary embedded (though not uncontested) within the local Berlin (and also national) regime of contemporary governmentality. While most protagonists in the creative milieu in the city see this as being eroded on a daily basis, its existence allows us to draw some conclusions about how a post-industrial cultural strategy for employment looks when it is not wholly dominated by a vocabulary that sings the joys of entrepreneurship and that simply conveys happy images of young people living in urban lofts and cycling to work. At the same time it has not been the aim of this chapter to flag up Berlin as a kind of haven for anti-capitalist livelihoods. Tensions open up across the sector and particularly in fashion and crafting between the policy-makers and advisers who want to see stronger business plans and sustainable enterprises and the creative actors who resist this call of commerce. The stumbling block is always the question of subsidy, although the fact that the *Creative Industries in Berlin Report* (2008) states the need for a 'good well-functioning, focused and efficient public support system for the creative industries' serves as a reminder that social democratic thinking survives, albeit with a shrunken power base. The presence too of an older social democratic imaginary dating back to the late 1970s forms something of a bulwark against the modernizing zeal and the anti-welfare rhetoric of the modernizers who, following the example set by former SPD Chancellor Gerhard Schroeder and the *Hartz IV* policies, seek constantly to reduce public spending. Nevertheless we found through the course of undertaking these interviews that the female subjects of these prevailing norms that combine in uneasy harmony social democratic values with the role of the business plan, themselves acted as critical and engaged citizens interested in extending a neighbourhood ethos through seeing female economic activity as a dynamic visual aspect in the streets and shopping areas of this particular *kiez* or location. As J. K. Gibson-Graham says, feminist academics need to pay more attention to 'a practical politics of strengthening the sustainability of community economies'. These authors also remind us of the 'inter-generational durability of local cultures, practices of sociality and emplaced liveli-hood strategies that support community economies' or in other words the ideal of feminist 'post-Fordist place-making strategies' (Gibson 2002; Gibson-Graham 2003; Colomb 2012). The final points to emphasize here include the reality of modest incomes on the part of the social entrepreneurs, the designers themselves and the fashion makers and crafters, indeed almost everyone across the fashion sector in the city. As Esther Perbandt said, 'No one is making money.'[33] This in turn raises the question of what makes for a reward-ing working life without the prospect of a large salary but with other compensatory rewards, such as a neighbourhood community that provides enjoyment and the pleasures of active citizenship and some sense of decision-making capacity and self-directed work. There is also something of a political momentum in these social enterprises, which in turn enhances the meaning of work, an idea of the social good and of taking part in the expansion of opportunities for women. While some critics might explain this female-led anti-economy and lack of competition and reluctance about the business plan as a privi-lege based on Germany's relatively intact welfare system, my own emphasis here is on the idea of 'the work' being done 'for its own sake', a theme that will be more developed in the final chapter of this book under the heading of a 'good job done well'. Others might add that in this case the social democratic element within this regime of the Berlin creativity *dispositif*, along with the more specific address to women's employment makes such a style of governmentality all the more successful when it is translated into a technology of the self. Here the call to 'be creative' is all the more appealing because of this social effect and without the demonization of welfare so recurrent in US and UK systems. And, lo and behold, the women work long hours for relatively little pay. Last and by no means least, Ulrich Beck, writing on the Eurozone crisis reminds his readers of the domi-nant place occupied by Germany among member states thanks to its stronger economy; this in turn ensures some degree of social protec-tion in work and in life, something Beck in a re-distributive move, argues needs to be extended equitably across the countries of the EU. In my argument the economic activities that I have provided an account of, could be seen as containing at least the seeds of a counter-capitalistic ethos. They envisage and retain an image of socially useful work, something that is unusual in itself when we look at the fashion world today. In this sense, fashion as a third sector economy, revives and updates previous radical traditions in the city, notably the radical activities of the counter-culture, which also contained job creation strategies. This connects with an idea of artistic practice as oppositional, and there is a downgrading of commerce in favour of social values.

6

A Good Job Well Done? Richard Sennett and the New Work Regime

An eagle-eyed reader will notice that the word creativity appears in this book as little as possible. (Sennett 2008, p. 290)

[F]lexible forms of underemployment meet increasing interest among (young) men and women, in fact are virtually demanded of them in order to balance wage labour and family work, work and life more equitably. (Beck 1996, p. 143)

In Praise of Ordinary Work

A consistent and original dynamic in the writing of Richard Sennett is the attempt to deflate the current emphasis on all notions of exceptional achievement in the world of work including leadership, success, creativity and genius. There are four themes in this body of writing, which also allows us the opportunity here to develop further the critique of the creativity *dispositif*. These are (a) the 'corrosion of character' wrought on subjects of the new work regime, (b) time, memory and narrative in working life, (c) the value of craft, and (d) 'respect' in the urban environment. Taking into account also some of the limitations of this Sennett *oeuvre*, I will later in the chapter make a more specific argument about how his thinking offers an intellectual bridge between old and new ways of working, and that his historical sociology provides also an ethical voice that can speak directly to those already enmeshed in the thick of the new culture industries, not least because the writing, though highly erudite, is uncomplicated by theoretical vocabularies. Sennett's elegiac literary style brings him

closer to the ranks of American novelists of his generation or older.
When he seems to be writing specifically about work or the city, he
is actually writing about America, indeed a strand of American life
that is often narrow-minded, conservative and moralistic. Aware,
indeed exasperated by some of these voices, Sennett insists they are
listened to if we are to understand the impact of changes in everyday
life. While admirable, this also has shortcomings, especially when
considered through the lens of gender, for the reason that many of
the men he talks to are self-evidently patriarchal and regretful of
changes. Often they seemed to have walked right out of a novel by
John Updike or Philip Roth. I will also suggest in the course of this
chapter that, though deeply egalitarian in outlook, Sennett's argument about the dignity of labour, as relevant today as in the past,
leads him ironically to endorse a rather elevated notion of craft. He
sees the highly skilled craftsman at his work-bench, engrossed in the
process of making. Or else drawing on his close attachment to the
world of classical music, his ideal craftsman or woman is one who
is constantly practising for what may be a relatively modest role, in
the violin section of the city orchestra, or in the *corps de ballet* at the
Paris Opera. This kind of work, requiring a commitment bordering
on obsession is, however, far removed from the women crafters of
today, producing items from home for sale on Etsy.com. With the rise
of digital media, the realm of craft has opened up far beyond the
realms of concentration and attention to detail described by Sennett.
This raises questions about gender and new hierarchies within the
'arts and crafts' of the present-day cultural economy.

Sennett's favourite topics are in fact so deeply entangled with one
another as to be hard to prise apart. By lifting creative work from its
pedestal and focusing on the mundane dimensions of the process of
making, Sennett brings creative work closer to the more ordinary jobs
and occupations that have also recently been transformed, or are
being destandardized (as Beck puts it) so as to concur with the
requirements of the new regime of flexible labour. Alongside this, he
advocates a more integrated and egalitarian methodology for urban
research, which in the context of creative economy discussion has
been more or less exclusively concerned with the young people who
congregate in city spaces more typically inhabited by poor and disadvantaged social groups, including ethnic minorities, migrants and
an indigenous working class. He provides a strong counter-current
to the writing of Richard Florida, talking to old and disenchanted
workers from many occupations. Sennett has investigated the everyday life of cities over many decades and has been drawn to unremarkable people. Like Florida, he is listened to by governments, not

because he offers a kind of magic formula for building creative sectors
in rundown urban districts but on the basis of deeper and more sustained ethical concerns, such as why the giving of respect to disadvantaged people is both important and complicated. Sennett also
enquires into what happens to people when their jobs become projects, and when their workmates become team members? When rosters
bring in different groups of people who don't talk to each other and
who simply come in and leave, who are employed on different kinds
of contracts, and who, with the impact of new technology become
operatives rather than people with distinct skills?[1] Creative work
often seems far removed from the kinds of activities Sennett is interested in. Indeed the old jobs disappear as the new ones emerge. But
in fact there is a new middle ground, where new technology and
social media impact across the lives of young and old alike, where
flexible working means different working rhythms, where more
people seem to be at home during times in the day, when in the past,
residential areas would only be busy with mothers and children, or
with the retired and the unemployed. In reality most sectors of the
working population are affected by changes in work regimes. It is my
intention here to draw these strands together in a bid to think in new
ways about the creative industries. I will assess how far Sennett's
concept of craft helps us to develop a less inflated and overblown
vocabulary for thinking about the rise of the creative sector. Can it
provide the basis for a kind of everyday ethics of work, and a counter
to the prevailing individualism of the so-called talent-led economy?
How well does it function in fields of activity that are socially necessary but unpaid or under-paid, such as domestic work, childcare and
care of the elderly? If, following Beck, we need to be looking at
investing in areas of hitherto unpaid labour, e.g. 'family work', that
could, in the light of under-employment, become a source of value
and enrichment, how does craft replenish the kind of jobs that have
always carried connotations of drudgery or of monotony (Beck 1996,
2000)? There is a sense in which craft in Sennett's thinking seems to
have the power to make all work rewarding and interesting, as long
as the craftsman has patience, concentration and a desire to see a
good job well done. Sennett makes his case against the writing of
Hannah Arendt on this subject. Often he seems to be saying there
need be no such thing as drudgery, all work can have life-enhancing
qualities. Certainly, by downgrading the spectacular aspirations of
creative work, craft provides a kind of calmness and a steadfastness
in the relation between the worker and his often recalcitrant object.
Sennett is of course alert to feminist questions and his use of the word
craftsman is carefully rehearsed and gender neutral. Still, I am left

wondering about the recalcitrant child and the tired mother, who may also be trying to keep her freelance work and flexible job in the creative sector viable, while also having a clean and tidy house, or at the other end of the spectrum, the stressed-out young woman who is also a freelancer, let us say a web-designer, and who cannot consider taking time out to have a baby for fear of losing her network and who becomes depressed and drinks too much.[2] Can the high level of craft skill involved in web design compensate for the wider structural factors determining the economic viability of reproduction and the bringing up of children? Work here replaces life. Sennett's comments on parenting as craft may well also disguise a feminist deficit, which points to a political weakness in his analysis. The repetition he values so highly in the process of, let us say, practising a musical instrument, has an entirely different meaning for the mum at home changing the tenth nappy of the day and trying to work out how she can re-enter the labour market and afford childcare. Likewise he overlooks the toll new creative labour takes on the young, so that it is not only the old and seemingly displaced or redundant for whom there is loss and displacement. Does Sennett's idea of 'corrosion of character' imply that young creatives who have grown up with the new entrepreneurial ethos and been trained in it and so know nothing else, are in effect tainted in advance by this process of corrosion? Are their work-based friendships contaminated by the politics of projects? Does this mean that it is next to impossible to envisage a turning away from the apolitical individualism endemic in creative circles, or might this process be reversed and a new spirit of co-operation emerge? Sennett certainly provides a challenge to the frenetic speeded-up and then burn-out mentality currently experienced by 'young creatives'. He does not claim for his writing an explicit political agenda, nevertheless, the question has to be raised, does craft have purchase, as an ethics of work, to be of assistance by way of offering an alternative to those caught up in the anxieties of multi-tasking and a future of short-term multiple job holding? While the benefits of patient labour are palpable, the ability to implement such practices seems increasingly distant and this may call for a more substantial overhauling of the politics of work, in the light of the rise of both creative labour but more generally of destandardized work. In this chapter therefore I aim to see how we can address the new creative work, not by isolating it and lifting it out from the routines of everyday working lives, and thus making it exceptional, but quite the opposite. I seek to re-embed creative work, so that it can be viewed alongside other kinds of jobs not associated with the aura of inspiration, and not requiring this magic ingredient of creativity. I also want to re-embed it spatially so that we can consider these kinds of working lives within the context of the everyday life of the city. I want to find a way of countering the romance and emphasizing more the ordinary rewards in the sense of a 'good job well done'. Richard Sennett helps me to move in this direction (Sennett 1993, 1998, 2003, 2006, 2008). Instead of the existing models of success and failure, of euphoria or of burn out and new psychopathologies of anxiety, depression, panic and worthlessness, as examined by Berardi, there is another possibility connected to a radical downgrading of exceptional work (Berardi 2009). If the work is less important the worker can detach and invest less of a sense of self-value in its outcomes. He or she can perhaps 'clock off' at the end of the day and relax with the children at the weekend. Sennett also provides a counter to the assumptions of youthfulness, by insisting on a longer view. His own research traces occupational dynamics over the long term. He re-visits and interviews again people who were the subjects of his research into work and organizations thirty years ago. He also integrates discussion of new kinds of flexible working within a wider remit, which means that his focus spans jobs that are far removed from those connected narrowly with the new creative economy. He considers the working practices of bakers, and computer programmers, of bar-owners and of musicians. Sennett is best known for his research on cities, architecture and urban space, and this too permits a widening of the current perspectives on urban creative economy for reasons that will be examined later in this chapter.

The search for exciting jobs, or those promising rewards connected with the aura of creativity, invariably means that other jobs lacking these possibilities are cast aside as, at best, something to fall back on if all else fails. I am thinking here of jobs within the realm of possibility for arts and humanities graduates, e.g. librarian, benefits office manager, publishing assistant, social worker or youth worker etc. Even when such jobs promise regular pay, promotion and benefits and entitlements, they are frequently discounted. Why is this the case? Today we live in a world of collapsing boundaries and with the intensification of the working day, working lives nowadays merge with leisure time and with non-work activities, so these kinds of creative careers are especially desirable because they promise a social life as part of the job. Work is entirely entangled with life itself. Not long ago one of my own final-year students, who had gained high passes in all of her assessed work and who considered herself politically radical, explained to me why she was hoping to turn her ongoing part-time job in the night-time economy into a more promoted full-time career in party and social network management. During her degree she had worked as a hostess for an events management company that was dedicated to bringing young single professionals together not for dating but for exchange, intelligent conversation, for company and an enjoyable night out. My student's job was to be an ice-breaker and keep the flow of conversation and sociability flowing. The company had opened branches outside London and she was hoping to run one in the northern city in which her extended family lived. When I commented on the shallowness of party management work, she agreed that a socially valuable job with, let us say, disadvantaged youngsters, would be something to consider, but not for the present.

Ulrich Beck has reminded us that there is less regular and full-time employment available (Beck 1996). For the affluent countries of the West stable work has been shrinking over the last two decades. Many young people now work within the shadow of threatened unemployment. Indeed, Beck's analysis of under-employment is absolutely central to a fuller understanding of creative work, despite, indeed being inextricably bound up with the anxious and frenetic pace of multi-tasking. Institutionalized long-term under-employment can be seen as a way of managing and holding at bay, the impact of actual unemployment. It also serves to suspend the periods of 'rest', or the time between projects, as true unemployment. Instead these periods have to be planned for and covered financially by the ongoing projects, so that they become short holidays, or time to devote to domestic obligations, or else time for pitching for new work. Projects are symbolically central to the rise of under-employment and downtime; they are often under-funded or barely funded, which means that while they signal to the outside world a confident buzz of endless activity, they are significantly under-renumerated and so frequently hardly count as paid work at all. But still, busy under-employment bears no stigma, and the constant stream of projects serves a kind of social face-saving function. At the exact same time, working under the shadow of unemployment brings the seemingly privileged new creatives closer to other social groups experiencing the hard consequences of de-industrialization, the de-standardization of work, and the disappearance of traditional jobs (Beck 1996). The slimming down of the gigantic bureaucratic structures, which, as Sennett reminds us, created inflated layers of work, means that old jobs are lost (Sennett 2006). The growth of new communications technologies, where machines and computers replace people, limits the opportunities for lifetime work for many people across the world, and in poor and slowly developing countries unemployment levels regularly encompass the majority of the population. In the former communist states of east Europe there is high unemployment, which leads to the exodus of young people to the more prosperous cities of the West, often in search of work in the field of social care. In third-world countries the flow of people out of the country of origin, creates whole new social strata of migrant labour seeking work in the service sectors of the developed world and sending money or remittances back home to support family and kin who are unable to become mobile in the same way.

These forces of change can mean that in the context of the large urban environments there is a collision of new cosmopolitan populations in and across many of the sites of work. This is especially noticeable in London in flexible labour markets appealing to young people. Another female student of mine tells me her part-time job, held onto through all the years of study, is in a well-known chain of coffee shops. Here she works alongside what we might call the truly precarious, who are often young migrant men and women (from Algeria, Brazil, Egypt) trying to earn a basic subsistence income. The coffee chain knows that this young woman is a student and they offer her an additional role writing press releases and working on brand development, while also serving from behind the counter. The coffee chain might even offer the student a managerial job after she graduates but her sights are set on her career as a freelance writer and journalist, and member of a band, so it is unlikely she will take up this option. Instead she will carry on with her shifts and hope that her real career takes off. City department stores also provide work opportunities for equally diverse groups of young people, since in retail there has also been a marked reduction in traditional full-time jobs, which would have recruited relatively low-qualified working-class young people and offered some of them longer-term prospects and a way of moving into retail management. Here too there is a new mix, smaller numbers of full-time school leavers are taken on, and much larger numbers of young people, some of whom are spending time in a big city like London, having come from east Europe, and hoping they can eventually find a way of gaining more of a foothold in the labour market, while others are working part-time while engaged either in study, or in pursuing another more prestigious career.[3] In effect the retailers can only benefit from this shift to employing flexible and better-educated and less invested personnel, for whom they will not be fully responsible as employees. For a start they lower their costs for training. Today many young people working behind the counter in stores like *Cos*, or *Gap*, or *agnès b*, have other aspirations, in much the same way as waiters and waitresses in upmarket restaurants are typically understood to be actors or models who are working between jobs. Sennett might propose we investigate what the outcome of this transformation of retail is for those for whom such work remains an end in itself, rather than a temporary way of paying the rent. These days it seems few such personnel still exist.[4]

Different layers of the workforce and different kinds of workers are responding to similar macro-social processes. Greater emphasis is now put on self-reliance and on inventiveness in creating jobs for oneself. An underlying argument across all the chapters of this book is that the arts and the creative sector embody an economic space for novel forms of job creation, or for creating a piecemeal livelihood, from a range of ever-changing projects, which have become a defining feature of the lives of well-qualified young people across the West and the affluent world. (What this means overall is that in the affluent countries of the West, the younger middle classes are being re-stratified and forced to become less reliant on the infrastructure of welfare and the institutions of the public sector that were defining features of the social democratic post-war state.) As we have seen in previous chapters the energetic meanings attributed to such jobs, that they are exciting and desirable, occur within a biopolitical landscape overseen at government and employer-level, in the light of the diminishing opportunities for work. The key instrument is entrepreneurialism. This functions to solve the problems thrown up by the decline of the employment society for an aspirational sector of the workforce. While the prevailing value system celebrates the growth of the creative economy and the rise of talent, the talented themselves are working long hours under the shadow of unemployment in a domain of intensive under-employment, and self-activated work. But this does not mean such young people are pushed down into the ranks of what in the past would be called the proletariat. In Chapter 3 of this book the weaknesses of the proletarianization argument have been addressed; in contrast to this Ulrich Beck makes a point about 'Brazilianization' – the way the informal or popular economies of the street,[5] are now extended to include middle-class self-employment practices in the West (Beck 2000). He is right in one crucial respect, but is at risk here of comparing the patchwork of emergent work cultures in Western affluent countries, which are nevertheless underpinned by a residue of welfarism, with cities suffering from extremities of violence and destitution and characterized by massive populations living in abject poverty. More apposite is his analysis of work destandardization as a 'risk-fraught system of flexible, pluralized, decentralized underemployment, which, however, will possibly no longer raise the problem of unemployment in the sense of being completely without a paid job' (Beck 1996, p. 143).

Behind the Counter

What Sennett's *Conscience of the Eye* contributes to my attempt to bring creative labour down to a ground level so that it can be analysed alongside and in the context of more mundane activities, is this, and here I choose selectively. Attention is paid to the cityscape and the neighbourhoods where people are going about their business, Sennett remarks on unremarkable economic activities such as the Indian and Pakistani shopkeepers. 'The shop owners stand in their doorways in summer, making jokes or comments' (Sennett 1993, p. 128). The rhythms of the neighbourhood and its architecture point to the intersection of working and non-working lives, in unspectacular ways, and his walks up and down the grids of New York, undertaken in the spirit of Baudelaire's *flâneur*, allow him to make an argument about impersonality and the subjective life of the city. Sennett aims to develop a visual anthropological method for urban analysis, a 'conscience of the eye' in regard to the complexity of power and powerlessness in the city spaces. He wishes to retrieve sympathy and self-expressiveness in the city across diverse social groups, and to encourage exposure through 'mobilizing...artistic energies in everyday life' (Sennett 1993, p. 149). This is a proposal for artists to become more outward-looking and more energetic in their civic life. Sennett looks at shops and small shopkeepers on 14th Street in New York, which is run down, but where there is a kind of solidarity in the various attempts to hold the mafia with their demands for protection money, at bay. The weak borders and porous boundaries of working-class neighbourhoods offer scope, he claims, for more than just impersonal co-existence. The jarring discontinuities, the differences and the disorientations, could become the basis for binding people together in new more politicized ways. Sennett brings into the current discussion of urban creative economies the idea of locale, of neighbourhood, of the diverse people living and working there, alongside each other. He urges us to consider what the shops and pubs look like inside and who the people are who are working behind the bar.

What then if we were to consider the artists and creatives who seek out spaces for living and for showing and selling their work, or for setting up a bar or a café as a mini-business to support the art, in rundown or under-resourced areas, where they also act as local shop-keepers? They open small shops, they present their objects and collections for sale to a passing as well as to an invited public. They play their part in the expressive life of the street, alongside the other small entrepreneurs. The shop acts as a critical interface between the creative activity behind the scenes and its public exposure. The public front, the space of creative display, the craft shop, the design outlet, the shop that doubles up as a bar or café or place for launch parties, these are all highly valued spaces for those working in the creative economy. Perhaps they can be conceptualized alongside and in solidarity with what A. M. Simone calls the 'popular economies' of migrant shopkeeping (Simone 2010). These newcomers need not necessarily be seen or see themselves as gentrifiers, they could instead become community activists, they could feed into a wider revival of local politics. With the exception of Doreen Jakob and Sharon Zukin this shop-keeping function has not been closely considered in most recent accounts of the growth of this sector (Jakob 2009; Zukin 2010). Jakob considers the city-funded initiatives that allow young creatives to set up shop in rundown parts of the city of Berlin. But she only fleetingly considers the relations between the artists and the locals. Doubtless this is because of the loftier aspirations typically associated with the world of the arts, which would separate out the newly opened gallery from the internet café next door. Nevertheless the reality for so many creative economy people is that they are also doubling up as shop-keepers of sorts and in some of my own other writing the reader will find various references to young people who are simultaneously running a bar or a café or who have started off with a space that is also a local café and a gallery at the same time.[6] So we could propose that this is one way of re-embedding artistic economies into the normal everyday life of the city. It is a weakness of existing accounts that other people in these urban milieus are faded into the background, only visible as local colour. And as was apparent in the previous chapter, women, especially mothers who must remain put in the city they live in for reasons of schools, and childcare, often seem the best placed people to develop what we referred to as female 'post-Fordist place-making' strategies, in this case through local creative economies (Colomb 2012).

Urban Autobiography

Across most of Sennett's recent work, there is a strongly autobiographical current. This is most vivid in *Respect* where he reflects more directly on neighbourhood and social class, and where he describes his own early years in one of Chicago's housing projects, the Cabrini estate where he lived with his mother who went on to train as a social worker (Sennett 2003). Through these personal reflections Sennett provides a way of thinking about creative work itself, or art working, in a less grandiose way, which is a counter to the highly individualistic notions of inspiration, genius, talent and competition. He gets to this by describing his own training as a child in classical music and how he was thwarted in his intended career by an accident that meant that his left hand was no longer able to play his instrument at the level that would have been required for a highly successful career. He was forced to give up his dreams and re-consider his options. This personal tragedy permits a changed relationship to art and to playing music where the qualities of craft, rather than the brilliance of individual performance come to the forefront. It is a matter of reconciling oneself to a life among the ranks of the chorus or the *corps de ballet*.[7] What is important here is that the work itself continues, the musician has to practise for many hours each day, regardless of what position he or she occupies in the orchestra, as does the dancer. It is what is needed to ensure a good job well done. And this in turn becomes the focal point for satisfaction and reward. Such close attention to the craft of playing an instrument well, as a 'good job well done' also permits a different relation to career and to working life, one that is less competitive and no longer defined in terms of great success or abject failure. A craft approach means being able to work all the time with failure, with material and instruments that will not easily do what the craftsman hopes or wishes they will do. There is constant struggle, there is patience and slowness, rather than the glamour of speed, there is a kind of quietness and concentration. Sennett also sees this idea of craft as something within the reach of most people. It is both an accessible and an abstract concept, a template for working across the range of activities that gives dignity and self-value to the person engaged in this way. Craft lifts the individual out of the 'space-time compression' of contemporary capitalism and its overcharged rhythms, restoring a sense of tranquillity and quiet, but not as some backward looking nostalgic idyll. It is more about the ability to work in a way that is not flashy, not spectacular or flamboyant but that entails attention to detail, and to the value of trial and error. This ethos can be seen as a counter to the dependency on seemingly innate talent. There is something much more rewarding about constant practice and then seeing improvement or finding a solution to a problem. Here is a more modest and down-to-earth idea of a working life in the creative sector.

'No Long Term'

Sennett makes us think about the temporality of the flexible city, where the patterns of working life no longer focus round the office, but are less fixed, often based round meetings that can take place in cafés or bars. Streets in these neighbourhoods become busier places when the people are no longer hidden away in their office blocks. This idea of placeless work has been associated, thanks to the influence of Richard Florida, with intense gentrification, with young people working on their laptops from coffee shops in newly fashionable areas of town. Few urban creative economy writers focus on mothers and children, on grandmothers and older women, on play parks or on local amenities such as swimming pools or public libraries. Old people seem to fade out of view, as do aggressive youths or young teenage mums pushing prams. Even the critics of gentrification duplicate this selective vision, and few urban sociologists or commentators on the new creative economy stop to talk with the ordinary people going about their business. Rarely is there a focus on the people in these neighbourhoods whose daily movements are indicative of their irregular work. In areas of long-term working-class unemployment, the daytime streets are often crowded with men, perhaps more men than women, for the reason that their female counterparts are more likely to have jobs, e.g. Neukœlln and Wedding in Berlin; Partick in Glasgow; Brixton and Finsbury Park in London. These men are also increasingly joined by the under-employed creatives who are also out and about. Sociologists tend to focus on how the arrival of the middle classes results in old spaces being re-claimed for more upmarket uses, with the original inhabitants being at best screened out by various filtering processes and at worst being evicted. This often has the ring of deadly inevitability. But if the policy language of the new creative economy had not been cast in such deeply individualistic terms and had instead been concerned with questions of how artists and creative people could work in ways that would be valuable to others, and with how they could engage in pressing social and urban issues, the current self-conscious hipness and the distance from the normal life of the working-class or migrant city would not have been so acute.[8] Working-class culture and its institutions would have been better protected, anti-racist community politics would have impacted on opportunities for youth in the area, and so on. In effect there would have been plenty for the new creative workers to do in their downtime, some unpaid, some potentially rewarded in the longer term. Sennett does not spell this out, but some traces of earlier waves of urban activism along these lines in New York echo in his writing.

It is hard to slot Sennett into current trends in social or cultural theory. His sociological training combines conventional American social psychology and psychoanalysis with (pre-Marxist) organizational sociology. He is influenced by Hannah Arendt and familiar with all the Marxist traditions. He espouses the US tradition of pragmatism. One also wonders if it is this that limits the political imagination in his recent work. It is hard to see exactly how craft might be taken up as a force for change in the world of work. Those already working as artists or designers may welcome the attention Sennett gives to the sheer difficulty of working with materials and objects and the endless processes of trial and error. But the patient labour of craft is likely to remain a distant ideal for freelancers working on a piece-rate system and having to cut corners. In *The Corrosion of Character* Sennett isn't going for so many walks, but he does provide, in an elegiac tone, a series of accounts or sketches of the dramatic changes in the working lives of a handful of respondents with whom he built up lasting friendships. It is hard not to think of great American dramatists like Arthur Miller and David Mamet who, like Sennett, allow their characters, ordinary men and women, to ruminate about work, the organization, and personal life. Sennett writes movingly about Rose, a bar-owner who gives up her job in mid-life to try her hand in advertising, only to return to her 'Trout Bar' some years later chastened. In this new America there is a sundering of ties, 'no long term'. Flexible capitalism gives rise to fleeting and impermanent relations. In the past when men could gather in the pub after work, even though the work itself might have been routine, they could tell their stories of their jobs and colleagues often over a lifetime. This narrative capacity is depleted with team work, and with the requirement to display a kind of shallow friendliness at all times. As Sennett says 'teamwork is the group practice of demeaning superficiality' (Sennett 1998, p. 99). Discussing how new technology appeared to create efficiency, he writes, 'Computerized baking had profoundly changed the balletic physical activities of the shop floor. Now the bakers make no physical contact with the materials or the loaves of bread', this produces 'weak work identity' and a 'lack of attachment' that is also 'coupled with confusion'. Looking back at the age of the bigger institutions and the legacy of bureaucracy, Sennett suggests that one of the great strengths here for ordinary people was 'the gift of organized time' (Sennett 2006, p. 36).

Artists, Craftsmen, Mothers, City-Dwellers

Sennett proposes the revival of the idea of craftsmanship as a counter to the prevailing ethos of creative work and the wider environment of speeded-up flexible labour. This is also a much expanded notion of craft. '[It] cuts a far wider swath than skilled manual labour, it serves the computer programmer, the doctor and the artist; parenting improves when it is practised as a skilled craft, as does citizenship' (Sennett 2008, p. 9). It is not simply a matter of extending craft values to professional activities however. Sennett is emphasizing the value of those jobs that could be seen as monotonous or mundane, and here he challenges Arendt, who envisages transcending the drudgery of sheer repetitive work undertaken to fulfil basic human needs, in contrast to more stimulating work where men use their brains and imaginations: something that can only be done when the hard manual labour is completed or carried out by someone else. In an admirably egalitarian spirit, Sennett refutes this division. But is he right to do so? The two are admittedly frequently bound and are mutually dependent on each other, requiring deep concentration and producing pleasures and satisfactions from getting it right. In a kind of post-feminist move, Sennett's writing serves to re-valorize housework, cooking and childcare and on several occasions he refers to the craft of parenting. And yet, although nowadays often carried out by both mothers and fathers, both housework and childcare remain dispro-portionately women's work. It is hard to read Sennett's work as a feminist and not think about the work of the domestic sphere. Its temporality lies outside the time relations of capitalism (as 1970s feminists argued, if such work was subjected to market forces and had to be paid for, the cost of nanny-time would be exorbitant); its space is often the home or the local public facilities of park, swimming pool, library, football pitch. The idea of a good job well done, takes the form of emotional satisfaction, and the deep but often overlooked pleasures of motherhood. In the late 1970s Julia Kristeva discussed 'women's time' (Kristeva 1981). Despite numerous and often cited objections, notably from Gayatri Spivak, it has value for its notion of a different temporality imposed on women's lives through their primary responsibility for looking after children and the home (Spivak 1981). We could add to this that in many if not all respects children cannot be speeded up, the time of getting on or off shoes and outer garments is not easily reconcilable with the need to multi-task on various paid projects. But can women's work looking after children be really upgraded and incorporated into the realm of craft?

Craft remains too closely tied to the image of the solitary male worker, engrossed in the task at hand, which entails an object. And the frustrations he may experience when things go wrong are quite far removed from the frustrations and tiredness of doing the same thing each day with pre-school-age children.

Some of what Sennett finds important in the idea of craft can arguably be seen to exist in the bringing up of children. Both exist outside the time relations of speeded up capitalism, both bring body and mind together; one must handle a child with the same care as does the craftsman, and with a constant eye and relentless concentration. Here too there is improvisation, and there is also the entrenched inter-generational passing on of knowledge and advice between mothers, and indeed between women. So where does this lead to? Does Sennett's concept of craft subsume the rewards of mothering and of parenting? As mothers, women have always been flexible workers. Close to home and community, both under-employed and over-employed with wildly irregular hours, they have also relied on female friendships and support networks, which refute the mentality of the 'no long-term' ethos. Their narratives, just like those of the older male workers to whom Sennett listens in great detail, also give sustenance and maintain social bonds. But housework in itself is not part of paid labour, so it cannot be considered alongside the traditional jobs now being eclipsed or left to die. There may be an increasing demand for jobs associated with motherhood such as cleaning and care work, which are now part of the new service sector. These are frequently low-paid jobs performed by migrants who are desperate to get a foothold in the labour market. Caring for the elderly may well bring some rewards but repetitive cleaning and caring are more often associated with monotony and exhaustion. This marks the egalitarian limits of craft. Where it may be fruitful to downgrade the dizzy expectations of artists and creative people so that they can sit alongside others, and benefit from the time-slow pace of a mode of working that gratifies on the basis of the job being done for its own sake, it proves more difficult to upgrade some stubbornly unrewarding jobs such as domestic cleaning.

What Sennett calls the 'new culture of capitalism' has the opposite effect of reducing social ills. In regard to the new creative economy it resurrects social hierarchies and disconnects the young people inhabiting the spaces of the urban cultural economy, from their neighbours and from the other people making a living in these same spaces. Often these are poor and disadvantaged communities dominated by informal or irregular economies (fruit and vegetable shops, cab companies, internet shops, small cafés, cheap clothing outlets etc.). The

artists and creative people are also led to believe their work is exceptional and unique through the prevailing vocabularies of coolness and
hipness that pervade the various forms of media which report on
the rise of the talent economy. Hence this creative work is understood
to have nothing in common with more ordinary people trying to
make a living in difficult circumstances. This disaggregating ethos
also serves to further de-politicize creative work, lifting it out of any
obvious connection with other more mundane work and separating
out people by means of complex 'dividing practices', which allows
for the creation of new, more competitive social hierarchies. Likewise
in the often rundown and hence relatively cheaper areas of the
cities in which such young people often live, there too they are iso-
lated from others and dependent instead on their own party network
and club scenes. Such a scenario, although immediately recognizable,
is not inevitable. As discussed in previous chapters, it is a sign of
the success of the strategy embarked upon by New Labour under its
Cool Britannia agenda that we now think of graduates of art schools
as largely apolitical and individualist with little concern about
the urban environment other than as a 'site specific' showcase
for their own talents. There has been a very determined strategy to
sever the connections between the creative economy and the social
democratic and radical values that have historically underpinned the
provision of education and training for this sector through the post-
war years. We could see this as an attempt, through the insertion of
neoliberal vocabularies, to disconnect a sector of the middle classes
who in the past, through their cultural and creative training and
expertise, would often have aligned themselves with radical political
perspectives such as anti-racism, multi-culturalism, feminism, anti-
poverty issues etc. The new generation of city dwellers is also disconnected from, or seemingly disinterested in, the histories of urban
activism of past generations.[9] The question is, can this be reversed?
Is it possible that by re-visiting the history of how feminists, anti-
racists, artists and creative people have, in the not so distant past,
involved themselves productively in many forms of urban and neighbourhood politics, the hype around creativity as 'network sociality',
and on the artist as manager of his or her own brand, may be
eclipsed?[10] There is scope for developing a more critical perspective
so that the Florida-led euphoria could be interrupted with an insistence on a vocabulary that refuses hyperbole, glamour and excitement and that brings into play topics such as under-employment,
craft, dedication, public-mindedness, social care and the retrieval of
time and space from the speeded-up creativity-machine. We could say
that contemporary neoliberal values seek to extol the importance of

entrepreneurial activities in the cultural and creative sector as a means of re-stratifying sectors of the educated middle classes so that this group are weaned off reliance on the public sector, which used to provide a 'job for life', while also seeing their seeming privileges maintained through the idea of pleasurable or self-expressive work, even when this entails a shift to dependency on over-stretched family economies as part of the new rhetoric of human capital. This is effected through the injecting of positive and exciting meanings into a terrain of work that is precarious and insecure and often poorly paid. Because the arts and culture have long enjoyed high status and prestige, this further enhancement through glamour and the encouragement of talent is particularly appealing and has become a mode of self-government, a disciplining of the self through the extraction of creativity from some inner sources of the soul, the psyche or the heart. The value of Sennett's work is to demote creativity and to emphasize craft. Likewise his writing on the urban landscape permits a potential for new radicalism within and beyond the dictates of the flexible city.

The New Crafters

Sennett provides a strand of thinking that complements and extends one of the key theses in this book. Readers will recall that I have suggested (in a context of strong biopolitical power aimed at producing happily creative subjects) a capacity for resistance to the new work regime as something that, although seemingly individualized and internalized, is nevertheless carried on, or embodied, through memory and family history. The children of the working class, or of immigrant parents, will retain something of their hardship and their striving to improve the lives of their offspring and this intergenerational transmission often surfaces in complex, unpredictable, symbolic forms. With the growth of the creative economy and the extension of arts education in the UK through the primary and secondary as well as higher education system, such expressions of resistance on the part of formerly working-class and now putatively middle-class young people, take aesthetic rather than subcultural forms. That is to say, they shape up in the form of arts or more recently in crafting. What Sennett provides is the testimony from the 'parent culture', albeit from an American location. He insists on the importance of history and duration. Contemporary neoliberalism in the UK urges social forgetfulness especially in regard to the history of social democratic policies and the values of old-fashioned municipalism in the cities of the UK and elsewhere. It was for example not so long ago that, under the auspices of the radical GLC in London, young graduate fashion designers including some of those whom I interviewed for my 1998 study, were eligible to apply for live/work housing with subsidized rents in newly set up Housing Associations designated for artists and other creative persons (McRobbie 1998). The setting up of such associations took a good deal of time and political energy on the part of the urban activists of the mid 1970s through to the mid 1980s, by which point they had grown tired and the political tide was decisively turning against them. The artists and crafters of today could do well by investigating this kind of urban history in a bid to restore these ideas to contemporary debate. Sennett also retrieves topics that currently have no place in art and cultural worlds such as the role of social work and the importance of youth clubs and facilities for disadvantaged young people in the city. These are key themes in at least two of his works, *Respect* and more recently *Together* (Sennett 2008, 2012). Throughout this book I have been launching something of an appeal to young creatives to engage with their neighbours and re-discover the history of earlier community activities, which as self-organized initiatives frequently led to funding and jobs for organizers as well as for others, making these activists precursors of today's 'social entrepreneurs'. However Sennett's historical sociology also empathizes (while also disagreeing) more wholly with the social conservatism of many of his male respondents. If character as 'the long-term aspect of our emotional experiences' also has the capacity to lead to the insular and even racist resentments of some of the figures in his book *Corrosion of Character*, then we must surely be open to how inter-generational transmission of family memory works its way down from parent to child (Sennett 1998, p. 10). We cannot hold out for memory as inherently radical, as the first story told by Sennett about Rico, the son of Enrico, clearly shows. Both father and son in different ways embody aspects of patriarchal, white Italian–American immigrant conservatism. Enrico, the hard-working janitor father, 'disliked blacks', while his son's anti-welfare stance led Sennett to comment that he 'loathes social parasites' (Sennett 1998, pp. 17, 27). This leads me to refine further the thesis about 'lines of flight' based on family memory offering a potential for resistance, or at least it forces me to acknowledge just how contingent such possibilities are, how easily emotional attachments to a parent culture can lead to right-wing as well as left-wing outcomes. Once again artists such as Damien Hirst and Tracey Emin, both educated in public-funded institutions but having also imbibed the spirit of Mrs Thatcher, fulfil this idea of contingency. They could have gone in one direction and emerged as leading artists with radical and socially engaged ideals, but instead one makes diamond skulls as a kind of jokily ironic celebration of global capitalism, while the other bemoans having to pay tax to the UK government as a high wage-earner. These fine lines between moving to the left or right are strong indicators of life under contemporary capitalism; there is a constant tussle and what may seem like a radical or progressive force for change is almost instantly co-opted or re-appropriated for more conservative ends. As Boltanski and Chiapello show, from the mid 1960s on, capitalism learnt how to benefit from borrowing and incorporating ideas from some of its most trenchant critics on the left as well as from the ranks of the artistic and cultural professionals (Boltanski and Chiapello 2005). These forces, constantly on the look-out for what is new, can also be seen clearly at play in the current rapid rise of the craft movement. Even though such micro-enterprises as these sit in a small corner of the contemporary economy, still we can detect so many cross-cutting currents, which show just how much the micro is now at the heart of the macro. What this high visibility also points to is the way in which, since Sennett's book on craft first appeared, and in so-called austerity times, small-scale and often home-based working has come to play an important role on the basis of new digital technology and social media.[11] In order to draw this chapter to a close, with a set of arguments that point to the seeming inevitability of craft economies departing sharply from Sennett's vision and being subsumed instead by the new vocabularies of social enterprise, start-ups, or else by the insatiable demand for 'innovation', we will take a brief look at some issues relating to craft and gender and then at craft in the new business environment.

What runs right through the craft scene is a strong generational consciousness. The new crafting movement emerges as a product of the last decade, having accelerated since the economic crisis of 2008 while also expanding alongside the many other forms of e-commerce. Interestingly most of the academic material relating to the rise of crafting has come from feminist sociologists and historians. As we shall see, their crafters are typically women and often 'amateurs', which itself is something quite different from Sennett's highly skilled man at his work-bench passing on the techniques of glass blowing or stonemasonry. Among the multiple aspects of female crafting is a vivid attempt to impregnate urban spaces with traces of colourful feminine activity, a good deal of which re-writes or re-invents former feminist art practices dating back to the 1970s when leading feminist artists consciously re-discovered otherwise overlooked female domestic skills such as quilting, knitting, lace-making and crocheting.

However, and to stress the point about the ambivalent political valency of these practices, when public knitting first emerged as a signature of hipster visibility in the city it was adamantly non-feminist in tone; indeed many young women in the Shoreditch area of London aligned themselves to, with a dash of post-feminist and postmodern irony, the old-fashioned homesteading Women's Institute. This gesture also worked well as a publicity stunt as many journalists flocked to witness this interesting intersection of old and new femininities. The rise of knitting circles summed up a transitional moment when feminism was still repudiated by younger women drawn to the hipster scenes (referred to in Chapter 2) and instead looking to *Vice* magazine as a style guide, and then just two or three years later the new wave of feminist activity brought to bear a much more assertive and proud re-claiming stance, a willingness to take up the word feminism once more, and doing this precisely through referencing feminist history rather than consigning it to oblivion or deliberately forgetting it. We can turn then to recent articles by Luckman (2013) and Wallace (2012) for the insight they offer on the new phenomenon of female crafting. In these accounts attention is paid to the historical connections which make the present-day craft economy progressive in character, such as the emphasis on 'amateur labour' as something that marks out gender hierarchies and women's domestic roles, there is claims Luckman a 're-articulation of (largely) women's domestic work' in this resurrection of craft, since it makes the links apparent with the radical tradition of the arts and crafts movement of the nineteenth century (Luckman 2013, p. 249). Digital culture, she argues, allows craft to re-emerge in a global virtual world. In effect it permits not just a resurgence but a wider making public of women's ordinary and not exceptional skills. Bringing back into circulation the 1970s feminist uptake and critique of William Morris's 'paternalistic socialism' serves a useful function in the debate about the place for women's crafting today. Luckman also reminds us of how the 'pleasures of the hearth', which were so central to the original arts and crafts movement in England came to be seen as the source of a kind of authenticity for a younger generation today, for whom such home-based activities also offer an alternative to the consumer culture of contemporary *Walmart*-led capitalism. Likewise for women angered by the way in which the fashion industry caters almost exclusively for slim-sized women, the attraction of home dressmaking is that it allows for diversity as well as personal style. Luckman rightly mentions the nostalgia that accompanies the return to domesticity. This is something that in fact pre-dates the new craft scene, and was associated with, for example, the ironic elevation of the housewife of the 1950s, which finds commercial expression in the

success of homespun companies such as the *Cath Kidston* range of
domestic products and kitchenware. Here there is an ironic yearning
for the seeming simplicity or uncomplicated pre-feminist times of
affluent and white 1950s America when men were men and women
were women. Indeed 'gender re-traditionalization' pervades significant parts of the crafting and hipster outlook (Adkins 2002). The
'homey' gingham style of young women standing behind the counter
of their authentic 'hausgemacht' bakeries in Neukoelln or in London's Hoxton resurrects an idyll of domestic femininity as a challenge
to some common-sense idea of feminism. Likewise the appearance of
old-fashioned 'Mom and Pop' stores in rapidly gentrifying areas such
as Peckham, South London, looks back to a time of family businesses
prior to the rise of the supermarket.[12] Then again, at the opposite
end of the scale we see the move on the part of new crafting female
artists to appropriate city spaces and decorate them with colourful
and peaceful interventions, which involve such things as knitting
items to fit onto lamp-posts or nineteenth-century horse water-
fountains (in Berlin) or in festooning parked bicycles with knitted
wheels or handlebars. Here feminism is unashamedly re-claimed,
with strong references, as Wallace points out, to the otherwise disparaged activities of the women of Greenham Common (Wallace 2012).
And as Wallace also shows, this new wave of feminist crafting openly
adopts the language of political activism including 'yarn bombing',
with the aim of advocating peace as part of the various current anti-
war struggles conducted on city streets across the world. Here there
is an active feminist re-invoking of women's history and role in both
public and private life and struggle, and less of an emphasis on craft
as means of making a living.

Crafting, however, cannot be seen in isolation from the many
strands of more commercially driven activities, which accompany the
growth of small online businesses and start-ups. Thus even in Berlin
where, as already referred to, there are neighbourhood-based social
enterprises that seek to develop the skills of women from ethnic
minority backgrounds who are poor and want to find ways of earning
a living on the basis of these skills, within these same new craft-
oriented enterprises are design graduates hoping to develop partnerships and collaborations with luxury fashion houses in Milan, and
who are also marketing the uniqueness of these traditional handicrafts
to celebrity clients. In effect, different forms of capitalism, including
strands of anti-capitalism, fold into one another. The most commercially focused craft activity, which is closely interwoven with
e-commerce and global markets, is to be found within the field of
fashion for menswear and male accessories. Here the emphasis is on,

as Zukin discusses in her most recent book, the idea of authenticity (Zukin 2010). This means uncovering and resurrecting past techniques for making, in particular searching out old, obscure, small-scale manufacturers in far-flung locations, often the mid West, which are almost out of business but still producing, for example, high quality leather belts based on an expertise in saddlery. Or it means transforming an old forgotten piece of quality clothing, such as the Canada Goose jacket (carefully crafted from down and feathers alongside various hardwearing textiles) and worn by workers exposed to freezing temperatures and bringing it into circulation as a unique collector's item for those who are 'in the know' (Burrell 2014). Craft then is subject to a revivalist fervour, including, especially in menswear, the selective re-issuing of 'classics'. The old is associated with high quality craft skills no longer found in this sector and so it accumulates value on the basis of past exclusiveness in comparison to contemporary mass produced and especially 'fast fashion'. This re-birth of craft within the trend-setting milieu of menswear is in fact grounded and founded in the spaces of new social media, in blogs, on Instagram, and in the editorial brief of the online style magazines, which orient themselves to this select readership of subcultural fashion menswear insiders. For example, if the reader takes a close-up look at the four copies a year magazine *Inventory*, which comes out from a small base in Vancouver and reaches in hard copy the shop windows of art-oriented stylist outlets in London, what can be seen is a connoisseur approach to well-crafted objects that have long since fallen out of fashion.[13] While the commercial potential here lies originally in the expansive, if select, market for vintage or second-hand items (itself accelerated by online 'pre-owned' specialist sites such as www.covetique.com, or the luxury vintage business titled www.therealreal.com/) the business acumen reaches much further, so that the value of these old-fashioned companies can be brought to the attention of mainstream fashion companies or indeed private equity firms looking to launch a new initiative. In this context craft becomes a major site of innovation. The best current example is the *Shinola* ('Shinola – Where American Is Made') brand, which was, before it shut down, based in Detroit producing small hardware items and has recently been rescued as a craft factory producing watches, bicycles, and leather goods in the same old building shared with and overseen by an Art School.[14] This then would be the unexpected outcome of the slow, quiet, unobtrusive rhythms of craft as examined by Sennett, finding a niche place in the fast-paced world of fashion and lifestyle. Upcycling, re-cycling, second-hand and vintage pieces, or *Brew To Bikes* – these too come under the spell of social media and Instagram (Heying 2011). Alongside the social agenda and good intentions environmentally, and often relying on support provided for setting up a social enterprise model, the well-crafted items eventually find their way into the showrooms and the department stores where they add 'authenticity' to the existing collections.[15]

Many participants with diverse interests now engage in the development of craft scenes. At a distance, are the private equity companies ready to invest, and there are also major international corporations such as *LVMH* who will often subsidize seemingly 'indie' ventures as a way of maintaining close connections with sources of ideas and innovation as well as gaining insight into emerging youth markets. As Susan Luckman argues, 'pro-am' makers are part of the creative economy, drawing on the new business culture of the internet, whose outlook is one of serious professionalism (Luckman 2013). That said, crafting also includes women, often mothers knitting from home and hoping to sell just a handful of jumpers through Etsy.com or in the local craft or 'pop-up' shop. Overall we can see some irony in the slowness of craft, which to Sennett marked out something of its value as a counterfoil to the speeded-up and flexible time of post-Fordist capitalism, being uncovered as a possible authentic source for that same just-in-time regime. (The signs did perhaps appear more than a decade ago when vintage clothes were introduced as concession spaces in central London's flagship *Topshop* store.)

None of this invalidates the overall contribution of Sennett, which is to insist on the historical knowledge of craft production being remembered, and the importance of process as well as outcome. The value of historical sociology to develop a better understanding of the modern work economy remains the defining feature of Sennett's contribution. Perhaps Sennett is also saying that overall we have too high expectations of 'careers'. It has become too strongly a mark of self, as though everything depends on it. The routine work of making bread, long since replaced by computerized ovens and screens for selecting types of loaf to be made, gave Sennett's bakers a time and space for the creation and exchange of narratives. They, like the computer programmers who were made redundant when the company they worked for did not move fast enough in the world of PCs and laptops, could tell long-winded stories about their working lives in a context where such stories would be listened to and valued. The loss of this is what disturbs Sennett so greatly. His idea to re-instate a history of times of sociality and mutuality and of labour organization chimes well with the aims of this current book. There remains some lack of clarity in Sennett's writing about which jobs must surely remain unrewarding, though the drift of his thinking is to suggest that it is the current organization of work, the rosters and casualization, which is what makes them so. Sennett is not naive in this respect and it is neither his aim, nor mine here, to tackle the much bigger intractable questions about how contemporary low-paid or poorly rewarded work could be better rewarded, how workforces could be encouraged to form or join unions, and how employees' rights could be better protected. Extending these concerns into the ranks of the part-time or freelance workforce or to those who are self-employed would require a rather different kind of debate. The point at which we can see a more socialized vision of work, however, may well lie in those jobs that badly need to be done and that have in neoliberal times lost their appeal and their status. These would be jobs that help to enrich and empower the lives of vulnerable or disadvantaged people, often living in unpropitious circumstances in poor housing in rundown urban neighbourhoods. There is no shortage of jobs to be done in improving the fabric of urban life, and if we agree, albeit reluctantly, that there is unlikely to be a return to the days of well-staffed social services along with sufficiently resourced family and youth professionals, then we at least have the option of exploring the ways in which creative economy can be perhaps re-defined in this direction under the auspices of social enterprise. Such an option, to be explored by way of a conclusion to this book, opens up a discussion, in the spirit of Sennett, about what is at stake in positing community-building and the idea of social care as objectives for a new culture industry.

Youth exchange trainee from Berlin in Spoleto craft workshop. Photo: Monika Savier

Conclusion: European Perspectives[1]

Incongruous though it may seem to use the conclusion of this book to embark on some new explorations, I want to look beyond the contours of the UK and its creativity *dispositif*, and offer a series of critical reflections on two inter-connected topics. The first of these provides some observations and insights from two projects funded by the European Commission.[2] The second, more briefly, serves as a *finale* through looking at the version of 'social enterprise' that has come to prominence in the UK, with many ideas imported from US business schools. I ask the question: What other forms of social enterprise could be imagined within the frame of the culture industries? The European Commission has of course for several decades financed programmes designed to tackle urgent social issues such as youth unemployment and urban disadvantage in member states, and in this respect it merits a full-blown study of the modes and specificities of the governmentality at play within the many instruments and toolkits devised to deliver a more 'integrated' European citizenry. Across the member states and in Brussels itself there are thousands of people employed as dedicated professionals, so much so that they constitute a kind of parallel academy to the entire pan-European university system and their job is to plan, devise, administer and implement programmes and initiatives devoted to a 'social agenda' with budgets that run into billions of euros. If these departments of government, along with the institutions and organizations that have grown up alongside them, mark out the parameters of 'social and regional Europe', we might well ask the question of how they transform themselves according to the political direction required of them by the EU itself, especially in times of austerity and economic crisis. In this chapter I refer to two instances of what in UK parlance would be called 'job-creation schemes' although in reality they were much more than that. The projects described below were part of a tier of major initiatives to encourage youth employment, something that had become more of a priority with the enlargement process following the collapse of the Soviet Union. In both projects culture, the arts and media occupied a much more prominent place than would have been the case in similar initiatives less than a decade ago. (The transition could be pinpointed to the moment at which digital and social media and arts activities were introduced as part of the curriculum for those enlisted on job creation or simply citizenship and employability schemes.) For this reason, it could be important to follow through such developments as these within the terms of labour reform. This would be to extend the concerns of this book into a wider European frame, in order to see how arts and creativity are being mobilized to create employment for young people (in the context now of mass unemployment and widespread underemployment) and simultaneously to create jobs that have the advantage of cutting costs to the employer or firm through being short-term, or project-based or freelance. If such a conjecture transpired to be the case, then an argument could be made that within the complex institutional infrastructures of the EC here too could be seen subtle ways of transforming work as we know it, with the aid of 'creativity', away from the idea of a job with career progression, workplace entitlements and a pension, towards something altogether more risk-laden and precarious. Of course, in reality things are always more complicated and the results of my own investigations laid out below show this to be a more contested process, with the impact of neoliberalism as an EC instrument for reform making itself felt more specifically at the organizational level. It was in effect the units for delivery of programmes that were most effected by the changes. In the longer term they could only be swallowed up by bigger wealthier institutions such as the newly 'entrepreneurial' universities. For now, I just want to flag this space up for further debate and analysis, with a view, in the future, to understanding the specificities and nuances of working lives in the 'cultural economy' as defined by the EU. In the meantime it may nevertheless be useful to draw attention to some minor developments. For instance we can point to the gradual erosion of social democratic values in the context of 'youth in action' initiatives conducted within the framework of various EU programmes, and their transformation into more fully neoliberalized endeavours (Mitchell 2006). Even a rather cursory glance across the landscape of two or three projects running from 2006 to 2012 opens up such a discussion and permits a European perspective on the deployment of the creativity *dispositif*. The official documentation for these programmes displayed an interesting hybrid of social democratic elements combined with the newer vocabularies associated with entrepreneurship and as a result the training programmes found themselves in transition. An old framework was forced to co-exist and find some common ground with a new one. A stubborn residue of social democratic values remained more or less in place, for the simple reason of the personnel in place, but was conjoined with ideas about self-employment, innovation and the value of creativity. It is to the credit of the project managers that they found ways of translating the new to make it more compatible with the old, in effect humane, egalitarian and aware of issues about gender, multiculturalism and social inequality. Thus there were visible tensions running through both projects as they progressed. Overall what could be seen was a shift away from the social towards the cultural, with this tapping into young people's enthusiasm for art as self-expression alongside media production and creative activities in general. Consequently the social element was frequently in danger of getting lost and had to struggle to retain a key position. 'Culture', again, within this regime of European governmentality, was being made to function as a conduit for some perhaps small, but not insignificant aspect of labour reform. The two projects reported on below involved multiple layers of actors all of whom found themselves subjects of these new vocabularies, and who were required to implement them at ground level. The younger professionals in their thirties were able to adapt to this transition, and sought to find ways of radicalizing it in their practice, while the older '68'ers' who were the programme directors and senior managers, had more overt reservations about this new requirement to 'be creative'.[3] Each programme had connections with Berlin, although the actual field of activity was in Italy, one in Palermo in Sicily, the other in Spoleto in Umbria. (There were no UK partners for these particular projects.) Both initiatives were undertaken and managed by social enterprises or non-governmental organizations. They found themselves having to respond to a new kind of language, one that was results driven and dominated by benchmarks, in a context of decreased budgets and fierce competition for new awards from either bigger organizations, which could carry the high costs of the co-funding mechanism,[4] or from the new NGOs, which had sprung up across east Europe and which had much lower labour costs. In addition the initiatives took place against a background of high unemployment for young people across member states, something that was amplified many times over with the onset of the Euro-crisis of 2008.

STEP in Palermo, PIA/IDA in Spoleto

There are various different institutions and infrastructures for the training of the creative labour force and thus for the exercising of the creativity *dispositif*. So far in this book attention has been drawn to the role of the art school and the 'creative' university, this latter marking in effect a new transformative configuration for the arts, humanities and social sciences. However, by examining two small European projects, it is possible nevertheless to discern how the voluntary sector, the world of professional non-governmental organizations often founded with a brief to implement policies aimed at tackling social inequalities and serving disadvantaged social groups has become involved in this same process of creative self-entrepreneurialism. What follows, then, is an attempt to briefly sketch out two EU-funded programmes. While projects such as these are typically devised and developed within primarily social democratic frames of reference, what could be seen happening in the course of these activities was their gradual replacement by a more visibly neo-liberal agenda (see also Mitchell 2006). Increasingly present was a vocabulary of deliverables, benchmarks, and at the *finissage* of the projects, the expectation to provide 'feelgood' happy stories as evidence of the success of the undertaking. With this there was also a squeezing out of the time and place for critical recollection and animated debate. In effect both projects could be seen as transitional, the older ideas of best practice were giving way, in the context of reduced budgets, to an agenda for evaluation that precluded wider critical discussion. The speeded-up temporality of project-working meant that by mid-way through the duration of one project the key actors were already searching around for new 'calls' for which they could apply and by the time an existing project actually ended little time or energy was left to do anything more than organize a press event in order to gain the required publicity as evidence of a good job well done. This intensification of labour, the idea that there is never enough time to see a job through to its successful conclusion, becomes a defining feature of social and cultural work receiving some form of public funding within the 'risk society' (Beck 1992).

The Palermo project[5] was a significant undertaking with funding streams from the EU as well as from the Municipality of Palermo in Sicily. It was led by a not-for-profit organization and consultancy based in Berlin, which had at that time several branches across Europe, stretching from west to east, including Brussels, Palermo, Budapest, Moscow and elsewhere. These offices were all staffed by highly qualified social scientists who had long mastered the intricacies of European Commission funding applications falling under various programmes such as the social fund, the sixth and seventh frameworks, alongside the well-established *Grundtvig*, *Erasmus*, *Tempus* and *Leonardo* initiatives. During this time the vocabularies that were still intact concerned citizenship for young people, multi-cultural community-building, integration for asylum-seekers, anti-violence initiatives, personal development, curriculum development and most often training schemes for meaningful employment for disadvantaged people including migrants and ethnic minorities. The Palermo activities stretched out (with several stops and starts) over four years and were directed to a cohort of about thirty to forty young people in the city who had no job or else were partly employed.[6] Some were graduates, others had college-level qualifications and a few had no qualifications at all. Where in the recent past meaningful jobs for a group of youngsters like this would have meant social and community work, or environmental programmes or else work with socially marginalized people such as the homeless or those with addiction problems, the way this particular project evolved meant it had a more cultural and media-oriented focus. The reason for this was that the economy in Palermo, already a city with historically high unemployment and poverty, was confronting even higher levels of youth unemployment.[7] Policy-makers in the city were already working to re-invent and expand the service sector, to build on the tourist economy and to create new forms of work that incorporated the famous history and heritage of the region and its well-known arts provision and museums.[8] This was the context for providing the participants with various short courses within a range of media and arts topics with an emphasis on creative practice. The project was based in a former church in the old quarter of the city and here the youngsters could get involved in almost any area of the arts and culture, from music-making to performance art, from photography to film-directing.[9] The question that arose, however, was how could this eventually turn into something that would bring in an income? In Southern Italy, being a graduate or having school-leaving certificates has meant doing something other than setting up a café, even if it has a gallery, since this was the kind of small business undertaken by parents who wanted their children to do better than they had done. As an adviser to the project, I had the role of offering some perspectives, to the participants as well as to a wide range of professionals in the region including teachers and social workers, on how the creative economy debate has developed in the UK.[10] This could be done with a critical and analytical perspective, also drawing attention to ongoing European debates about 'mini-jobs' and precarious labour. As it happened the 'club to company' option (described in Chapter 1) did not have much attraction for the youngsters themselves, because what was wanted by them was a full-time job in arts administration (e.g. in the theatre or opera) or with the cultural department in the Municipality. If such jobs as these were few and far between and often in Sicily seen as being given to people who were already connected through nepotistic or *Mafioso* family networks, then why not, in a context of widespread under-employment set up some kind of cultural project that could create income? With some misgivings, bearing in mind the critique of Florida in Chapter 2, suggestions were made that involved a local oral history of the region including photography projects. The value of this would be in generating an inter-generational dialogue. While the cash-flow or monetary value might admittedly be uncertain, it was not entirely unrealistic to presume some small trickle of income. Across both the projects referred to here and a few others undertaken simultaneously by the NGOs based in Berlin, it was often my role to provide an account of current developments in parallel fields in the UK.[11] The biggest difference between the UK and these European schemes was the speed with which privatization had spread in the UK across the 'providers' for training courses for unemployed adults and young people (with the trainers having few if any formal qualifications, such initiatives as these thus suggesting more or less wholescale de-professionalization of the sector) and the introduction of more overtly disciplinary approaches with sanctions for failure to attend.[12] Loïc Wacquant, writing in the context of the US and France, has referred to this as the 'punitive upsurge' (Wacquant 2009). In contrast the Palermo and Spoleto initiatives were distinctly non-punitive.

These kinds of EU projects, underpinned by many decades of social democratic principles, offer some good examples of egalitarian and sanction-free programmes of job creation. In the Palermo case the ideas about oral history, working with museums and archives would have taken a lot longer to get off the ground, and in the event the programme director, with many years of experience came up with a faster (and effective) strategy, which was a mobility exchange scheme. In fact the concept of 'exchange visits' has been fundamental to EC social programmes for many years, hinging around the personal and economic benefits to individuals able to take part in inter-cultural dialogue across the member states. Exchange is at the very heart of the self-identity of the European Union. And this particular idea, proposed by the director chimed with comments made by the German Chancellor Angela Merkel (and widely reported) about labour mobility as a key instrument for job creation across recession-hit Europe. The exchange scheme functions then as a form of job training or job preparation based on mobility of labour and as such it remains a cornerstone for the EC. In this Palermo context the training and learning agenda was not just a matter of going to where the jobs were, but a process of learning from different work and employment environments. The youngsters were found job placements in Berlin for up to six months. Hostels and travel had to be booked, occupying many hundreds of hours for the project administrators and, even more time-consuming, meaningful internships had to be arranged by the director herself who sat on the phone night and day calling up her contacts. Of the cohort, more than half took up this opportunity and the informal evidence through the various networks and Facebook pages pointed to the benefits of such a scheme. Being exposed to how creative economies worked in Berlin gave to the young people a more dynamic idea of how they could themselves find work in similar ways. Indeed these opportunities exposed the participants to the actual experience of on-the-ground small-scale cultural entrepreneurship, although of course terms like this (e.g. cultural entrepreneurship) are in effect imported from government, policy-makers and other sources and imposed onto what would otherwise and in the past have been seen as jobs in arts administration or simply as professional activities (such as being a film-set and prop designer). One young woman got a placement in a theatre design workshop in Berlin, another in a feminist bookstore, while another worked for the press department of a sexual advice clinic, and several others worked in events management. The director of the programme instinctively inserted the 'youngsters' inside such organizations as these. Most returned home after the exchange but some stayed on.

These projects did not actually include an 'action research' element. The standard practices at the end of the project were 'evaluation' and 'lessons learnt for future good practice'. Had there been more time it would have been important to weigh up the balance of forces between embedded social democratic elements, which drove the thinking of the team, young and old, and the new ideas appearing essentially from a range of sources within the EC about 'deliverables', competition for the knowledge economy, entrepreneurialism, and also about new models of project management. The team in contrast were driven by a kind of idealism, which sought to find ways of supporting young disadvantaged people, some overwhelmed by problems at home, beyond their control, others simply finding it impossible to get a job. The pedagogy was very much tilted towards appealing to the interests of the individuals while also providing small group learning of new skills. There was also a focus on personal development and on seeing a wider enthusiasm grow more naturally on the part of the participants. (The absence of a sanction-led approach could also be explained perhaps by the subjects of the programmes being designated as 'youth' or 'youngsters' or even 'teenagers' and at the time of running the project such terms signalled juvenile status and the need to support and nurture, in contrast for example with the more negative terms in UK parlance such as NEET – i.e. not in education or employment.) Or, more bluntly, we could argue that under the auspices of European Social Funds, disadvantaged people of whatever age and background enrolled in programmes are still treated with respect, in contrast to the new regimes in place in the UK and importing many of the so-called tough love strategies associated with US welfare-to-work systems, which are marked by a distinctive lack of respect, even down to slang nomenclature (at worst 'welfare queens') and more often 'claimants' or 'benefit seekers' (Sennett 2003).

Overseeing the project were three teams, one comprising older vocational training professionals based in Palermo, the other younger graduates brought in from elsewhere in Italy to run the project at ground level, and above these were the director and two or three senior EC experts and advisers all of whom had a lifetime of experience on such projects as this. For all of these project managers the nature of the job itself was undergoing transformation, as the financial realities of NGO work made the existing organizations increasingly unviable. Other kinds of lighter more flexible or networked structures clearly had to be conceived of, but how, within the bureaucratic heavy-weight of EC programmes? In effect, huge swathes of time had to be spent 'back-stopping' the complicated time sheets and payment procedures that in turn involved submitting claims for work done to the EC for re-imbursement so that people could actually be paid. The young graduates most closely involved in running the project occupied the exact same precarious status as their counterparts in the new creative economies in London and Berlin; however, in each of these cities there was potential for supplementing one low-paid but interesting and rewarding job like this with others, working two or three days a week on other similar projects, even on a kind of moonlighting basis (e.g. leaving one job for a couple of days to earn cash in hand on a film crew as a guaranteed way of paying rent). But in Palermo no such possibilities were available and the team of three, despite having subsidized accommodation in the city during the project, were still paying rent back in their own home towns. In addition the long hours needed to mentor and get to know the students could not be counted within the spread sheets of 'working hours' in much the same way as teaching preparation time, plus after-hours sessions with students in the pub cannot be costed into the hourly contracts for university visiting tutors. In effect for a 'good job to be done', the true costs of running a project like this could not be met by the overall grant. The other more senior people working on the project were employed at most on a one-day-a-week basis, even though in reality the overseeing and management and planning often took up more time than a full time job, especially when problems arose. For the remaining days of the week these people were engaged in other parallel projects, some requiring just two or three days a month, others needing more full time attention. In line with emerging patterns in recession-hit Europe the actual salaries held by the senior managers of this project were stagnant, while the hours had intensified to breaking point. This meant that social project management and grant application became a kind of labour of love, especially where there was a requirement from the start for co-funding, for instance where the grant-holder (in this case the NGO) had to under-write the activities by providing 20 per cent of the funding. There were, then, multiple layers of job creation being sustained. For those at the top this was a prestigious contract to have won under fierce competition, but in reality the financial returns were hardly sustainable, the highly qualified graduates could consider the job as part of their portfolio, prestigious and good for the CV as evidence of having worked on a major European grant. The take-home pay was small, but the status accruing was considered vital in the search for the next job, and for the recipients of this activity, the 'youngsters', this was a foretaste of things to come, part of a welfare-to-work agenda in a context where Italian welfare was virtually non-existent, and something of a cultural shock to lower middle-class or working-class young Sicilians for whom university or further education had promised something more secure and more conventionally professional than the jobs their parents had done. In effect most of them yearned for a job in the local state; they had expected to become bureaucrats or senior administrators, with a salary and a pension, but this seemed increasingly unrealistic.

The second project, titled BEKORE,[13] was indeed a labour mobility project again funded by the European Social Fund along with the *Arbeitsagentur* in Berlin. In this case the director lived in Berlin, where she was involved in a not-for-profit skills and training agency and for this initiative she brought in as partners organizations based in Hilversum in the Netherlands, Malta and again in Spoleto in Umbria. I myself had a very occasional role in this project, involving meetings with some of the Berlin people while they were in Umbria taking part in the exchange, and then giving a talk at the *finissage* event. The Italian participation was led and managed by the NGO director based in Umbria.[14] This was, to British eyes at least, an unusual undertaking. With a typically German emphasis on *ausbildung* rather than on actual outcomes, such as a job, a group of the long-term unemployed in Berlin (up to 102 persons in total) were provided with the chance to go either to Malta, Italy (Umbria) or Hilversum in Holland for up to three months, where they would be provided with a high-quality work experience programme in either gastronomy (culinary arts), cultural tourism, or arts administration (see also Briedis and Minks 2007) [15] Among the group who chose to go to Umbria was a Berlin-based Chilean artist who was offered the chance to work on a mural project for the annual prestigious Spoleto Festival. There was also a Russian young woman who got a placement in one of the Umbrian regional arts festivals and who planned to gain experience in event management, having spent a lot of time in Berlin clubs, and there were also twelve single mothers who came with their children (nineteen in total). Indeed a defining characteristic of the initiative was to give single mothers the kinds of chances for labour market participation through providing intense training and support in a new cultural environment. Once again, there were many layers of administration and accountancy for the allocation of the budget alone, along with the finding of accommodation, and kindergarten places for the children of the mothers, all of which amounted to an astonishingly high volume of hours and work. Like the STEP project in Palermo the disciplinary element of PIA/IDA was more subdued than would be the case with any UK welfare-to-work programme. (Apart from a handful of British voluntary organizations teaming up as partners on similar EC-funded projects, there is little comparable to these programmes in the UK.) The participants were treated with great respect and as equals, with no sense of the stigma of being 'on benefits'. The ethos across the team was one of intercultural exchange with the mentors and trainers exuding friendly enthusiasm. In fact, dozens of people were involved on the ground in Spoleto, the guests had to be ferried around by shuttle service, rooms had to be found for them, and timetables drawn up. They had to become familiar with bus routes and with the location of the childcare centres, and they had to find their way to the language classes. Over time they settled in and could be seen drinking coffee in a local café or else rushing across the beautiful hillside town *en route* to the library where the mural project was based, or over to Castel Ritaldi to the annual festival there. For perhaps obvious reasons, the mothers found the experience more challenging, especially when a child fell ill and had to see a doctor. Certainly, the difficulties faced by mothers taking part in such an exchange tell us a good deal both about the exigencies of normal working in the flexible cultural economy in one familiar location, never mind how this may be magnified in a foreign country, albeit one within the European Union. At the same time the positive features of such an adventurous project should be flagged up. Why should only middle-class students benefit from EC exchanges such as the Erasmus programme? Why must single mothers find themselves more or less excluded from jobs in the new culture industries such as event management for reasons of 'network sociality'? (Wittel 2001, and Chapter 1 of this book.) If hundreds of thousands of undergraduates across the member states can take part in such schemes as these and enjoy the benefits of a foreign environment with all the stimulation and the various life-chances this offers, why not extend this experience to the ranks of the socially disadvantaged such as unemployed single mothers? To British ears such projects as these are literally unthinkable, even before the onset of the current economic crisis. In the UK, wide-scale political forgetting of the value of social democratic projects has been intensified with more than a decade of demonization of people on benefits, and for this reason any idea of sanction-free 'provision' is regarded as a waste of public resources. Nor are there many people who would listen to arguments about the overall benefits to the person of travel and work experience in a different country unless the outcome was indeed a full-time job with no additional costs 'to the taxpayer'. In other words there is no current rationale or support for 'redistributive welfare'.

However the programme itself was not without its critics from inside. In one document the director in Umbria drew attention to the space for misunderstanding between the Italian small companies where the visitors were placed and the central office back in Berlin, the issue being the welfare ethos in Germany having no counterpart in recession-hit Italy (Beck 2013). This led to some debate about insufficient consideration being given to the reality of Italian culture and economy, as though they were merely the more passive partners and hosts for job insertion.[16] So there were some questions raised about the fine details of 'inter-cultural dialogue'. Such internal debate was nevertheless part of the egalitarian basis upon which the whole programme was run. The Chilean woman artist who also attended the *finissage* in Berlin spoke about how much she had learnt and how, even though she had not found a permanent job, the experience had been enriching. Other participants gladly came forward to vouch for the value of the programme.[17] At the same time the sheer scale of the undertaking and the working hours needed to ensure its success far outweighed the level of funding allocated to the professionals to oversee the day-to-day running. As the project moved to a conclusion the organizers were again burnt out. The elders expressed misgivings about carrying on with this kind of project management, while the younger people had no option but to drop the project abruptly as soon as the funds were depleted and were already working on new initiatives. For them the outcomes and the evaluation process could not be cast aside and forgotten about more quickly, given the harsh economic circumstances of not-for-profit multi-tasking environment and the urgent need to move onto the next project.

Project Working for All?

There have been few attempts to interpret more broadly changes taking place in social action programmes within the umbrella of EC funding. Mitchell for example offers an illuminating account of how under the Education and Culture Directorate ideas about social cohesion and the development of a democratic citizenry give way to more 'pragmatic' and individualized concerns about skills in a context of global competition (Mitchell 2006). She too points to the seeming abandonment of goals such as the encouraging of 'critical thinking' as an outcome for social action projects and a move away from the 'spirit of multi-culturalism'. Instead there is, she argues, across the many programmes of the type I already outlined, a focus on the production of 'flexible labourers' who are equipped with the competences needed for 'self-government'. Altogether this paves the way for the replacement of social democratic thinking by the newer ideologies of neoliberalism, in particular the giving up of 'redistributive policies'. In this case we might consider the German-led exchange scheme for the unemployed to learn new skills and broaden their horizons in Italy as 'redistributionist', something long since lost from policy-debate in the UK.[18] Mitchell also sees that while there can be some sort of co-existence (or residue as Stuart Hall in 2003 has put it) of social democratic principles alongside the pushing forwards of newer neoliberal criteria, in these many projects, it is nonetheless this latter that is in the ascendancy, even if just through the obstacles presented by budgets being cut and the increasing expectation of project managers that they work much longer hours for less tangible rewards (i.e. no time to think).

The overall focus, she claims, is for a workforce to be prepared to be more flexible and willing to adapt to the new demands of the labour market with a 'general abdication of welfarist principles and responsibilities' (Mitchell 2006, p. 398). In particular Mitchell singles out the idea of lifelong learning in order to show how it has undergone some profound changes. If in the past it entailed support to achieve some sense of 'ethical personhood and critical thinking' (itself of course also a form of self-regulation) it is now reduced to the acquisition of a skillset that complies with the requirement to be able to present a kind of summary CV on request. As was the case in the projects described above, Mitchell points to the reluctance at ground level among managers and teachers to be at the forefront of introducing such changes; there is, she claims, evasiveness and resistance on the part of those still more wedded to the earlier vocabularies. While this concurs with our own observations, these resistances do not, however, discount the fact that the pressure to implement the new policies also pushes the managers on the ground to the limits in terms of time and budget and frustration and this in itself means that the field of egalitarian working relations across different generations and levels of the workforce inside EC projects is itself compromised and transformed as older professionals feel the pressure to withdraw.

To sum up, here we see a field of activity that at ground level retains a stronger commitment to embedded principles of social democratic thinking in regard to unemployment and to those who often despite great effort have failed to find a job. We also see a firm commitment to re-distributionist welfare insofar as these schemes are both expensive and time-consuming and unlike many of their UK counterparts they are not devised on a 'pay by result' system. Indeed such a term was completely unknown in this European sector of vocational training managers. Overall, the way in which a neoliberalization process inside the Palermo and Spoleto projects functioned was to exert a high cost on the actors who were committed to defending the social value of a non-stigmatizing approach to unemployment, and for whom the principles of equality were played out in the humane and non-discriminatory way in which they interacted with the participants. This amounted to a cost in terms of health and well-being since in order to see a 'good job done' it was necessary to work long hours for very modest pay. In addition the small organizations could not bear the costs of such huge administrative loads. Ironically, and in line with the labour reform I have been chronicling, the only viable way to carry on with professional work in this European field was to break with the employment model, and for everyone to become more or less freelance, so that programme management was itself increasingly undertaken on a one-off project basis. A team comes together, on a temporary basis, undertakes a social project, along the same lines as would be the case for a film or TV documentary, and when it is finished, the team dissolves and people go their separate ways. This flexible network rationale increasingly becomes the only way of carrying out this kind of work, reflecting a client-based model in the commercial sector. The money that flows into the not-for-profit organization is not enough to cover the costs of staff 'between projects', and with this continuity, expertise and social relationships are lost. (And it would take a full-blown actor network theory model to track and analyse the movements, activities, budget-sheets, contracts drafted, personnel in and out over the course of a few years, office rented and spaces found, social networks mobilized to secure internships etc., all of which constituted a baggy assemblage of persons, objects, spaces and events, that together make up a 'project'.) In short, the sector of voluntary NGOs is squeezed almost out of existence, since only much larger wealthier institutions, such as big universities,[19] or increasingly major corporations working on a *pro bono* basis can bear the risk of covering costs between projects. And if there are no resources to keep people on between contracts they will simply leave or be 'let go'. The delivery of the kinds of projects described above, undertaken on a strictly non-punitive basis, and underpinned by egalitarian principles followed through as part of the everyday praxis of the initiatives, will therefore come under threat and may well disappear. Thus the fate of the small NGO within the logic of neoliberalism as it progresses within the EU is simply that of 'market failure', as larger more competitive organizations better able to develop innovative modes of flexibility step forward and prove themselves more attractive overall to funding bodies.[20] This new reality can be seen in operation within the EC *Youth In Action* programme more recently designated as ERASMUS+. A full panoply of reports reflects exactly the kind of thinking that was emerging in the two projects described above. One, titled 'Focus On: Youth Employment in Europe: Good Practice Projects' (2012) includes a wide range of cultural and creative activities across a range of European partners with Chapter 2 of the report titled 'Driven by Passion for Images' (Youth in Action 2012). An even more recent report from the same department of the EC is titled 'Focus on: Young People and Entrepreneurship : European Good Practice Projects' (2013), and here we find Chapter 6 titled 'Making Movies, and Making Movie Companies' (Youth in Action 2013). Most significantly however is the concentration of such programmes now inside the expansive university system.

The Social Enterprise Story: Payment by Results?

If one were to enquire of any of the directors of the NGOs and think tanks mentioned above, if, when setting up they had seen their activities as a 'business', based on a well-worked-through business plan, they would reply strongly in the negative (see also Feher 2007). This was not the point: the idea was that there was the chance to set up an organization that had a social role to play. The work to be done also connected with various forms of social activism, including feminism, green and urban politics and also the politics of multi-culturalism. There was also a situation where local or city councils, as well as national and extra-national bodies, wanted work to be undertaken in areas where these people had years of expertise and professional competence. There was no one else who could do such a job. Large institutions such as schools or colleges or social services had no resources for providing these training or citizenship projects, so the voluntary sector found itself occupying a key place, especially when the EU also increasingly saw the need for smaller organizations to run any number of youth in action or lifelong learning programmes. With enlargement these activities expanded enormously and as a result more and more 'social enterprises' sprang up in response. This is largely, however, a European story of the 'third sector' with such organizations scattered up and down the length and breadth of Italy, Spain, Germany and Holland in the first instance, and then in more recent times in Hungary, Romania, Bulgaria, Slovenia, Macedonia and Poland.[21] They have been points of gravity for generations of highly skilled graduates in social science, politics, economics, geography and urban studies. As suggested previously these form a kind of parallel to the academy carrying out applied social policy. However it is a very different picture in the UK. Of course there are all sorts of small voluntary organizations carrying out similar work, and even undertaking exchange programmes across the UK and especially in areas of high social deprivation.[22] Nevertheless there is a wide discrepancy between EC-funded-programmes in the UK, and the projects that win favour with the UK Coalition and before that the New Labour governments. This is the point, such bodies are quite at odds with each other in regard to political priorities for job creation and the task of reducing welfare. We do not have the time or space here to embark on any kind of meaningful comparison from a UK perspective with the projects I described above. Instead, it is apt and to the point of this entire book to focus simply on the highly charged vocabulary that has recently fallen into place in UK political culture around Big Society, and with it the rise of social entrepreneurship. This is timely because it also picks up on some of the threads from Chapter 3, where, as readers may recall, I pointed out that the Coalition government was a lot less thrilled, in times of economic recession, by the creative economy, than their New Labour predecessors. This continues to be the case, despite the occasional flourish in the direction of the creative industries.[23]

A recent article by Dowling and Harvie (2014) draws attention to the ways and means by which the question of 'the social' is currently dealt with in the terms preferred by the Coalition government. In effect, the UK Tories want to invent a neoliberal way of doing welfare that 'shrinks the state', massively reduces the costs of welfare, induces people to get into work somehow and off benefits, while at the same time inventing new, more profit-driven, and competitive ways of having these seemingly intractable social problems managed and overseen. One feature of such a programme is according to Dowling and Harvie the idea of 'social investment model'. This entails, for example, setting up a social programmes usually locally based where some sort of designated 'social problem' is visible, such as vandalism or youth crime.[24] The social entrepreneur would develop a plan for a small organization, which would become eligible for funds from the social investment bond (SIB) and he or she would enlist volunteers to carry out work (such as youth-work or advice work) that in the past would have been done by fully paid professionals. And then through some as yet obscure process such a social enterprise would gain further financial support if it could show success on a payment by result basis.

The notion of social enterprise has emerged as a kind of container concept that allows aspects of what were once areas of professional practice within the public sector to be undertaken by new small and self-organized businesses set up precisely to carry out work being privatized or being put out to competitive tendering. In effect the social enterprise model guarantees to introduce competition. As various authors have shown, this dates back to the times of New Labour and significantly was pioneered by the same adviser (Charles Leadbeater) who also championed the creative economy. Author of *The Rise of the Social Entrepreneur*, Leadbeater can be credited with inventing a hybrid political discourse, which combined the heroic entrepreneur figure much loved by US Business Schools, while harnessing this to the idea of the social good (Leadbeater 1996). But in fact social enterprises in the UK take many shapes and forms and, sadly, there is no space here other than to point to those features that are relevant to the discussion of creative economy and the experience of work within this emerging sector. In this respect we can flag up the simple fact that as the official definition released by the UK Cabinet Office states, a social enterprise 'is a business with primarily social objectives whose surpluses are principally reinvested for that purpose in the business or community, rather than being driven by the need to maximize profit for shareholders or owners' (UK Cabinet Office Social Enterprise Action Plan 2006). As a UK phenomenon this idea of social enterprise has been seen as a possible avenue for renewed social engagement in communities and regions (the democratic potential) and also as a way of shrinking the state through a business-oriented strategy that typically hinges round a rhetoric of heroic and charismatic individuals who are able to 'make a difference'. If we were to follow through the critique of neoliberalism as the project of the UK Coalition government, we could point to a discomfort zone in the management of poverty and disadvantage, which surfaces in the vocabulary of social enterprise. This comes about through the importation of the US business school and 'start-up' model that Gina Neff has described in detail, and its application to so-called 'social problems' (Neff 2012). Most sociologists, myself included, would say that the heroic individuals who litter the literature of success in start-ups and entrepreneurship and who always have a happy story to tell, cannot do anything other, in their guise as 'change-makers', than demean the reality and everyday existence of what Pierre Bourdieu called 'social suffering' (Bourdieu 2000). This points to an inevitable clash between the social scientist community and the business school model. The former would see an element of disrespect coded into these same vocabularies, regardless of what happens when they are actualized on the street (Sennett 2003). Certainly, not all social entrepreneurs in the UK conform to this model, which ultimately seeks to 'financialize social reproduction' (Dowling and Harvie 2014). But the overall thrust of policy-thinking in this domain is to make 'social-work' pay through the visibility of results. This can include prisoner re-habilitation or working with children in the care system. Across the board, a process of de-professionalization can be seen, as newcomers and business-people are welcomed for their experience in other worlds, and not those of the public sector.[25] From the point of view of government the key question, as Dowling and Harvie point out, is how to measure the success or not of such projects. This gives rise to all sorts of new instruments and toolkits and the need for 'success stories'. In their bid to make an argument about the ultimately monetary impulse behind such projects these authors quote the Schwab Foundation for Social Entrepreneurship, which says that 'Big Society Capital will make investments with risk and return characteristics comparable to the broader financial market' (Schwab Foundation quoted in Dowling and Harvie 2014).

The Creative Business School

It would be tempting to make an argument in the light of the above discussion that where the UK goes, with seemingly inventive and self-evidently neoliberal ways of tackling social issues, increasingly by cultural means, the EC with a good deal of reluctance at ground level, follows. Or alternately a case could be made that the balance of forces within EU Social Fund programmes retains a stronger presence of social democratic principles than is the case in comparable UK political discourse. This drift can be seen most tangibly in the Youth in Action programmes referred to above where the cultural and creative economy is drafted in to encourage creative self-employment in a landscape of unprecedented levels of youth unemployment across Europe. We might then surmise that just as the UK university sector including the new universities, with their enormous former 'art school' provision, increasingly sweeps into dominate this entire terrain, so also will the extensive European university system follow suite. What can be seen in the UK in the last decade is the university system move to a centre stage position in regard to the so-called 'new economy' (Thrift 2001). The pinpointing of education as the key site for the creativity *dispositif* to become embedded is something that has been referred to across the pages of this book (Banks and O'Connor 2009). And for this reason the 'creative business school' and the tensions that come into play around such an entity mark the right spot for this book to end. This idea comprises an assemblage of institutional practices that stretch the length and breadth of the university system with particular resonance within the arts, humanities and social sciences. It is a transformative project that seeks to maximize the value of creativity by means of human capital and self-entrepreneurship. The subjects of this new society model are expected to be endlessly flexible and fleet of foot when it comes to opportunities and possibilities in what is now not so much a business environment as a cultural world. This is a way of producing a new workforce for the precarious creative economy. The point of capture at which it functions most successfully is where often well-educated young but job-less Europeans (and students from southeast Asia) embark on Master's and other pre-Master's courses, which bring them into this creative scene. Here they are provided with a vocabulary which in a sociological way helps them to make sense of their own structural position in the global economy. The university also becomes a place of contesting discourses in the form of curriculum design. From Critical Management Studies to Business Models for the Creative Industries, from Social Innovation Studies, and the New Sociology of Work, to Getting Set Up for Start-Ups and so on. Master's students will use their time back inside the university system to network, re-draft their CVs, look for internships, start a blog and all the time apply for jobs in London, the global city *par excellence*. Or of course other key cities such as New York. Most importantly they will learn how to differentiate themselves so as to demonstrate their uniqueness and the distinct package of skills they bring to the table of prospective employers or commissioners of projects.[26] I am myself deeply inscribed within this 'teaching machine'. And I have to find ways of justifying the various pedagogic *dispositifs* which I wield on a week-to-week basis. If the official objective is to create new behaviours and to shape up individuals so that they can survive the slings and arrows of economic misfortune, which may well rain down on them, this is in itself a matter of pragmatism and expediency. Thus, as ever, the official discourse that imagines happy and fulfilled young creatives enjoying the business potential of their own inspiring ideas is offset and perhaps undermined by those actors, trainers, teachers, academics and intellectuals who crowd out the space of implementation, making it a new zone for dissent and for contestation, and for whom in dialogue with a younger generation there is often found the wherewithal for social action, protest and for pursuing new sets of rights and entitlements for welfare-in-work rather than welfare to work.

In a prescient article of 2001, Nigel Thrift offers an account of what we could construe as the background to this creative business-school model (Thrift 2001). Here is found an analysis of the rise of the spirit of 'romance', which permitted the development of new business styles that in turn played an integral role in the creation or invention of what he calls a 'new economic form', i.e. the 'new economy'. It became imperative to be 'passionate' about business and this paved the way for the kind of 'mass motivation' that could then be rolled out as the essence of newness across the business school environment. We have referred to this kind of ideological incitement to find pleasure in work across the pages of this book, with some of its earliest diagnosticians emerging from the Collège de France and Foucault himself in the decade before he died in 1984. So recurrent is this theme of happiness at work for this present book that it is timely to return to it at the end. Thrift points to the rise of the new

economy company as one based on small-scale mobile flexible entrepreneurship, ICT, venture capital and the requisite amounts of
passion. The youthful/relaxed/charismatic/prescriptive mode of pedagogy (best seen in the TED talk genre) that underpins a good deal
of this business school approach comprises, as Thrift sees it, of a
'grammar of business imperatives' (Thrift 2001, p. 416). This then
became a mantra of sort for a new stratum of managers mostly in
the US and replacing the more heavy-handed technocrats of the
so-called 'new managerialism'. 'The heavy bureaucratic hand was
replaced by the light touch of the "change agent"' (Thrift 2001,
p. 419). And as he continues, 'However efficacious they may or may
not be, the fact is that teams and projects are now regarded as the
main way in which bodies can be aligned to produce creativity'
(Thrift 2001, p. 420). Acknowledging that this managerial brand of
passionate work was heavily tilted towards the male workforce,
Thrift shows how appealing this was as a way of injecting the bohemian values of artists into what had previously been the drab environment of the office. This 'new style of doing capitalism', which in
the first instance centred around new media entrepreneurs, the various
emerging ICTs and the availability of venture capital along with an
expansive press and media circuit to chronicle the ups and downs of
Silicon Valley was, as Thrift sees it, 'a new received economic doctrine
of the elite masquerading as a democratic or even aesthetic impulse'
(Thrift 2001, p. 428). Across the pages of this book an argument has
been made that sees the extension of the 'new economy' into the
spheres of culture and creativity where the seductions of passionate
work have an even more natural or comfortable habitat. The creativity *dispositif* is activated inside the seminar rooms and lecture theatres
of the creative business school. By this means a new middle class of
educated young persons is being 'made up' to withstand and prepare
for a world of seemingly self-directed work often interrupted and
relatively unprotected. For this precarious generation, in particular
those who have grown up in Europe in the last two decades, the
challenge will be to draw on their creative and political resources in
order to invent new forms of social protection for themselves and
others alongside them. In short, compassionate and socially re-inflected
job creation must become an imperative for young people across
Europe and the world in the years to come.

Notes

Introduction: Pedagogical Encounters and Creative Economy

1   This is a subtle point on the part of the film director and scriptwriter who has signalled her indebtedness to Richard Sennett's writings in published interviews following the release of the film. There is also something of a gesture to the new 'post-feminist' way in which marriage or partnership take on the form of a seemingly impregnable economic unit. To dissolve the marriage has much greater repercussions than would have been the case in the era of welfare.

2   Ottinger's trade-mark and painterly use of clear blue sky is used to great effect in *Bildnis* and in several of her other films, such as *Madame X*, where it forms a skyline of avant-garde embrace and of gay/queer-oriented women now eventually inhabiting the world with an exciting sense of their own female sexuality. *Eine Flexible Frau* deploys the same device as homage, including the gesture to lesbian encounters, but also to mark out some landscape greyed with disappointment.

3   Paulo Virno (2005) points to the often-cited Milan Women's Bookstore as an example of collectivist socio-economic enterprise. But there is a history to be written about the thousands of feminist undertakings that grew out of various forms of local community organization such as women's photography projects or workshops for young women to learn non-gender-specific skills such as camera operating. These radical ventures date back to the mid 1970s in the UK and across western Europe. Their informal histories are replete with narratives of 'failure' or closure after a limited period of time. This is not the point, since many undertakings like these had and have a short life but nevertheless serve an

important function on the basis of the attempt to work collectively as a counter to unemployment or to limited available employment options.

4 This can have a divisive effect within the universities, with the older elite universities downplaying this role, or pushing it into some less prestigious corner, and the newer universities seeing the rise of new invisible hierarchies according to the nature and level (technical/ practical/managerial) of courses offered.

5 This issue also requires some breaking down of the idea of creative economy into its constituent parts including sectoral dimensions; e.g. if a national TV organization like the BBC partly re-locates to Glasgow or Salford, this has some noticeable impact on each city; however this is a public sector corporation. The fashion sector is something quite different, as is the music industry.

6 See the 'teddy boy' menswear collection from Hedi Slimane for Saint Laurent http://www.theguardian.com/fashion/fashion-blog/2014/jan/20/hedi-slimane-saint-laurent

7 Cultural studies is not the only site for this intensification of pedagogy. There is also the 'educational turn' and 'theoretical activism', which have grown up within and alongside the European *précarité* movement and which emerge more directly from within the field of art and visual culture (Rogoff 2010; Lorey 2015)

8 The word *dispositif* is often used interchangeably with apparatus in Foucault's writing and intervious; for a fuller definition see p. 38 of this book.

9 At the time of writing (20 February 2015), the BBC in partnership with other UK government agencies is launching a Get Creative campaign with film clips of Kate Moss and other celebrities describing the pleasures of such activities as making your own clothes from second-hand vintage hunting etc. see http://www.get-creative.com

10 See http://www.thewestminsterforum/fashion /Made-in-Britain

1 Clubs to Companies: Notes on the Decline of Political Culture in Speeded-Up Creative Worlds

1 This is taken from the guest list for the September 2000 meeting of the Cultural Entrepreneurs Club attended by 325 people and hosted at Channel Four.

2 For London as a global city see Sassen (1991), for cultural economies an urban areas see Scott (2000).

3 By 'independents' I mean small-scale micro-economies primarily in music and fashion and related fields, which emerged as post-punk phenomena in the mid 1980s also in response to unemployment and to government endorsement of 'enterprise culture'. Generally, these groupings presented themselves as radical, critical, innovative and loosely

collective – e.g. the fashion duo Body Map, the 'indie' record label Rough Trade, the magazine *The Face* in its early days.

4   The DCMS Mapping Document of 1998 indicates employment rates in culture and communication at over one million persons; the DCMS Mapping Document of 2001 puts the figure at 1.3 million.

5   In an earlier article on this subject I quoted a hairdresser interviewed in the *Independent* who said he was 'classically trained' (McRobbie 1999).

6   This kind of comment is emerging from current interviews with respondents working in the cultural sector. They repeatedly tell me of small companies undercutting others by offering virtually no cost for jobs that will help their profile.

7   Another respondent currently runs one tiny TV production company, another a media consultancy and alongside this she also teaches two days a week.

8   Rave culture is a much cited influence on the entrepreneurial activities of artists, including Damien Hirst.

9   Personal communication from former MA student, Goldsmiths College London.

10   Young women are increasingly encouraged to consider work and employment as lifelong activities, as husbands can no longer be relied upon as breadwinners.

11   The Minister for Culture, Media and Sports the Rt Hon. Chris Smith said to me in a panel debate (Royal Television Society February 1999) that the young people working in the industry 'do it because they love it, they know what they are letting themselves in for'.

12   An unexpected consequence of my study of UK fashion designers is that I have been visited by a stream of aspiring young fashion graduates who have come across the book, and as a result seek my advice.

13   Cultural Entrepreneur Club (September/October/November 2000) is comprised of a majority of white males from 'good' universities.

14   This point is made clearly in 'Good Character and Dressing for Success' by Jesh Hanspal (2000).

15   This is the result in my study McRobbie (1998).

16   At the above-mentioned Cultural Entrepreneurs Club I was introduced to a trained architect working as a time-based arts agent, a photographer working as a curator/administrator and a graphic designer working as a web-site editor.

17   Again, on both the occasions I attended this club I was the only academic present. Unlike the business mentors and venture capitalists also present, I found no immediate role to play other than to 'chat' with former students.

18   The nominations for the Turner Prize 2000 included three non UK artists, one German, one Dutch and another Japanese, all based in London, and two of whom trained in London art colleges. In fact a pattern is emerging, where European and overseas students train in UK

art colleges and then go on to enjoy better support for their creative activities from their own governments than is available in the UK. Hence the prominence of the new Dutch, Belgian and South Asian fashion designers.

2 Unpacking the Politics of Creative Labour

1 See Initiative Media Survey June 2014 where across nineteen countries over 9,000 young so-called Millennials reported that the tough financial climate was engendering an ethos of self-employment and the need to think and act creatively, www.initiativemediasurvey/ 2014.

2 Efforts are quickly made to regularize this new informal economy, for example the setting up of the Deutsche-Italienische Start-up Forum der Botschaft Italian. The *Berliner Morgenpost*-12 November 2013 reports Mattia Corbetta, the Italian ambassador based in Berlin, as saying 'innovative Unternehmen können ein Neuanfang für eine gemeinsame Zukunft sein'. 'Italiens Grunder knupfen Kontakte nach Berlin' (Stuber 2013, p. 6).

3 Bourdieu of course comments on several occasions about the raising of expectations among young people from working-class backgrounds through the opening up of access to higher education, only for them to be let down on finding themselves part of the now more highly educated but nevertheless unemployed strata (Bourdieu 1984).

4 The 'routes and roots' of UK black music in the last decades could also be read through these kinds of narratives; see Melville 2005.

5 We could illustrate the shifting nature of institutional power operating upon lines of flight by considering the different municipal ethos prevailing on art-oriented school leavers from disadvantaged social backgrounds from the late 1970s to the early 1990s, for whom access courses and the wavering of the need for conventional qualifications provided a direct route into otherwise wholly middle-class fine-art educational institutions. This non-standard entrance pathway helped countless young people who, like Jarvis Cocker, subsequently went on to become well-known artists and musicians. With the introduction of fees based on substantial loans, as well as the virtual disappearance of the discourses around 'access', these equalizing avenues fade into non-existence.

6 Broadcasting, Entertainment, Cinematograph and Theatre Union.

7 A fuller analysis of this shift would mean looking beyond the debate simply about the creative industries led by DCMS Minister Chris Smith, to the Department for Trade and Industry and the various policies favoured by Peter Mandelson, which aimed at limiting the power of the trade unions and isolating their activities.

8   Trying to raise questions about low pay, or unpaid internships at that point in time, proved to be an unpopular move. My own attendance at round-table seminars at the DCMS in the early 2000s showed this to be the case. On one such occasion a DCMS spokesperson said to me that I was a 'bleeding heart liberal', and that young people had to learn to 'sink or swim'.

9   The bearded young man behind the counter in *J Crew*, a mid-market fashion chain not typically part of the hipster landscape, spots the vintage 1960s Italian shoes my daughter is wearing and, instead of commenting on what she is buying from the *J Crew* stock, initiates a conversation instead about the best vintage stockists in town.

10 Kepplova (2013) makes a similar argument on the basis of her study of club culture, raves and parties in post-socialist Slovakia.

11 For example Angela Merkel the German Chancellor, addressing an EU conference in 2007, mentioned Florida's work as a model for growing the creative economy (Merkel 2007).

12 This point was made forcefully by the well-known UK film director Danny Boyle who also created the Olympics Opening Ceremony in July 2012. The narrative that ran through the entire ceremony was the social value of state-funded institutions such as the National Health Service. In interviews regarding the opening event, Boyle repeatedly drew attention to his own working-class upbringing and to his successful career made possible by free education.

13 In November 2011 a group of people working for the Rosa Luxemburg Foundation in Berlin (attached to Die Linke party) invited Jamie Peck to deliver a short version of his forceful critique of Florida to an audience of about 300 in the lecture theatre, which was then duly reported in the local press; see www.rosa-luxemburg-stiftung

14 Centre for Contemporary Cultural Studies under the directorship of Stuart Hall.

15 See *Inventory Magazine* from Vancouver

16 For example London Fashion Week 13 September 2013, as reported by the *London Evening Standard*, Louise Gray is held up as a leading young designer whose signature is 'subculture'.

17 The self-consciously hipster publication *Shoreditch Twat* demonstrated this point, eschewing all ideas of ethical or political responsibility, while the *London Evening Standard* led the bandwagon of celebrating the spiral in house prices and the windfall this has brought to homeowners and landlords alike.

18 See the documentary film by John Akomfrah (Smoking Dog Films 2009) *Saturn Returnz* about the mixed-race music performer, composer and producer Goldie.

19 Paul Willis of course was the only CCCS writer to consider labour, however his focus was on the few remaining of industrial working-class jobs that awaited the 'lads' he studied as they got ready to leave school and enter factory employment (Willis 1978).

3   The Artist as Human Capital: New Labour, Creative Economy, Art Worlds

1   Department of Media, Culture and Sport
2   Ian Birrell, writing in the *Guardian* (10 April 2014, following the resignation of the Minister at the DCMS, http://www.theguardian.com asks the question 'Does Britain really need a ministry of culture?...the ministry itself has almost ceased to exist. After slashing staff budgets, the department was shunted last year from its own office into the treasury, where it sits squashed onto one floor beside the nation's tax collectors'.
3   See for example 'Beyond the Creative Industries: Mapping the Creative Economy in the UK', NESTA, February 2008. See also the special issue of the *International Journal of Cultural Policy* 'After the Creative Industries' 15 (4) (2009).
4   Chris Smith himself authored a book titled 'Creative Britain' in 1998 (Smith 1998).
5   McRobbie 2002.
6   NESTA (National Endowment for Science, Technology and the Arts).
7   See *Staying Ahead* (Work Foundation 2008).
8   This book (originally a report to the Gilbenkian Foundation) drew on ongoing research by various cultural studies academics on subjects such as vintage clothes markets, DIY music production etc.
9   The *New Times* (1989) collection came out of earlier versions of short, journalistic essays published in *Marxism Today*, and it was because the format was accessible and less academic that it received coverage across the UK press. In effect *Marxism Today* functioned as a kind of think-tank alongside Demos and the IPPR.
10 Other countries, in particular Germany, found ways of bringing the TUs on board on a number of policies arising from the shift to a new post-industrial economy with the concept of flexicurity (see Wilthagen and Tros 2004).
11 Personal email communication with Stuart Hall, 12 June 2012.
12 See the profile written by Suleman Anaya (15 August 2013) of Andy Rogers at Fred Perry, www.thebusinessoffashion.com/the-creative-class-andy-rogers-brand-director.
13 'Tories Are the Only Hope for the Arts', 16 May 2011, www.theguardian.com/culture/culture-cuts-blog/may/arts-emin.
14 Michael Craig-Martin, former Goldsmiths Head of Art and mentor to the Young British Artists, in conversation with current Head of Art Dr Richard Noble, 24 January 2013, www.gold.ac.uk/YouAre/Alumni/goldlink magazine/24/01/13.
15 One of Bill's students says 'we have all worked crazy hours [...] I don't even want to speculate how many. We have been living it, eating it, sleeping it. It has been insane' (Bill 2012, p. 52).

16   This intensity has been defined by Banks recently in terms of 'being in the zone' (see Banks 2014).
17   I would like to thank Stephanie Tayler for sending me the manuscript of her co-authored book. At the time of reading for this chapter no page numbers were available.
18   Many of these artists have been connected with Stuart Hall and with cultural studies and post-colonial theory; see e.g. McRobbie 2005 and forthcoming McRobbie 2016.
19   Isaac Julien, personal communication (email), 18 March 2014
20   Chila Burman, personal communication, 14 May 2013.
21   Yinka Shonibare, personal communication.
22   Isaac Julien, personal communication (email), as above 18 March 2014.
23   Marion von Osten, and myself have collaborated on joint projects, including Atelier Europa: Be Creative, from which I borrow the title for this current book; warm thanks to Marion von Osten; see also von Osten and McRobbie http://www.ateliereuropa).

4   The Gender of Post-Fordism: 'Passionate Work', 'Risk Class' and 'A Life of One's Own'

1   It is relevant to this discussion that the site for the masquerade in Rivière's account is the workplace, indeed the lecture theatre where the professional woman is delivering a lecture to her male colleagues (Rivière 1928).
2   E.g. Britain's Got Talent , The X Factor, The Voice, The Apprentice and indeed Young Musician of the Year Awards (BBC 4)
3   CREATe interview with UK fashion designer Margaret Howell on Scottish knitwear factories, 1 May 2014.
4   See for example Hardt and Virno (1996); Hardt (1999, pp. 89–112); Lazzarato (1999); Hardt and Negri (2000); Virno (2005).
5   All the years of debate about the problems of class reductionism in the writing of Stuart Hall in the 1970s and 1980s and also Ernesto Laclau and Chantal Mouffe, have no place here. Nor is there any sense of a need to interrogate class as a cultural and a political signifier, a space where relations of power and powerlessness are pursued across the sites of everyday life, for example in the school playground. See Willis (1978); Bourdieu (2000).
6   Many of these kinds of workplace now carry requirements that female staff have regular manicures, to maintain a perfectly groomed appearance at all times; while male staff will also be subjected to rules about hair and overall appearance, these will be less extensive than those applied to women.
7   See for example Bott 2006 in *Feminist Review*.
8   Gutierrez Rodriguez writes 'With the term precariousness, Precarias describes a form of material and immaterial destabilization. This is

determined by axes of time (stress, excess, instability, impossibility to plan) axes of space...axes of income...axes of conflict, of hierarchies, of risks and bodies...These...express...the suffering and violence of new ways of living and working conditions', but also 'point to a precarious release of new ways of connection, work and life' (Rodriguez 2008, p. 39).

5 Fashion Matters Berlin: City-Spaces, Women's Working Lives, New Social Enterprise?

1 'The city is home to around 600 fashion designers whose spectrum ranges from haute couture to streetwear' (Wowereit 2008, p. 72).
2 The *Creative Industries Report* 2008 suggests over 400 small fashion enterprises
3 See Wowereit (2008) for an account of the available resources and support mechanisms for arts, culture and creative sectors in the city.
4 This point was made by Daniela Fleig and Sabine Huelsebus during a visit to the NEMONA studio, 22 April 2012.
5 NEMONA has been supported by European Social Funds see http://www.nemona.de
6 See for example LIFE EV http://www.life-online.de
7 There is no space here to offer a brief reflection on the history of these kinds of organizations in Berlin and elsewhere in Germany, save to say they have often functioned as satellites for the social state taking the form of local *sozial-arbeit* projects, e.g.with vulnerable youths etc. This is a different historical trajectory from the UK social enterprises set up as part of the process of modernization and of new managerialism of state functions through privatization of public services by means of competitive tendering, something that developed through the Thatcher years and gained momentum during the times of New Labour.
8 In a *Guardian* article, Wood (2012) reports a 30 % jump in profits as *Zara* has become 'Spain's biggest company', see also Burgen (2012).
9 Interview with Michael Sontag, 20 June 2014.
10 E.g. the so-called Spandauer Vorstadt, an areas of Mitte that include Torstrasse, Linienstrasse, Oranienburgerstrasse and Auguststrasse.
11 See http://www.RIXPACK.de
12 The listings magazines *Tip* and *Zitty* provide extensive coverage of the many forms of urban anti-gentrification activism.
13 See for example http://www.arbeitsagentur.de, http://www.arbeitsagentur .de/ein-euro, or http://www.caritas.de/glossare/ergaeenzendearbeitslosen geld/aufstocken
14 'In Berlin women working in the artistic and creative professions earn less than their male colleagues' (Wowereit 2008, p. 87).

15   See D'Ovidio and Pradel's account of resentment on the part of young Italian designers as they are passed over in favour of UK and US-trained graduates (D'Ovidio and Pradel 2012).

16   See the famously run-down and shabby pop-up store *Lil* on Torstrasse stockist for *Comme des Garçons*: http://www.lil.com

17   The question of IP and Copyright for independent Berlin designers is currently being investigated by the author see http://www.create.ac.uk

18   Efforts are made on the part of the city fathers to stifle this anti-capitalist reputation for fear of putting off investors (while also, if reluctantly, attempting to use it as a quirky branding strategy).

19   This marks an extension of research I carried out in London some years ago and was initially prompted by casual observation that in Berlin young designers could indeed set up with their own labels, and have a retail space from which to sell direct, located at the front of their work-shops (McRobbie 1998). In London this has long since been impossible due to the high cost of space. From 2012 this Berlin research has been funded by the AHRC CREATe grant see www.create.ac.uk

20   Derya Issever, interviewed 6 November 2013.

21   Interview with Michael Sontag, 20 June 2014.

22   This comment comes from an animated conversation with sociologist Anja Schwanhaeuser (1 November 2011). In her recent work she has described this kind of economic activity as specifically 'Berlin capital-ism', pointing to the lasting influence of youth culture in the city (Schwanhaeuser 2010).

23   See Ahlfeldt (2010) for the various accounts of citizen opposition to the re-development of key sites such as the MediaSpree.

24   Fashion Matters Berlin at September Galerie Kreuzberg, 28 June 2012, Fashion Matters London, Berlin and Milan, Goldsmiths University of London and AHRC CREATe, 12 June 2013.

25   Tanja Muehlhans attended the event at the September Galerie in 2012 and also agreed to be interviewed in person in June 2013.

26   In Berlin these are Universität der Künste and Weissensee Kunsthochschule.

27   Majaco were interviewed for this study on 15 July 2014 as part of the CREATe project.

28   Interviewed in Berlin, 7 July 2014, and follow-up comments on email, 24 and 25 August 2014.

29   These showrooms have been part of the attempt led by Tanja Muehl-hans to create a wider market for Berlin fashion.

30   Oliver MacConnell, discussion, 12 February 2014.

31   If I admire the style of Turkish–German teenagers as they hang about the U-Bahn stations in the neighbourhood, for example girls with thick Amy Winehouse-like eyeliner, and colourful headscarves loosely wrapped around high pony tails, is my gaze colonizing or is it something else – the feminist looking at beauty beyond the narrow categories of the front pages of fashion magazines?

32 To be precise, these include Reuterstrasse, Friedelstrasse, Pflugelstrasse, Wesenstrasse, Burchenerstrasse and the postcode of Berlin 14117.
33 Interview with Esther Perbandt, 7 July 2014.

6 A Good Job Well Done? Richard Sennett and the New Work Regime

1 The remarkable film by German film director Nikolaus Geyrhalter (2005) *Our Daily Bread* shows the isolation of the operative in a chicken-rearing factory who now works alone all day, and even has her tea breaks alone, because advanced technology has depleted the need for other workers.
2 See the Introduction of this book and the discussion of the film *Eine Flexible Frau* (dir.Turanskyj 2010).
3 One Goldsmiths student undertook research on her own place of part-time work, a well-known fashion store, for her dissertation. She reported divisions between the small number of full-timers, who were more subjected to traditional labour discipline and managerial control, in contrast to the part- timers who worked shifts and had no interest in a longer-term career. Another student working for a similar retailer in central London reported that as a part-timer over several years she had never been encouraged to apply for promotion or to pursue a manage-rial job; instead it was assumed all part-timers would leave sooner or later.
4 I know of no current research that examines the extensiveness of casual jobs in comparison to secure full-time work in urban fashion retail.
5 Perhaps such activities appear more unusual to Beck for the reason that their existence in German cities is more hidden. There are greater restrictions on opening up 24-hour local shops and convenience stores, and small internet shops doubling up as cafes and latenight groceries are only to be found in neighbourhoods with high migrant or Turkish–German populations such as Kreuzberg and Neukölln in Berlin.
6 See interview with Richard Hedges of The Hales Gallery (McRobbie 2004).
7 See the documentary by Frederick Wiseman *La Danse* (2009).
8 See, for example, the profile in *Vogue Italia* on Dalston, East London, 'Benvenuti a Dalston' by Chiara Zampetti, May 2009.
9 In this same spirit, in an interview in the *Guardian*, Thursday 16 October 2014, the musician Thurston Moore of Sonic Youth, now living in Stoke Newington London N16 says 'That history (of the counter-cultural presence in the neighbourhood) has been deleted ... from the streets of Stoke Newington ... You should know where you live ... I find that to be a certain responsibility'. Interview with Dorian Lynskey; see www.theguardian.com/music/2014/sonic-youth-thurston-moore.

10   The artist Isaac Julien's life history, as a young black boy growing up in east London in the late 1970s and early 1980s, and also many aspects of his art works, tell one version of this alternative story. Further back to the mid 1970s every city in the UK had artists, musicians, film-makers and writers who were deeply invested in the urban culture around them and committed to defending disadvantaged people in these areas from social injustice, aggressive policing and from various forms of mistreatment on the basis of poverty and powerlessness.

11   See the *Daily Mail* report ('One in Ten of Us Makes Our Hobbies Pay') by Louise Eccles (18 October 2014) that the so-called hobby economy is now worth £8bn annually. She writes 'Hobby entrepreneurs working in design earned the most at £3,200 a year.' Arts and craft work brought in on average £1,443; see www.mailonline/18/10/2014/. See also Calhoun C. and Sennett R. (2007) especially Chapters 2 and 7.

12   Thanks to Aida Baghernejad for drawing attention to the ironic hipsterism of the General Store, Bellenden Road in Peckham, South London.

13   See www.inventorymagazine.com, and for a similar ethos see also *Huck* at www.huckmagazine.com/.

14   For a fuller history of the re-birth of *Shinola* see www.shinola/detroit.

15   The UK's most successful menswear designer Paul Smith has been staging this idea of the 'history of quality and craft' in his high-end stores for many years, including objects such as handmade toy trains, or cigar holders or old-fashioned briefcases alongside the clothes, but more recently we can see a similar engagement with craft in the London headquarters and showroom of fashion designer Margaret Howell, whose clothes have been laid out around and 'in conversation with' rescued and restored pieces of Ercol furniture; see www .margarethowell.co.uk/.

Conclusion: European Perspectives

1   Many warm thanks to Monika Savier whose permission I needed to write this chapter.

2   For a working definition of creative economy in the EU context I have referred to the European Commission's KEA The Economy of Culture in Europe Report (2006). This includes both an 'industrial' sector meaning products such as books and films, which have large circulation and audiences and also 'non-industrial' goods, which includes events and activities such as art galleries and museum sector, theatre, ballet, opera etc. However within these definitions there is no consideration given to the workforce in this creative world.

3   The senior managers had generally been educated in social work or social pedagogy with a strong emphasis on the 'practice', or the 'Prak-tikum', which meant developing and continually assessing action

programmes with disadvantaged social groups such as young offenders, teenage mothers, sex workers, or drug users. The philosophical and conceptual framework they worked with continued to be informed by feminist theory, anti-racist thinking and radical approaches to poverty and inequality, while in reality these ideas were being replaced by the EC's versions of training for the knowledge economy, and increasingly for the cultural economy.

4 The requirement is for hosting organizations to provide 20 per cent of finance as co-funding for programmes as a condition of eligibility for participation. When new social enterprises enter this terrain, which are able to divide their activities into a profit and a not-for-profit sector, this co-funding mechanism can be costed in, and covered, indeed such organizations can even afford to see the not-for-profit EC activities as loss-makers but good for the image or the overall brand of the company. By this means a more competitive environment for all players is fostered.

5 Funded and supported under the EQUAL call (see http://ec.europa.eu/ employment social-equal consolidated/), now no longer existing, having been replaced by a variety of Lifelong Learning Schemes. The programme started in 2007 just before the onset of the economic crisis, and was completed in 2011.

6 The recruitment process in itself took several weeks and a good deal of negotiations with existing charities and street organizations working with youth. The most at-risk youth proved to be the most difficult to enlist, instead it was a better qualified cohort who formed the majority of participants.

7 Since the end of this project and especially in the light of the Euro-crisis and subsequent recession and austerity across the Eurozone, there has been a good deal more attention to Sicily and indeed to Palermo. For youth unemployment in Italy the most recent figures show 41.3 per cent (Inman 2013). In relation to Palermo as a city of now self-defined 'precarious workers' see 'Palermo is a Laboratory for the Precariat' in OpenDemocracy 14 September 2014 (Mackay 2014).

8 While adjusting to this new horizon of arts and culture as job creation proved unproblematic for the young team who provided a good deal of the courses and day-to-day training, and who were all social science graduates but already familiar with media and cultural studies, and the ideas of 'media practice' and 'creative entrepreneurship', for the older managers who had been schooled in working with socially marginalized persons such as delinquent youth or sex workers, and also with training new generations to carry on this tradition, the shift to providing for the idea of cultural work or creative labour was more difficult for the reason that the social dimension was less visible, instead it was mediated through the technologies of film, video or through performance art etc.

9 Some of the final outputs for the programme included theatre pieces and performances, short films and musical recitals.

10   One of the key events took the form of a day conference for the young people and for cultural workers and teachers in the city, as well as for various political figures including the head of Vocational Training Research (ISFOL) from Rome, the Mayor and the Vice Chancellor of Palermo University. The day culminated in performances by the participants, including an art exhibition, a film show and live music.

11   On another occasion hosted in Palermo there was a panel event with an economist from the Department of Labour Research (ISFOL, Rome), myself (McRobbie) and Monika Savier (Head of the NGO BBJ/ShareIt). To an audience of professionals from job centres across Europe, we each offered commentaries on the future of work, ISFOL argued strongly for the Made In Italy approach to protecting the big industries and trade unions. Monika Savier discussed the tight fiscal rules being drafted by Berlin following the banking crisis and the consequences for Italian unemployment and I gave an account of the growth of freelance work and cultural economy in the UK and diminishing role of the trades unions.

12   These points of difference were made clear to an audience of about fifty people in Berlin at the *finissage* for the IDA/PIA project managed by the NGO BEKORE. On this occasion I compared the approach to job-training undertaken by the European colleagues on the IDA/PIA exchanges with the new regime of unemployment training provided by privatized agencies in the UK such as A4E (Action for Employment). This new style was also vividly portrayed in the Channel Four 'Reality TV' (2010) series called *Benefit Busters*, which showed a female director of a privatized training agency (called Hayley Taylor) assume a combination of hard (dominatrix-type) style of management of the unemployed in their search for work, with an almost flirtatious soft approach (emotional labour) as she cajoled the clients with up to several phone calls daily to check up on their attendance etc. at interviews. With the aid of clips from the TV series (which critics in the UK describe as 'poverty porn' (see Biressi 2013), this talk indeed provided a jolt of incredulity to the serious-minded social democrats in the audience, since of course the TV series was also designed to have 'entertainment value' in order to attract audiences and hence advertising revenue. Of note also is the fact some months later the CEO of A4E Emma Harrison was accused of mismanagement of government funds and hastily resigned.

13   Berufliche Kompetenzentwicklung & nachhaltige Ressourcennutzen in Berlin, Praxis im Ausland 2010–12.

14   Thanks also here to Tatjana Freygang and Rita Eichelkraut for this invitation.

15   See the final report titled 'Bekore! Bericht' : Durch Auslandpraktika zu neuen beruflichen Perspektiven' (Freygang 2012).

16   In her response to the project made on the part of the Italy partner, Monika Savier comments on how the processes of individualization

impact on professional practice. Since the groups chosen for the exchange shared nothing in common other than their residency in Berlin and their unemployed status, the more usual forms of group work had to be replaced by more time consuming one-to-one case-work, which in turn made it more difficult to draw any wider generalizations from the project. This change also reflects the new agenda for 'assistance for individual cases', which has entered the EC vocabularies having already been established in UK welfare-to-work schemes for many years now. Savier comments that this in effect de-professionalizes the team overseeing the project because they are unable to apply 'pedagogic standards'. With such heterogeneous groups it becomes arbitrary whether or not the provision of activities and job placements actually work and the participant finds a job on their return home (Savier 2012).

17 The final report includes statements from several participants who testify to its value; e.g. one young mother says, 'Thanks to my time in Spoleto working at the kindergarten I have decided to train in social work', another says, 'This Praktikum has improved my emotional intelligence, my inter-cultural competence and my language skills', and one other says 'The experience has helped me reach the decision to work as a teacher in Guatemala' (Bekore! Bericht 2012).

18 A small aside, it would be important to see how Scotland, Northern Ireland and Wales act in regard to these job-training provisions overseen by the EC.

19 See for example the Innovation Incubator Luephana at Lueneburg University, which is funded by EU Regional Development Funds, or the URBIS programme based in Paris.

20 Of course the unspoken question is how large organizations including universities can themselves absorb the costs of 'winning' a multi-million euro contract where overheads and co-funding mechanisms almost immediately absorb up to 50 per cent of grant income.

21 See for example Evers and Laville (2004).

22 For example the European Social Fund Report, which states that the Liverpool in Work Scheme allowed 'job seekers in deprived communities the chance to set up their own businesses 'with the scheme hoping to see 650 new start-ups' as the outcome (www.eu/esf/liverpool-in-work).

23 E.g. the establishment in December 2014 of the Creative Industries Federation see www.creativeindustriesfederation.com.

24 It is a mark of the business school approach to adopt a rather light-hearted and hence trivializing attitude to deep-rooted social issues, the origins of which lie in many years if not decades of deprivation, high male unemployment and ill-health. In such vocabularies as these, the words social inequality do not exist or have any salience as such. Instead appeals are made to prospective social entrepreneurs to 'become a change-maker' or to take part in a field where it is possible to 'solve social problems'.

25 On having a question put from the floor about accountability regarding newly privatized sectors of the public domain, the Labour MP Margaret Hodge, who is Chair of the Public Accounts Committee, replied that where there could be no 'turning the clock back', the key issue for Labour was to enforce high standards of provision and to install news systems of checks and balances across the field of service providers (M. Hodge MP in conversation, 12 December 2014, fund-raising dinner, London E4).

26 See the opening section of the Introduction to this book.

References

Aage, T. and Belussi, F. (2008) From fashion to design: creative networks in industrial districts, *Innovation and Industry* 15(5): 475–91.

Adkins, L. (2002) *Revisions: Gender and Sexuality in Late Modernity*, Open University Press, Buckinghamshire.

—— (1999) Community and economy: a retraditionalisation of gender, *Theory, Culture and Society* 16: 119–41.

Adkins, L. and Devers, M. (2014) Housework, wages, money, *Australian Feminist Studies* 29: 50–66.

Adorno, T. (1991) *The Culture Industry: Selected Essays on Mass Culture*, Routledge, London.

Adorno, T. and Horkheimer, M. (1976) *Dialectics of Enlightenment*, Herder and Herder, New York.

Ahlfeldt, G. (2010) Blessing or curse: appreciation, amenities and resistance around Berlin 'Mediaspree', *Hamburg Contemporary Economic Discussions* 32.

Akomfrah, J. (2009) (dir) *Saturn Returnz*, Smoking Dog Films.

Arvidsson, A. and Malossi, G. (2010) Customer co-production from social factory to brand, D. Zwick and J. Cayla (eds) *Inside Marketing*, Oxford University Press, Oxford.

Arvidsson, A., Malossi, G. and Naro, S. (2011) Passionate work: labour conditions in Italian fashion, *Journal for Cultural Research* 14 (3): 295–309, www.ricercaurbanamilano.com.

Auge, M. (1995) *Non Places: Introduction to an Anthropology of Supermodernity*, Verso, London.

Bader, I. and Scharenberg, A. (2010) The sound of Berlin: subculture and the global music industry, *International Journal of Urban and Regional Research* 34 (1): 76–91.

Bandinelli, C. (2016) Social entrepreneurship: ambiguities within and beyond neoliberalism, PhD dissertation, Goldsmiths, University of London (forthcoming).

Banks, M. (2010) Craft labour and creative industries, *International Journal of Cultural Policy* 16 (3): 305–22.

—— (2014) Being in the zone of cultural work, *Culture Unbound* 6: 241–62.

Banks M. and O'Connor J. (2009) After the creative industries, *International Journal of Cultural Policy* 15 (4): 365–73.

Bauman, Z. (1990) *The Individualised Society*, Polity, Cambridge.

—— (2000a) *Liquid Modernity*, Polity, Cambridge.

—— (2000b) *The Individualized Society*, Polity, Cambridge.

Beck, U. (1992) *Risk Society: Towards a New Modernity*, Sage, London.

—— (2000) *The Brave New World of Work*, Polity, Cambridge.

—— (2013) *German Europe*, trans. Rodney Livingstone, Polity, Cambridge.

—— (2014) Transformation/Metamorphosis, Annual lecture delivered at the London School of Economics, February, London.

Becker, H. (1982) *Art Worlds*, University of California Press, Berkeley CA.

Benjamin, W. (2009) *One Way Street*, Penguin, London.

Berardi, F. (2009) *The Soul at Work: From Alienation to Autonomy*, MIT Press, Boston.

Berlant, L (2010) *The Female Complaint*, Duke University Press, NC.

Bernt, M. and Holm, A. (2005) Exploring the substance and style of gentrification, in R. Atkinson and G. Bridge (eds) *Gentrification in a Global Context*, Routledge, London.

Bernt, M. and Holm, A. (2009) Is it or is it not? The conceptualisation of gentrification and displacement and its political implications in the case of Berlin-Prenzlauer Berg, *The City* 13 (2–3).

Bill, A. (2012) Blood, sweat and shears: happiness, creativity and fashion education, *Fashion Theory* 16 (1): 49–66.

Biressi, A. (2013) The virtuous circle: social entrepreneurship and welfare programming, http://www.academia.edu/3999737/_The_virtuous_circle_social_entrepreneurship_and_welfare_programming_in_the_UK.

Birrell, I. (2014) Does Britain really need a ministry of culture? *Guardian*, 10 April.

Bodirsky, K. (2012) Culture for competitiveness: valuing diversity in EU-Europe and the 'creative city' of Berlin, *International Journal of Cultural Policy* 18 (4): 455–73.

Boltanski, L. and Chiapello, E. (2005) *The New Spirit of Capitalism*, trans. G. Elliott, Verso, London.

Bott, E. (2009) Migrant British women producing selves through lapdancing, *Feminist Review*, 83 (3): 32–41.

Bourdieu, P. (1984) *Distinction*, Routledge, London.

—— (2000) *The Weight of the World*, Polity, Cambridge.

—— (1993) *The Field of Cultural Production*. Blackwell, Oxford.

Braham, P. (1997) Fashion: unpacking a cultural production, P. Du Gay (ed.), *Production of Culture/Cultures of Production*, Sage, London, p. 119.

Breward, C. and Gilbert, D. (2006) *Fashion's World Cities*, Berg, Oxford.

Briedis, K. and Minks, K-H. (2007) Generation Praktikum – Mythos oder Massenphaenomen? HIS: Projectbericht Bundesministerium fuer Bildung und Forschung. Available at http://www.uni-bamberg.de/fileadmin/uni/fakultaeten/ggeo_lehrstuehle/volkskunde/Dateien/organisatorisches/praktikum.job/Generation_Praktikum_HIS-Studie_April_2007.pdf.

Brown, W. A. (2011) Industrial relations in Britain under New Labour: a post-mortem, *Journal of Industrial Relations* 53 (3): 402–13.

Burgen, S. (2012) Jobs, a social conscience and big profits: what's not to like about the world's biggest fashion store? *Guardian*, 18 August, p. 27.

Burrell, Ian (2014) Canada goose: from arctic utility to urban chic. *Independent*, 11 October, http://www.independent.co.uk/life-style/fashion/features/canada-goose-from-arctic-utility-to-urban-chic-9780145.html.

Cabinet Office UK Government (2006) Social enterprise action plan. Available at http://webarchive.nationalarchives.gov.uk/20070108124358/http://cabinetoffice.gov.uk/third_sector/documents/social_enterprise/se_action_plan_%202006.pdf.

Calhoun, C. and Sennett, R. (eds) (2007) *Practising Culture*, Routledge, New York.

Campbell, C. (1987) *The Romantic Ethic and the Spirit of Modern Consumerism*, Blackwell, Oxford.

Cochrane, A. and Jonas, A. (1999) Reimagining Berlin as world city, national capital or ordinary place, *European Urban and Regional Studies* 6 (2): 145–64.

Colebrook, C. (2002) *Understanding Deleuze*, Allen and Unwin, London.

Colomb, C. (2012) Pushing the urban frontier: temporary uses of space, city marketing and the creative discourses in 2000s Berlin, *Journal of Urban Affairs* 34 (2): 131–52.

Cosse, E. (2008) The precarious go marching, *In the Middle of a Whirlpool* http://www.inthemiddleofawhirlpool.

Cuenca, A. L. (2012) Artistic labour, enclosure and the new economy, *Afterall* 30 (Summer) http://www.afterall.org/journal/issue.30.

D'Ovidio, M. and Pradel, M. (2012) Social innovation and institutionalisation in the cognitive-cultural economy: two contrasting experiences from southern Europe, *Cities*, August 2012.

de Peuter, G. (2014) Beyond the model worker: surveying a creative precariat, *Culture Unbound* 6: 263–84.

Deleuze, G. (1987) *Negotiations*, University of Minnesota Press, St Paul's MN.

Department of Culture, Media and Sport (2001) Creative Industries Mapping Document, DCMS, London.

Department of Culture, Media and Sport (1998) Creative Industries Mapping Document, DCMS, London.

Donzelot, J. (1991) Pleasure in work, in G. Burchell et al. (eds) *The Foucault Effect: Studies in Governmentality*, Harvester Wheatsheaf, London, pp. 251–81.

Dowling, E. (2007) Producing the dining experience; measure, subjectivity and the affective worker, *Ephemera* 7 (1): 117–32.

Dowling, E. and Harvie, D. (2014) Harnessing the social: state, crisis and (big) society, *Sociology* 48 (5): 869–86.

Du Gay, P. (1997) *Production of Culture/Cultures of Production*, Sage, London.

Emin, T. (2011) Tories are the only hope for the arts, *Guardian* 16 May, www.theguardian.com/culture/culture-cuts-blog/may/arts/emin.

European Commission (2006) KEA: The Economy of Culture in Europe, Report. Available at http://ec.europa.eu/culture/library/studies/cultural-economy_en.pdf.

—— (2012) Youth in Action Programme: Focus on Youth, Employment: European Good Practice Projects. Available at http://eacea.ec.europa.eu/youth/tools/documents/youth_employment_brochure_2012.pdf.

—— (2013) Youth in Action Programme: Focus on Young People and Entrepreneurship: European Good Practice Projects. Available at http://eacea.ec.europa.eu/youth/tools/documents/youth-entrepreneurship.pdf.

Evers, A. and Laville, J-L. (eds) (2004) *The Third Sector in Europe*, Edward Elgar, Sussex.

Exner, M. (2011) Fashion and the city: how the built environment mediates Berlin's rise as a fashion capital. Master's thesis. London School of Economics.

Feher, M. (2005) Self-appreciation: or, the aspirations of human capital *Public, Culture* 21 (1) 21–43.

—— (ed) (2007) *Non-Governmental Politics*, MIT Press, Cambridge MA.

Fielding, H. (1996) *Bridget Jones's Diary*, Picador, London.

Florida, R. (2002) *The Rise of the Creative Class*, Basic Books, New York.

—— (1988) *Technologies of the Self: A Seminar with Michel Foucault*, L. H. Martin et al. (eds) University of Massachusetts Press, Cambridge MA.

—— (2008) *The Birth of Biopolitics*, Palgrave Macmillan, Basingstoke.

Freygang, T. (2012) Bekore! http://www.life-online.de/publications/download

Foucault, M. (1980) *Power/Knowledge: Selected Interviews and Other Writings*, 1972–77, ed. C. Gordon, Harvester, Brighton.

—— (2008) *The Birth of Biopolitics: Lectures at the Collège de France 1978–9*.

Gandini, A. (2014) The Reputation Economy: Creative Labour and Freelance Networks, PhD, University of Milan.

Garnham, N. (2005) From cultural to creative industries: an analysis of the implications of the 'creative industries' approach to arts and media policy-making in the United Kingdom, *International Journal of Cultural Policy* 11 (1): 15–29.

Geyrhalter, Nikolaus (director) (2005). *Our Daily Bread*. Austria.

Gibson, K. (2002) Women, identity and activism in Asian and Pacific community economies, *Development: Journal of the Society of International Development* 45 (1): 74–9.

Gibson-Graham, J. K. (2003) Enabling ethical economies: cooperativism and class, *Critical Sociology* 9 (2): 123–61.

Giddens, A. (1991) *Modernity and Self-Identity: Self and Society in the Late Modern Age*, Polity, Cambridge.

Gilbert, D. (2011) World cities of fashion, in L. Welters and A. Lillethun (eds), *The Fashion Reader*, Berg, Oxford, pp. 237–42.

Gill, R. (2007) Technobohemians or the new cybertariat, new media work in Amsterdam a decade after the web, Institute of Network Cultures, Amsterdam.

Gillick, L. (2010) The Good of Work, in J. Aranda et al. (eds) *Are You Working too Much? Post-Fordism Precarity and the Labour of Art*, Strenberg Press, Berlin, pp. 60–73.

Gilroy, P. (1987) *There Ain't No Black in the Union Jack*, Routledge Classics, London.

Gregg, M. (2011) *Work's Intimacy*, Polity, Cambridge.

Gržinić, M. and Reitsamer, R. (eds) (2008) *New Feminism: Worlds of Feminism, Queer and Networking Conditions*, Locker Verlag, Vienna.

Hadjimichalis, C. (2006) The end of Third Italy as we knew it? *Antipode* 38 (1): 82–106.

Hall, S. (1988) *The Hard Road to Renewal: Thatcherism and the Crisis of the Left*, Verso, London.

—— (2003) New Labour's Double Shuffle, *Soundings*, 15: 10–14.

—— (2011) The Neoliberal Revolution, *Cultural Studies*, 25 (6): 705–28.

—— (2013) Common-sense Neoliberalism, *Soundings*, 55 (13): 9–25.

Hall, S. et al. (1987) *Policing the Crisis: Mugging, the State and Law and Order*, Macmillan, London.

Hall, S. and Jacques, M. (1989) *New Times: The Changing Face of Politics in the 1990s*, Lawrence and Wishart, London.

Hall, S. and Jefferson, T. (eds) (1976) *Resistance through Rituals*, Hutchinson, London.

Hanspal, J. (2000) Good character and dressing for success. MA thesis, Goldsmiths College, London.

Hardt, M. (1999) Affective labour, *Boundary 2* 26 (2): 89–100.

Hardt, M. and Negri, T. (2000) *Empire*, University of Harvard Press, Boston.

Hardt, M. and Negri, T. (2006) *Multitude, War and Democracy in the Age of Empire*, Penguin, London.

Hardt, M. and Virno, P. (eds) (1996) *Radical Thought in Italy: A Potential Politics*, University of Minnesota, MN.

Hark, S. (2014) Vom Erfolg uberholt?: Feministische Ambivalenzen der Gegenwart, in D. Haenzi (ed.), *Konstellationen und Paradozien einer gesellschaftlichen Leitorientierung*, Leviathan, Sonderband, pp. 76–91.

Hauge, A. and Hracs, B. J. (2010) See the sound, hear the style: collaborative linkages between indie musicians and fashion designers in local scenes, *Industry and Innovation* 17 (1): 113–29.

Hebdige, D. (1978) *Subculture: the Meaning of Style*, Methuen, London.

Hesmondhalgh, D. (2005) Media and cultural policy and public policy: the case of the British Labour Government, *International Journal of Cultural Policy* 11 (1): 95–109.

—— (2010) Normativity and social justice in the analysis of creative labour, *Journal for Cultural Research* 14 (3).

Hesmondhalgh, D. and Baker, S. (2011) *Creative Labour: Media Work in Three Cultural Industries*, Routledge, London.

Hesmondhalgh, D. et al. (2015) Were New Labour's cultural policies neo-liberal? *International Journal of Cultural Policy* 21 (1): 97–114.

Hewison, R. (2011) Creative Britain: myth or monument? *Cultural Trends* 20 (3/4): 235–42.

Heying, Charles (2011) *Brew to Bikes: Portland's Artisan Economy*, Ooligan Press, Portland OR.

Hochschild, A. (1984) *The Managed Heart: The Commercialisation of Human Feeling*, University of California Press, Berkeley CA.

Inman, P. (2013) Eurozone youth unemployment reaches record high of 24.4%, *Guardian*, Friday 29 November. Available at http://www.theguardian.com/business/2013/nov/29/eurozone-youth-unemployment-record-high-under-25s.

Jakob, Doreen (2009). *Beyond Creative Production Networks: The Development of Intra-Metropolitan Creative Industry Clusters in Berlin and New York*, Rhombos, Berlin.

Kalandides, A. (2014) Report submitted on Berlin fashion micro-producers CREATe, AHRC, University of Glasgow, Scotland.

—— (2007) For a stricter use of the term gentrification, *Geographies* 13: 158–72.

Kepplova, Z. (2013) The beat of cool capitalism: how Slovak club culture helped make the new middle class, PhD, Central European University, Budapest.

Klein, N. (2000) *No Logo: Taking Aim at the Brand Bullies*, Picador, New York.

Komurcu, O. (2015) Postmigrant theatre and cultural diversity in the arts: race, precarity, and artistic labour in Berlin, PhD, Goldsmiths, University of London.

Kosnick, K. (2012) Out on the scene: queer migrant clubbing and urban diversity, in G. Stahl (ed.) *Poor but Sexy: Reflections on Berlin Scenes*, Peter Lang, Frankfurt.

Kristeva, Julia (1981). Women's time, *Signs*, 7 (1): 13–35.

Lane, C. and Probert, J. (2009) *National Capitalisms, Global Production Networks: Fashioning the Value Chain in the UK, US and Germany*, Oxford University Press, Oxford.

Lange, B. (2012) Value creation in the creative economy: the case of electronic club music in Germany, *Journal of Economic Geography*, 82 (2): 149–69.

Larner, W. and Molloy, H. (2009) Globalisation, the 'new' economy and working women: theorizing from the New Zealand fashion design industry, *Feminist Theory* 10: 35–59.

Lash, S. and Urry, J. (1994) *Economy of Signs and Spaces*, Sage, London.

Lazzarato, M. (1999) Immaterial Labour, www.generationonline/lazzarato/ immaterial labour.

—— (2012) *The Making of Indebted Man: An Essay on the Neoliberal Condition*, Semiotext(e) intervention series 13, Amsterdam.

Leadbeater, C. (1996) *The Rise of the Social Entrepreneur*, DEMOS, London.

—— (1999) *Living on Thin Air: The New Economy*, Viking, London.

Leadbeater, C. and Oakley, J. (1999) *The Independents: Britain's New Cultural Entrepreneurs*, Demos, London.

Lloyd, Richard (2006). *Neo-Bohemia: Art and Commerce in the Postindustrial City*, University of Chicago Press, Chicago.

Lorey, I. (2015) *State of Insecurity*, Verso, London.

Lowndes, S. (2003) *Social Sculpture: the Rise of the Glasgow Art Scene*, Luath Press, Scotland.

Luckman, S. (2013) The aura of the analogue in a digital age: women's crafts, creative markets, and home-based labour after Etsy, *Cultural Studies Review* 19 (1): 249–70.

McCarthy, T. (2011) Zara: the business of fast fashion, in L. Welters and A. Lillethun (eds), *The Fashion Reader*, 2nd edn, Berg, Oxford.

McGuigan, J. (2005) Neo-liberalism, culture and policy, *International Journal of Cultural Policy* 11 (3): 229–41.

—— (2010) Creative labour, cultural work and individualisation, *International Journal of Cultural Policy* 16 (3): 323–35.

MacKay, J. (2014) Palermo is a laboratory for the precariat, *Open Democracy*, 15 October 2014. Available at https://www.opendemocracy.net/can -europe-make-it/jamie-mackay/palermo-is-laboratory-for-precariat.

McRobbie, A. (1976) Working-class girls and the culture of femininity, in S. Hall and T. Jefferson (eds), *Resistance through Rituals*, Hutchinson, London.

—— (1988) Settling accounts into subcultures, *Screen Technician*, 34: 37–41.

—— (1989) Second-hand dresses and the role of the rag market, in A. McRobbie (ed.), *Zoot Suits and Second Hand Dresses*, Macmillan, Basingstoke.

—— (1998) *British Fashion Design: Rag Trade or Image Industry?* Routledge, London.

—— (1999) *In the Culture Society: Art, Fashion and Popular Music*, Routledge, London.

—— (2002) From Holloway to Hollywood: happiness at work in the new cultural economy, in Paul du Gay and Michael Pryke (eds), *Cultural Economy*, Sage, London.

—— (2004) Making a living in London's small-scale creative sector, in D. Power and A. J. Scott (eds), *Culture Industries and the Production of Culture*, Routledge, New York.

—— (2008) *The Aftermath of Feminism: Gender, Culture and Social Change*, Sage, London.

McRobbie, A. and Thornton, S. (1995) Rethinking 'moral panic' for multi-mediated social worlds, *British Journal of Sociology* 46: 559–74.

Mayer, M. (2004) New lines of division in the new Berlin, in F. Ulfers, G. Lenz and, A. Dallman (eds), *Towards a New Metropolitanism: Reconstituting Public Culture, Urban Citizenship, and the Multicultural Imaginary in New York City and Berlin*, Universitätsverlag Winter, Heidelberg.

Melville, C. (2007) 'London Underground': the multicultural routes of London's dance music cultures, PhD dissertation, Goldsmiths, University of London, London.

Merkel, A. (2007) Speech delivered to the European Parliament, Wednesday 17 January www.wikisource.

Mitchell, K. (2006) Neoliberal governmentality in the European Union: education, training, and technologies of citizenship, *Environment and Planning D :Society and Space* 24: 389–407.

Neff, G. (2012) *Venture Labour: Work and the Burden of Risk in Innovation Industries*, MIT Press, Cambridge MA.

Neff, G., Wissinger, E. and Zukin, S. (2005) Entrepreneurial labour and cultural production: 'cool' jobs in 'hot' places, *Social Semiotics* 15 (3): 307–30.

NESTA (2008) Beyond the Creative Industries: Mapping The Creative Economy in the UK NESTA London (National Endowment for Science, Technology and the Arts).

Nixon, S. (1993) *Hard Looks*, UCL Press, London.

Oakley, K. (2004) Not so cool Britannia: the role of creative industries in economic development, *International Journal of Cultural Studies* 7 (1): 67–77.

—— (2006) From Bohemia to Britart: art students over 50 years, *Cultural Trends* 18 (4): 281–94.

—— (2009) Include us out : economic development and social policy in the creative industries, *Cultural Trends* 15 (4): 255–73.

—— (2011) In its own image: New Labour and the cultural workforce, *Cultural Trends* 20 (3/4): 281–9.

Pasquinelli, M. (2010) Jenseits der ruinen der creativen stadt, *Skulpturenpark Berlin_Zentrum, KUNSTrePUBLIK*, Walther Konig, Köln, pp. 246–60.

Peck, J. (2005) Struggling with the creative class, *International Journal of Urban and Regional Research* 29: 740–70.

Phizacklea, A. (1990) *Unpacking the Fashion Industry*, Routledge, London.

Pollert, A. (1981) *Girls, Wives, Factory Lives*, Macmillan, Basingstoke.

—— (1988) Dismantling flexibility, *Capital and Class* 12 (34): 42–75.

Pratt, A. (2012) The cultural and creative industries: organisational and spatial challenges to their governance, *Die Erde* 143: 317–34.

Prime, S. and Exner, M. (2012) Kenne dein Geschaeftsmodell [Sian Prime interviewed by Maria Exner], *Der Tagesspiegel*, 21 July.

Pul, H. (2011) Resident experiences of encounters with tourists in Berlin-Kreuzberg, Master's dissertation, University of Amsterdam.

Rancière, J. (2012) *Proletarian Nights: The Workers' Dream in Nineteenth Century France*, Verso, London.

Rantisi, N. (2006) How New York Stole Modern Fashion, C. Breward and D. Gilbert (eds) *Fashion's World Cities*, Berg, Oxford.

—— (2004) The designer in the city and the city in the designer, D. Power and A. J. Scott (eds) *The Cultural Industries and the Production of Culture*, Routledge, London.

Raunig, G. (2013) *Factories of Knowledge, Industries of Creativity*, MIT, Press, MA.

Rivière, J. (1928/86) Femininity as masquerade, in V. Burgin, J. Donald and C. Kaplan (eds), *Formations of Fantasy*, Routledge, London.

Rodriguez, E. G. (2008) Sexual multitude and precariousness, in M. Gržinić and R. R. Reitsamer, pp. 31–40.

Rogoff, I. (2010) Turning in, www.e-flux.com?journal/turning.

Rose, N. (1996) The death of the social? Refiguring the territory of government, *Economy and Society*, 25 (3): 327–56.

—— (2008) *Governing the Present. Administering Economic, Social and Personal Life*, Polity, Cambridge.

Rosler, M. (2011) Culture class; art creativity urbanism Part 111 e-flux 25 May, http://www.e-flux.com/journal/culture-class-art-creativity-urbanism -part-III.

Ross, A. (2003) *No-Collar: the Humane Workplace and Its Hidden Costs*, Basic Books, New York.

Rubin, G. (1984) Thinking sex: notes for a radical theory of the politics of sexuality, in C. Vance (ed.), *Pleasure and Danger*, Routledge and Kegan Paul, New York.

Rushton, R. (2001) Fashion Feature. *i-D*, February.

Sandberg, S. (2012) *Lean In: Women, Work and the Will to Lead*, Vintage, London.

Sassen, S. (1991) *The Global City*, Blackwell, Oxford.

—— (2002) Urban sociology for the 21st century, in G. Bridges and S. Watson (eds), *The Blackwell City Reader*, Wiley-Blackwell, Oxford, pp. 476–94.

Savage, M. et al. (2013) A new model of social class? Findings from the BBC's Great British Class Survey Experiment, *Sociology*, 47 (2): 219–50.

Savier, M. (2012) Italian Reply to Bekore. Unpublished Paper.

Schwanhaeuser, A. (2010) *Kosmonauten des Berliner underground: ethnografie einer Berliner szene Frankfurt*.

Scott, A. J. (2000) *The Cultural Economy of Cities*. Sage, London.

Sennett, R.(1993) *The Conscience of the Eye: The Design and Social Life of Cities*, Sage, London.
—— (1995) *The Corrosion of Character*, Norton, New York.
—— (1998) *The Corrosion of Character: The Personal Consequences of Work in the New Capitalism*, W. W. Norton, New York.
—— (2001) *The Flexible City*, www.richardsennett.com.
—— (2003) *Respect: The Formation of Character In a World of Inequality*, Penguin, London.
—— (2006) *The Culture of the New Capitalism*, Yale University Press, New Haven.
—— (2008) *The Craftsman*, Penguin, London.
—— (2012) *Together: The Rituals, Pleasures and Politics of Co-operation*, Penguin, London.
Simone, A. M. (2010) A town on its knees? Economic experiments with post-colonial urban politics in Africa and Southeast Asia, *Theory, Culture and Society* 5 (27): 130–54.
Skeggs, B. (1997) *Formations of Class and Gender*, Routledge, London.
Smith, C. (1998) *Creative Britain*, Faber and Faber, London.
Spivak, Gayatri Chakravorty (1981) French feminism in an international frame, *Yale French Studies* 62: 154–84.
Springer, B. (2006) *Artful Transformations: Kunst als Medium Urbaner Aufwertung*, Kulturverlag Kadmos.
Stuber, J. (2013) Italiens grunder knupfen kontakte nach Berlin, *Berliner Morgenpost*, 12 November, p. 6.
Suleman, A. (2013) Andy Rogers profile the creative class, http://www.thebusinessoffashion.com/the-creative-class-andy-rogers-brand-director/.
Taylor, S. and Littleton, K. (2013) *Contemporary Identities of Cultural and Creative Work*, Ashgate, Kent.
Terranova, T. (2004) *Network Culture: Politics for the Information Age*, Pluto Press, London.
Thornton, S. (1996) *Club Cultures: Music, Media and Subcultural Capital*, Polity, Cambridge.
—— (2008) *Seven Days in the Art World*, Granta, London.
—— (2014) *33 Artists in 3 Acts*, Granta, London.
Thrift, N. (2001) It's the romance, not the finance, that makes the business worth pursuing: disclosing a new market culture, *Economy and Society* 30 (4): 412–32.
Turanskyj, Tatjana (2010) (director). *Eine flexible Frau*, Germany.
Van Heur, B. (2009) From creative industries to critique: comparing policies in London and Berlin, in J. Eckardt and L. Nystrom (eds) *Culture and the City*, Berliner Wissenschaftsverlag.
Virno, P. (2005) *The Grammar of the Multitude*, Semiotexte Foreign Agents Series, New York.
Von Osten, M. and McRobbie, A. (2002) Atelier Europa Project, funded by German Culture Ministry, see www.Atelier Europa/ von Osten and McRobbie.

Wacquant, L. (2009) *Punishing the Poor*, Duke University Press, North Carolina.

Walby, S. (1997) *Gender Transformations*, Routledge, London.

Wallace, J. (2012) Yarn bombing, knit graffiti and underground brigades: a study of craftivism and mobility, *Journal of Mobile Culture* 6 (3), online at http://wi.mobiities.ca/yarn-bombing.

Ward, J. (2004) Berlin, the virtual global city, *Journal of Visual Culture* 3 (2): 239–56.

Westwood, S. (1985) *All Day, Every Day: Factory and Family in the Making of Women's Lives*, University of Illinois Press, Urbana.

Willis, P. (1978) *Learning to Labour*, Saxon House, London.

—— (1990) *Common Culture: Symbolic Work at Play in the Everyday Culture of the Young*, Open University Press, Milton Keynes, Buckinghamshire.

Wilthagen, T. and Tros, F. (2004) The concept of flexicurity: a new approach to regulating employment and labour markets in Europe, *Transfer: European Review of Labour and Research* 10 (2).

Wiseman, Frederick (2009) (director). *La Danse*, France/USA.

Wissinger, E. (2009) Modelling consumption: fashion modelling in contemporary society, *Journal of Consumer Culture* 9 (2): 275–98.

—— (2007) Modelling a way of life: immaterial and affective labour in the fashion modelling industry, *Ephemera* 7 (1): 250–69.

Wittel, Λ. (2001) Towards a network sociality, *Theory Culture and Society* 18 (6): 51–76.

Wood, Z. (2012) Zara profits up. *Guardian*, 14 June, p. 30.

Work Foundation (The) (2008) Staying ahead: the economic performance of the UK's creative industries, The Work Foundation, London.

Wowereit, K. (2008) *The Creative Industries Report*, Berlin.

Wu C-T. (2003) *Privatising Culture: Corporate Art Intervention Since the 1980s*, Verso, London.

Zukin, Sharon (2010) *Naked City: The Death and Life of Authentic Urban Places*, Oxford University Press, Oxford.

Index